ETHICS IN RESEARCH
WITH HUMAN PARTICIPANTS

Chapter 1
p 134-135
142 (2.02)-144
153-157

ETHICS IN RESEARCH WITH HUMAN PARTICIPANTS

Edited by
Bruce D. Sales *and* Susan Folkman

American Psychological Association
Washington, DC

Fourth Printing, April 2010

Published by
American Psychological Association
750 First Street, NE
Washington, DC 20002

Copies may be ordered from
APA Order Department
P.O. Box 92984
Washington, DC 20090-2984

In the U.K., Europe, Africa, and the Middle East, copies may be ordered from
American Psychological Association
3 Henrietta Street
Covent Garden, London
WC2E 8LU England

Typeset in Century Schoolbook by EPS Group Inc., Easton, MD

Printer: Maple-Vail Book Manufacturing Group, York, PA
Cover Designer: Design Concepts, San Diego, CA
Technical/Production Editor: Emily Welsh

The opinions and statements published are the responsibility of the authors, and
such opinions and statements do not necessarily represent the policies of the APA.

This book is not an official statement of the American Psychological Association
(APA). Rather, it is an educational document that was written to stimulate an
awareness of; discussion about; and sensitivity to ethical issues, responsibilities,
and obligations in the conduct of research with human participants.

The official set of principles for psychologists is found in *Ethical Principles of
Psychologists and Code of Conduct*, which was published by APA in 1992 and is
included in this volume as appendix A.

Library of Congress Cataloging-in-Publication Data
Ethics in research with human participants / edited by Bruce D. Sales and
Susan Folkman.
    p. cm.
   Includes bibliographical references and index.
   ISBN 1-55798-688-6 (alk. paper)
    1. Human experimentation in psychology—Moral and ethical aspects.
   I. Sales, Bruce Dennis. II. Folkman, Susan.

BF76.4.S35 2000
174'915—dc21

00-032297

British Library Cataloguing-in-Publication Data
A CIP record is available from the British Library.

Printed in the United States of America

Contents

Contributors vii

Preface.. ix

1. Moral Foundations of Research With Human
   Participants... 3
   M. Brewster Smith

Part I: Ethical Concerns Across the Research Process 11

2. Planning Research: Basic Ethical Decision-Making 13
   Joan E. Sieber

3. Recruitment of Research Participants.................... 27
   Diane Scott-Jones

4. Informed Consent 35
   Marian W. Fischman

5. Privacy and Confidentiality............................. 49
   Susan Folkman

Part II: Ethical Concerns Within the Research Community........ 59

6. Other Responsibilities to Participants.................... 61
   Lorraine D. Eyde

7. Authorship and Intellectual Property 75
   Matthew McGue

8. Training 97
   June Tangney

Part III: Methods for Ethical Decision-Making 107

9. Identifying Conflicts of Interest and Resolving Ethical
   Dilemmas... 109
   Bruce D. Sales and Michael Lavin

Appendix A: APA's Ethical Principles of Psychologists and Code of
Conduct.. 129

Appendix B: Code of Federal Regulations: Protection of Human
Subjects... 161

Appendix C: The Belmont Report 195

Index 207

About the Editors 215

Contributors

Lorraine D. Eyde, PhD, U.S. Office of Personnel Management

Marian W. Fischman, PhD, Department of Psychiatry, Columbia University School of Medicine

Susan Folkman, PhD, Center for AIDS Prevention Studies, University of California, San Francisco

Michael Lavin, PhD, Department of Psychology, University of Arizona

Matthew McGue, PhD, Department of Psychology, University of Minnesota

Bruce D. Sales, PhD, JD, Department of Psychology, University of Arizona

Diane Scott-Jones, PhD, Department of Psychology, Temple University

Joan E. Sieber, PhD, California State University, Hayward

M. Brewster Smith, PhD, Psychology Department, University of California, Santa Cruz

Julie Tangney, PhD, Department of Psychology, George Mason University

Preface

Dramatic shifts have taken place in the contexts in which research occurs since publication of *Ethical Principles in the Conduct of Research With Human Participants* (American Psychological Association, 1973, revised 1982). These shifts, which include changes in research questions, settings, populations, methods, and societal norms and values, have generated new ethical challenges:

- Behavioral research is expanding into field settings and biomedical contexts where research priorities are being integrated with the priorities and interests of nonresearch institutions, community leaders, and diverse research populations.
- Increasingly, behavioral research involves a broad range of populations that may raise special concerns, such as children, elderly adults, gay men and lesbians, populations of color, inner-city populations, teenage mothers, runaway children, people with chronic or terminal illness, people with cognitive or emotional challenges, and people who abuse alcohol or drugs.
- Sensitive issues are being added to psychology's research agenda. For example, such areas as domestic violence, incest, and the sexual practices of various populations create a tension between rights to privacy and the need for careful research.
- Advances in electronic technologies for gathering, analyzing, storing, and sharing data have raised new ethical issues not addressed in earlier publications.
- More recent ethical codes published by the Office for Protection from Research Risks (1991) (see appendix B) and the American Psychological Association (1992) (see appendix A) need to be addressed.

In response to the manifold ethical issues raised by these recent changes, the American Psychological Association (APA) convened a Task Force in March 1994. Nominations for members were solicited from the APA's Committee on Standards in Research, announcements in the *Psychological Science Agenda* and the *Monitor*, and over the Science Leaders e-mail network. Nominations were also solicited from the presidents of all 52 APA Divisions, the Board of Scientific Affairs, and the Council of Science Advisors. The Board of Directors of the APA reviewed the nominations and selected six members to the Task Force. At its first meeting the Task Force, then comprising Marian W. Fischman, Susan Folkman, Matthew McGue, Bruce D. Sales, Diane Scott-Jones, and M. Brewster Smith, proposed that the American Psychological Society (APS) be invited to collaborate on this project. APS selected three individuals to join the Task Force—Lorraine D. Eyde, Joan E. Sieber, and June Tangney, although APS was not a formal partner in this project.

The charge to the Task Force was to address newly emerging ethical issues in the conduct of research with human participants and to create an educational, advisory document that would promote scientific rigor within an ethical context and suggest practical solutions to ethical dilemmas. The document is intended as an educational resource for undergraduates, graduates, faculty, basic and applied researchers in psychology and other disciplines involving human participants, and institutional review boards (IRBs).

We note that not all acts of systematic data gathering or applications of statistical techniques necessarily constitute "research," and not all systematic acts of data gathering require informed consent. Sometimes data are collected and analyzed for purposes of practice or in the provision of service to an organization. The distinction between data that are collected for purposes of practice or service as opposed to data that are collected for purposes of research is sometimes difficult to make. The Belmont Report (see appendix C) provides helpful guidance in making these determinations. This report defines *practice* as

> interventions that are designed solely to enhance the well-being of an individual patient or client and that have a reasonable expectation of success. The purpose of medical or behavioral practice is to provide diagnosis, preventive treatment or therapy to particular individuals. By contrast, the term *research* [italics added] designates an activity designed to . . . develop or contribute to generalizable knowledge (expressed, for example, in theories, principles, and statements of relationships). (Section A)

Some data collection in school, clinical, industrial, or organizational settings or surveys, for example, may fall under the rubric of "practice" or "service." This is not to say that such activities are exempt from ethical guidelines. Like any professional, practicing clinical, school, counseling, educational, human factors, or industrial–organizational psychologists are bound by APA ethical standards, but they may not be subject to the more specific demands that come with the collection of data for research purposes.

In preparation for their work, the Task Force conducted an extensive review of the literature, sought the advice of ethicists and scientists who were heavily involved in research and who were members of IRBs, and invited comments through the *Monitor*. The members of the Task Force drafted and reviewed chapters over a 36-month period. The editors at the APA, members of the APA Board of Scientific Affairs, and the Divisions of the APA reviewed several drafts of the document.

During the development and production of this volume, advances in digital technology led to the emergence of the Internet as an alternative tool and medium for the conduct of research in psychological science. Methodological and ethical issues surrounding research on the Internet have been gradually unfolding as the number of Internet-based studies in the behavioral and social sciences has proliferated. Among the ethical issues relating to Internet research projects are methods for: providing informed consent to participants, protecting the privacy and confidentiality of participants, ensuring that participants are adequately debriefed, and conducting careful analyses of the potential risks and benefits of a given project. Discussions of these and other issues have been initiated recently by the American Association for the Advancement of Science and the Office for Protection from Research Risks, and these discussions will continue as the frequency of Internet-based research increases. Unfortunately, these issues could not be addressed in the current volume due to production deadlines.

This publication, *Ethics in Research With Human Participants*, is organized in the following way. Chapter 1, "Moral Foundations of Research With Human Participants," introduces the issues addressed in the volume. It presents the broad ethical principles that underlie the decision-making process in planning and implementing research with human participants.

The four chapters in Part I review ethical concerns across the research process. Chapter 2, "Planning Research: Basic Ethical Decision-Making," reviews the ethical considerations that researchers consider when designing their research. Chapter 3, "Recruitment of Research Participants," reviews the ethical dilemmas in recruiting participants. Issues concerning coercion of potential participants are highlighted. Chapter 4, "Informed Consent," reviews the ethical and legal aspects of the informed consent process in research. Chapter 5, "Privacy and Confidentiality," defines the distinctions between privacy and confidentiality and provides an analysis of ethical issues associated with participants' interests in this regard.

The three chapters in Part II focus on specific ethical concerns within the research community. Chapter 6, "Other Responsibilities to Participants," discusses the treatment of participants in ongoing research. This chapter pays particular attention to the needs of special populations. Chapter 7, "Authorship and Intellectual Property," reviews the ethical issues surrounding authorship, including who may claim authorship, the ordering of authors, and ownership of research data. Chapter 8, "Training," covers ethical issues concerning the training of researchers and the use of research assistants.

The last chapter, in Part III, provides readers with practical methods of ethical decision-making. Chapter 9, "Identifying Conflicts of Interest and Resolving Ethical Dilemmas," first provides a review of the two main areas from which conflicts arise and discusses specific sources of conflicts of interest. Chapter 9 then provides a decision scheme for resolving ethical dilemmas. It reviews the potential conflicts that may arise by following the aspirational principles and enforceable standards of the APA ethics code, legal regulations, and the researcher's own ethical sense.

The intellectual and moral foundation for this volume is articulated in chapter 1. The subsequent chapters present an integrated and conceptual application of the principles described in chapter 1 to the ethical issues that arise in the conduct of research with human participants. Both the APA (see appendix A) and the federal government (see appendices B and C) have listed ethical principles and guidelines that should direct researchers as they conduct research. These sets of principles are easily summarized into five general ethical categories discussed in chapter 1 that underlie the ethical guidance provided in this book. We have also indicated how these five general categories match with the ethical principles found in the APA ethics code. In chapter 9, we discuss how ethical analysis should be used when addressing research problems. Because ethical analysis requires that individuals refer to specific professional ethical codes that establish mandatory behaviors in specific situations, this chapter refers explicitly to the APA code (1992). It is important to note that the process illustrated with the APA code is appropriate for ethical analysis within other disciplines for which professional codes have been established.

The change that has characterized the context of behavioral research during the past decade is going to continue, most likely at an accelerated rate. No advisory document can anticipate all the ethical issues that will arise in this environment, nor are there any easy ways to understand fully all the implications of a given ethical issue. Our goal for this volume therefore is to provide researchers with analytic tools for anticipating, understanding, resolving, minimizing, or circumventing ethical conflicts likely to arise in their research. We provide examples throughout to help the reader understand the issues and lessons of each chapter. The examples and ethical analyses are often simple extractions of more complex scientific dilemmas that we have selected in order to serve our pedagogical purposes; we do not provide an exhaustive listing of every possible instance of ethical concern in research with human participants. Finally, although we use the word *should* throughout the volume, we do so to raise the reader's consciousness, not to preempt the reader's own ethical analyses of dilemmas. Responsible decision-making is always predicated on the competence and expertise of the researcher making the decisions.

Acknowledgments

Order of editorship was decided by a coin toss.

Chapter 4 is based in part on the discussion of informed consent in R. J. Levine, 1986, *Ethics and Regulation of Clinical Research*. Baltimore: Urban & Schwarzenberg.

References

American Psychological Association. (1982). *Ethical principles in the conduct of research with human participants*. Washington, DC: Author.
American Psychological Association. (1992). Ethical principles of psychologists and code of conduct. *American Psychologist, 47,* 1597–1611.

ETHICS IN RESEARCH
WITH HUMAN PARTICIPANTS

1

Moral Foundations in Research With Human Participants

M. Brewster Smith

All scientific inquiry with human research participants necessarily involves ethical issues. For example, the pursuit of psychological knowledge about people is itself an ethical goal in the scientist's scheme of values. Psychological research that deals with central and sensitive personal issues, such as people's inner conflicts and their private victories and defeats, aspirations and regrets, inherently risks harming or offending the people that it studies. Researchers who seek to contribute to the understanding and amelioration of serious social problems like AIDS, youth or family violence, or substance abuse need to consider the rights and interests of the vulnerable people being studied.

An ethical perspective on research decisions inherently involves tension between responsible judgment and the rigid application of rules. The requirements of the law may conflict with ethical ideals, as may be conspicuously the case with some issues concerning confidentiality. The methodological requirements of solid research may conflict with the rights of individuals or with competing conceptions of the public good. Principles and guidelines can identify what is ethically desirable and what is clearly unacceptable, but there is a large area in which researchers are left to make their own decisions. These decisions can be ethically responsible when made on the basis of an ethically sensitized appreciation of the relevant considerations.

But what should be taught to engender such an appreciation? When the American Psychological Association (APA) took the lead in 1973 in promulgating *Ethical Principles in the Conduct of Research With Human Participants* (see APA, 1982), primary concern focused on problems such as the use of deceptive procedures in psychological research, the potentially coercive implications of departmental participant pools, and threats to confidentiality in academic investigations. Although these ethical issues remain important, they are no longer representative of the range of issues that many psychologists face in their research today, especially in biomedical and community contexts. In addition, with many behavioral scientists increasingly involved in biomedical research, guidelines for behavioral research also need to be compatible with guidelines developed in the biomedical areas.

Federal regulation has elaborated a legal and bureaucratic framework centering on institutional review boards (IRBs) that provides a salient context for the researcher's ethical responsibility, although it does not absolve researchers from making their own difficult ethical decisions (Office for Protection From Research Risks [OPRR], 1991). This admonition is important because some IRBs may lack appropriate behavioral and social science expertise. Further, the 1992 APA *Ethical Principles of Psychologists and Code of Conduct* includes principles and standards enforceable for APA members concerning the ethical conduct of human research that are found in Section 6 (Teaching, Training Supervision, Research, and Publishing) and elsewhere in the document.

Therefore, this book provides extensive discussion of ethical issues faced by contemporary researchers. This chapter is intended to introduce the reader to the broader moral considerations and ethical principles that underlie ethical decision-making for researchers studying human behavior. (Note that ethical considerations in research with nonhuman animals are dealt with in the *Guidelines for Ethical Conduct in the Care and Use of Animals,* APA, 1996.)

How Is This Ethical Approach Different From Others?

Moral or ethical judgment is a human universal, but systematic treatments of ethical principles obviously vary across religious traditions and schools of philosophical thought. Among Western schools of thought, for example, different ethical priorities are highlighted by the Kantian or "deontological" approach that emphasizes respect for individual autonomy and the "utilitarian" approach linked with John Stuart Mill that emphasizes the balance of harms and benefits to people. The deontological approach holds that the morality of an action is directly related to its intrinsic nature: Actions are right or wrong regardless of their consequences. The many variants of this approach share a common imperative: One's actions should strive to treat every person as an end and never as a means (Beauchamp & Childress, 1989; Bersoff & Koeppl, 1993). Respect for the dignity of the individual necessarily involves respect for individual autonomy. Conversely, utilitarianism, or consequentialist ethical theory, holds that the morality of an action is to be judged by its consequences, a perspective that highlights the balancing of costs and benefits.

Different religious and philosophical traditions propose different priorities and modes of analysis for determining what is the morally right course of action in a given situation. For example, most would agree that one should not take a life, but the determination of what comprises taking a life (e.g., abortion issues) or whether there are still higher principles (e.g., keeping society safe) differs among the traditions. This book does not aspire to resolve such differences in ultimate perspective. Rather, it seeks to promote good ethical practice in research with human participants by identifying consensually approved and consensually condemned research practices. Where there seems to be no consensus, or where ethical principles are in conflict, it highlights issues and approaches for researchers to consider. Federal regulations (OPRR, 1991)[1] are legally binding to those conducting research in this country; ethical standards such as those in the APA's 1992 code are obligatory for members of the professional associations that promulgate them. In contrast, the analysis and recommendations contained in this book are not binding. They are offered, rather, with the aim of raising the level of ethical awareness and practice of researchers.

The responsibilities of researchers can be sorted into four sets: responsibilities (a) to science; (b) to society; (c) to students, apprentices, or trainees in research; and (d) to the participants in the research. The primary focus will be on responsibilities to the participants in research. This focus will be balanced with the other three sets of responsibilities: to science—to do research that indeed extends knowledge or deepens understanding; to society—as in the case of determining how the results of research are used or publicized; to students, apprentices, or trainees—to contribute to their education in regard to ethical issues in the conduct of research.

Efforts in the biomedical and psychological research community to meet these responsibilities have involved both the utilitarian and deontological traditions as well as more concrete guidelines, such as the Belmont Report, *Ethical Principles and Guidelines for the Protection of Human Subjects of Research* (OPRR, 1979; see appendix C), the report of the National Commission for the Protection of Human Subjects of Biomedical and Behavioral Research that set the framework for federal regulation. Attention is also directed to the general principles included in the 1992 APA code (see appendix A).

Five basic moral principles underlie the ethical guidance provided in this book:

I.   Respect for Persons and Their Autonomy *
II. Beneficence and Nonmaleficence
III. Justice
IV. Trust
V.   Fidelity and Scientific Integrity.

---

[1]Federal agencies that have adopted the 45 CFR Part 46 as the Common Rule include the U.S. Department of Agriculture, 7 CFR Part 1C; the U.S. Department of Energy, 10 CFR Part 745; the National Aeronautics and Space Administration, 14 CFR Part 1230; the U.S. Department of Commerce, 15 CFR Part 27; the Consumer Product Safety Commission, 16 CFR Part 1028; the International Development Cooperation Agency/Agency for International Development, 22 CFR Part 225; the U.S. Department of Housing and Urban Development, 24 CFR Part 60; the U.S. Department of Justice, 28 CFR Part 46; the U.S. Department of Defense, 32 CFR Part 219; the U.S. Department of Education, 34 CFR Part 97; the Department of Veterans Affairs, 38 CFR Part 16; the Environmental Protection Agency, 40 CFR Part 26; the U.S. Department of Health and Human Services, 45 CFR Part 46; the National Science Foundation, 45 CFR Part 690; and the U.S. Department of Transportation, 49 CFR Part 11. The Office of Science and Technology Policy and the Central Intelligence Agency (CIA) accepted the common rule but did not publish it separately—the CIA having done so in response to an Executive Order.

These moral principles cover essentially the same ground as Ethical Principles B–F of the 1992 APA code, but as ethical principles, they are cast in terms especially relevant to research practice. Thus, Moral Principles I, II, and III are drawn from the Belmont Report. The relation of these moral principles to the aspirational ethical principles of the APA code is noted throughout the rest of this chapter. Because Ethical Principle A, Competence, of the code responds to a characteristic of the researcher and his or her work, judgments about competence precede review of ethical responsibility. Although competence is not listed as one of the basic moral principles, it is assumed to be essential for the design and conduct of responsible research. For example, decisions about risks and benefits of a specific research study are often best informed by expertise in the subject matter of the research. Competence of the researcher would imply expertise in the domain of the research.

Moral Principle I. Respect for Persons and Their Autonomy

Researchers respect the human participants in their investigations as persons of worth whose participation is a matter of their autonomous choice. Insofar as persons have diminished autonomy, whether because of immaturity, incapacitation, or circumstances that severely restrict their liberty, they require special concern. Guidance provided in subsequent chapters relating to informed consent, coercion, deception, confidentiality, and privacy relate to this principle, which corresponds to Ethical Principle D in the APA code, Respect for People's Rights and Dignity.

There is an intrinsic relation between Moral Principle I and Moral Principle II, Beneficence and Nonmaleficence. The interests of proposed participants who have diminished capacity or opportunity for autonomous choice need to be appropriately represented and assurance provided that they will not be at risk for harmful consequences. In many cases for such persons, informed consent should involve proxies (e.g., parents or spouse). Chapter 4 provides an expanded discussion of informed consent. Conversely, federal regulations do not require informed consent in connection with some categories of research that involve essentially no risk. The judgment of "no risk" may of course be problematic, and researchers should strive to ensure that such decisions are not self-serving. It is best to seek external validation for such decisions through consultation with colleagues or institutional resources (e.g., IRBs).

Moral Principle II. Beneficence and Nonmaleficence

In the planning and conduct of research with human participants, the researcher should maximize the possible benefits and minimize the possible harms from the research. Whereas Moral Principle I represents the deontological tradition, Moral Principle II represents the utilitarian tradition. In the APA code, it corresponds to Ethical Principles E, Concern for Others' Welfare, and F, Social Responsibility.

This seemingly straightforward principle becomes complex and ambiguous in application. Costs and benefits can seldom be estimated accurately in advance, and they can rarely be balanced against each other. In much psychological research, the conceivable benefit is to the science, and through the science, potentially to society at large. One cannot balance costs to the participants against benefits to the science, although psychologists should keep both in view in deciding whether to do the research. Because no simple summation of costs and benefits is possible, the researcher cannot avoid moral responsibility for the decision.

As already noted, the relation between Moral Principles I and II is critical. Because it is impossible to balance costs to the individual against uncertain gains to the science and to society, the imposition of any appreciable cost, risk, or harm from participation in research increases the ethical priority for obtaining the participant's autonomous informed consent or its equivalent from the participant's appropriately designated advocate or representative. Special considerations that apply when a scientifically required research design is incompatible with fully informed consent (as in the case of research involving placebo controls or deceptive instructions) are discussed in chapter 4.

A further complication in research concerns possible costs or harm to groups or categories of people or to social institutions. The question arises about whether official or unofficial representatives can or should give or withhold consent on behalf of such collective entities. Although there is little consensus on this issue, sensitivity to it is ethically desirable. Again, it is recommended that researchers seek consultation when making decisions about research risks.

Moral Principle III. Justice

The principle of justice states an ideal for research that is unlikely to be fully achieved in actual human societies that are never fully just. In the APA code, it relates most closely to Ethical Principle F, Social Responsibility.

Considerations of *distributive justice* (the proper distribution of benefits and burdens) arose saliently in medical research, in which risky new procedures were traditionally tried on ward patients, with benefits reaped largely by patients in private care. Threats to justice in research often arise from the almost inherent power differential between experimenter and research participant. For example, in some field studies, participants could be those who are weak and marginal rather than those who are socially and politically powerful and who thus can more readily guard their own interests. Members of ethnic minority groups may be especially vulnerable and likewise find their special concerns neglected. Traditional assumptions about gender have led to the underinclusion of women and their concerns in research. Such power differentials necessitate safeguards against exploitation, lack of representation or under-representation in scientific studies.

Concerns with *procedural justice* (the adequacy of procedures to ensure fairness) are relevant at every stage of the research process. For example, appropriate procedures need to be established in advance of the
research to ensure that research assistants and participants alike have
adequate access to mechanisms to address their possible concerns about
the research (e.g., issues relating to co-authorship by the research assistant or the adequacy of compensation offered to the participants).

Moral Principle IV. Trust

Researchers establish and maintain a relationship of trust with the participants in their research. Participation is based on explicit agreement
about what the participant will experience and its consequences and about
the researcher's obligations—for example, with respect to confidentiality.
Such agreements anticipate relevant exceptions such as legally imposed
exceptions to confidentiality.

This principle is closely related to Ethical Principle 1, Respect for Persons and Their Autonomy of the Belmont Report, and to Ethical Principle
C of the APA code, Professional and Scientific Responsibility. Ethical concerns arise when informing the prospective participant of the purpose of
the research or the details of the procedure when such disclosure compromises the validity of the research. Considerations involved in resolving
such conflicts are discussed in chapter 4.

The relationship of trust between experimenter and participant ought
to be reciprocal. In contemporary society, unfortunately, there is widespread mistrust of science and of public institutions, which fosters an unfavorable climate for the support and conduct of research. Overcoming
initial distrust is a frequent problem in the planning and conduct of research. Researchers therefore should exercise great care to avoid giving
occasion for increase in public distrust of behavioral and social research.

Moral Principle Versus Fidelity and Scientific Integrity

The researcher is committed to the discovery and promulgation of truth.
Recent criticism of "positivist" scientific epistemology that has challenged
the objective status of scientific truth in no way relieves researchers from
the obligation to do good science as that is understood in the research
community. Scientific integrity—truthfulness—is not open to compromise.
This principle corresponds to APA Ethical Principle B, Integrity.

Resolving Ethical Conflicts

Most research raises the potential for ethical conflicts (see chapter 9). The
chapters that follow include examples of ethical problems encountered in
the course of research and should help the prospective researcher under-

stand his or her responsibilities to science, society, students, and the research participants.

The approval of a research proposal by an IRB does not absolve the researcher from this ethical responsibility. IRBs differ in their composition, disciplinary expertise, institutional context, and interpretation of federal regulations. It may become part of the researcher's role to educate the IRB to relevant ethical considerations. Conversely, the IRB should alert researchers to ethical problems in their proposed research, and federal regulations require the researcher to defer to the IRB in matters of dispute.

In making ethical decisions about research, researchers should take into account the probable self-serving bias that can lead them to overestimate the scientific value of a proposed study and underestimate its ethical liabilities. Consultation with others less vulnerable to this bias, such as with colleagues experienced in the research area, is essential in compensating for it.

Conclusion

Five widely accepted general moral principles underlying the ethical conduct of research with human participants have been introduced to provide the basis for the more detailed guidance provided throughout this volume. Knowledge of these moral principles and consideration of the guidance provided here and in later chapters is important to researchers because merely following the requirements of law, federal regulators, and IRBs does not absolve the researcher from personal responsibility for resolving possible ethical conflicts that may arise in the conduct of their work. This volume is intended to facilitate ethical research practice by sensitizing researchers to the ethical issues encountered in contemporary psychological research with human participants. Finally, because the maintenance of high ethical standards is the shared responsibility of the research community, researchers typically communicate the substance of these principles' guidance through their roles as instructors, mentors, supervisors, reviewers, IRB members, and colleagues.

References

American Psychological Association. (1982). *Ethical principles in the conduct of research with human participants*. Washington, DC: Author.

American Psychological Association. (1992). Ethical principles of psychologists and code of conduct. *American Psychologist, 47*, 1597–1611.

American Psychological Association. (1996). *Guidelines for ethical conduct in the care and use of animals*. Washington, DC: Author.

Beauchamp, T. L., & Childress, J. F. (1989). *Principles of biomedical ethics*. New York: Oxford University Press.

Bersoff, D. N., & Koeppl, P. M. (1993). The relation between ethical codes and moral principles. *Ethics and Behavior, 3*, 345–357.

Office for Protection From Research Risks, Protection of Human Subjects. National Commission for the Protection of Human Subjects of Biomedical and Behavioral Research. (1979). *The Belmont Report: Ethical principles and guidelines for the protection of human subjects of research* (GPO 887-809). Washington, DC: U.S. Government Printing Office.

Office for Protection From Research Risks, Protection of Human Subjects. (1991, June 18). Protection of human subjects: Title 45, Code of Federal Regulations, Part 46 (GPO 1992 0-307-551). *OPRR Reports*, pp. 4–17.

Part I

Ethical Concerns Across the Research Process

2

Planning Research: Basic Ethical Decision-Making

Joan E. Sieber

The ethics of research with human participants deals with all entities involved in the research endeavor: the scientist, the research assistants, the institution where the research is conducted, the participants, and their community. It involves applying all of the principles discussed in chapter 1 in

- planning that maximizes such outcomes as respectful treatment of research participants, integrity of science, and benefit to all stakeholders (e.g., research participants, the community, researchers, the research institution, the funding sponsor, and society at large)
- planning that facilitates detection, understanding, and resolution of unanticipated problems.

Researchers can avoid many difficulties by integrating ethical considerations with scientific and practical considerations at the outset of the research planning. Negative consequences may result from failure to consider the social structures and relationships affected by the research, failure to remove avoidable risks, and failure to ensure respectful treatment and beneficial outcomes. This chapter emphasizes ethical elements of research planning and recognizes that ethical problem solving is an integral part of the larger, and often highly ambiguous, puzzle to be solved in the research process.

Research planning often begins with an inchoate but beneficent goal —to create useful knowledge about a specified topic via scientific means. The researcher then chooses tools for crafting a sound research approach. Flexibility and tolerance of ambiguity are important attributes at this stage of planning. The ethical problems inherent in a research plan—and possible solutions to those problems—may be obscure and subject to multiple interpretations. The realities of human nature and society often present the researcher with practical constraints and frustrating ambiguities. Researchers who are inflexibly wedded to a particular research design may be severely handicapped in designing a research plan that is scientifically and ethically sound.

Ethical planning in research typically involves a series of related decisions, in which one first identifies the general nature of the intended research and the ethical issues it is likely to raise. The researcher then considers plausible alternative specifications of the target research population, the research setting, the means of gaining access to research participants, the recruitment and screening, design and procedure scenarios and risks and benefits likely to be associated with each, the desirable kinds of communication with stakeholders in the research, training, and supervision of research assistants, and so on. This chapter introduces the major elements of this decision-making process. It reviews basic ethical and methodological issues likely to arise during the planning phase of the research process. The chapter goes on to consider examples of some plausible alternative research plans that would satisfy the rigors of both science and ethics, and reviews risks and social sensitivities likely to arise from research. Risks include those to research participants, the community, researchers, the research institution, the funding source, and society at large. Sensitivity to the vulnerabilities of these various stakeholders, in turn, helps produce a clearer understanding of how to benefit each. The chapter then considers what benefits can be created for research participants and other stakeholders in the research, and it considers whom to consult (e.g., colleagues, research administrators, representatives of the target population) when ethical questions remain. Finally, the chapter briefly reviews the kinds of specific agreements that need to be formulated at the outset, such as the informed consent statement, the protocol that is to be submitted to the institutional review board (IRB), agreements concerning authorship, publication rights and ownership of data, data-sharing agreements, and funding and administration of the project.

Researchers may find that it is sometimes difficult to follow one ethical directive without violating another; in such situations, the goal is to design the best feasible solution.

Assess Risk

Much behavioral and social research entails no or minimal risk. Yet, risk and safety are useful probabilistic concepts because they remind us that there may be some possibility of danger in our research and that to act without recognizing or being concerned about risk is problematic. For example, research on domestic violence cannot be guaranteed risk free for the participants, their families, or the researchers. In fact, there may be legal requirements to report child abuse that would preclude promising confidentiality in such studies. Nor is any research necessarily acceptable to all members of that research population, their community, or society at large. As with recent studies of the high-risk sexual behavior of adolescents, political and religious controversies often arise as to the value of the research and its effects on the public interest. Indeed, if research were limited to risk-free or uncontroversial projects, much serious research could not be undertaken. Thus, it is important that potential sources of risk be identified and that all feasible steps be taken to minimize risk and maximize acceptability.

Concerns about risk can affect choice of methods, research participants, recruitment procedures, research setting, and even the theoretical framework and hypotheses. Consider the example of designing a study to examine lifespan differences in complex cognition. The difficulty and duration of required performance tasks would be important considerations in selecting procedures to use with elderly participants. The screening procedures used when recruiting participants should ensure that reasonably healthy and cognitively intact participants are selected, to avoid the increased risk involved when dealing with frail or cognitively impaired elderly people. It also may be advisable to test the older participants in a setting close to their residence rather than in a university laboratory that is convenient for the experimenter but located far from the participants' homes. If testing certain hypotheses would place complex physical demands on the participants, given the increased risk inherent in using elderly participants in such studies, the researcher might choose either to modify the research design or not to test those particular hypotheses.

It is important to consider risk from various perspectives: for example, the researcher's own scientific perspective, the research participant's perspective, that of society, and perhaps that of other stakeholders as well. Risk here is less in the research topic and more in the social context of the research (Lee & Renzetti, 1993a). There are many types of risk, such as

- physical risk of injury or illness
- psychological risk, such as boredom, depression, altered self-concept, increased anxiety, or loss of confidence in others
- social risk, such as loss of important social opportunities or relationships
- economic risk, such as loss of opportunity for a job interview or opportunity to earn money
- legal risk, such as risk of being arrested or of having one's data subpoenaed.

These kinds of risk may arise in conjunction with three factors: (a) aspects of the research process, (b) particular vulnerabilities of the research participants, and (c) failure of the researcher to use appropriate risk reduction strategies. For example, some individuals may be at risk because of special characteristics (e.g., allergies, phobias, low self-esteem). Some may be at risk because of subjective factors (e.g., the research may cause them to have fears that are false but consequential nevertheless). (Chapter 6 discusses the relationship between risk and demographic characteristics of participants.) Some are at risk because the researcher failed to consider many risk reduction strategies in designing research, including strategies to ensure privacy and confidentiality, increase personal safety or well-being, ensure the validity of the research, respect autonomy, protect the interests of community leaders and others associated with the research, and ensure proper data management and use. For more detailed discussions of risk and risk assessment, see Sieber (1992).

Assess the Potential for Disrespecting or Harming Persons

Persons connected with the research may include the research participants themselves, persons who provide access to research participants, community members, and the research staff. Researchers should carefully examine how people might perceive the research and what might be in people's best interests in regard to it. The use of potential participants themselves to assess research risks is especially important when the researcher is studying persons from a demographic segment that differs from that of the researcher (e.g., different age, gender, sexual orientation, socioeconomic class, geographic location, ethnicity, and so on). Dialogue with participants from within that demographic segment might help identify potential risks that would not otherwise be considered had one consulted only with the research staff or university resources.

Research may involve significant psychological costs to research participants, such as guilt, shame, fear, or embarrassment, to which the researcher may not be sensitive. Research participants should have ample opportunity throughout the research process to withdraw so that they can protect themselves against such costs. Research participation may be psychologically neutral for some participants but highly threatening for others for reasons not apparent to the researcher. For example,

> A female student had moved, changed colleges, and taken an unlisted telephone number to escape an unbalanced ex-lover who stalked her. At her new college, she agreed to participate in an interview as part of a course requirement but later discovered that the interview contained questions about stalking that disturbed her. She terminated the interview and told her professor that she could not continue.

Research must be designed so that the participant feels completely free to terminate participation at any time and for any reason. Experimenters and research assistants need to be aware of the importance of the participant's freedom to end participation as a protection against increased risk.

Identify Possible Benefits to Participants and Others

Ethically, researchers are concerned with doing good or at least doing no harm. Scientific knowledge is a most appropriate benefit to give in return for research participation, but the results of the research are unlikely to be available immediately. Therefore, benefits of a more immediate nature should be offered. For example, the quality of the relationship between researcher and participant—the care, cultural sensitivity, rapport, communication, consideration, and courtesy with which participants are treated—is important. Benefits might also include referral to local services, providing relevant related information such as an annotated bibliography, money, food, medical or mental health services, and so on. Information and referrals should be offered without the implication that the participant is ignorant or needy.

Benefits to the community that is the site of the research might include developing networks and resources, finding a clearer definition of problems to be solved, developing new methods and approaches to solving problems, creating an opportunity for favorable media attention, and discovering an opportunity to continue the research relationship.

Much psychological research using human participants involves undergraduate students taking introductory psychology classes. A clear benefit of research participation for these students is that it can provide insight into the research process, depending on the quality of the post-study debriefing that describes the research and explains how psychological research is conducted.

Assess Design Elements

Considering Alternative Hypotheses

During the planning process, alternative hypotheses should be considered. The failure to consider alternative hypotheses can lead to serious violations of the principles underlying ethical research. An instructive example of scientists who failed to do this occurred during the 1920s. Distinguished scientists (psychologists and geneticists among them) speculated that Jewish, Russian, Italian, and Polish immigrants were mentally incompetent and would introduce a criminal element into American society. Intelligence tests administered in English to non-native speakers "proved" the theory about mental incompetence, and IQ tests to persons in prison "proved" that low-IQ persons are criminals (reported in Doris, 1982). Clearly, the investigators failed to consider the alternative hypothesis that it was skill in English as a second language rather than immigrant status that produced the correlational differences.

Choosing the Target Population

Sometimes the populations about whom knowledge is most needed are also the most difficult to reach because of cultural or language barriers or their unwillingness or inability to participate. Often, a researcher achieves access to populations that are difficult to reach only after much related community outreach activity and careful building of relationships with community leaders.

When studying elusive populations (e.g., people who abuse drugs, runaway children, victims of domestic violence) for which there is no sample frame or no ready access to all of the relevant subgroups (e.g., ethnic, linguistic), random sampling is impossible. The limits of generalization and possible confounding should be carefully evaluated beforehand to decide whether or how best to design the research. Ethical issues, such as difficulties in obtaining consent (see chapter 4) or assuring privacy and confidentiality (see chapter 5), as well as methodological issues, such as identifying or securing access to the appropriate population, may dictate modification of the original design.

Obtaining Consent for the Research

Obtaining the consent of potential research participants or others who hold the legal right to give permission or the moral right to assent can have an important impact on the conduct of the research. For example, researchers intending to study children or others who lack the competence or legal standing to consent to participation will need to obtain permission from those individuals or entities who are legally entitled to provide it (see chapter 4). In an industrial setting, consent may involve agreement by both the research participants and their employer or by just the employer in cases in which research participation is contractually a condition of employment. Where dual consent is required, researchers should be alert to the possibility of participants feeling pressured or coerced into consenting. Such a result may violate the principle of autonomy (see chapter 3).

Choosing Participant Identifiers

Data may be subpoenaed, accessed by a computer hacker, viewed by unauthorized persons, and so on. In addition, data matrices that are ostensibly anonymous may, in fact, contain information that permits *deductive disclosure*. That is, persons who know certain facts about a participant (such as his or her zip code, profession, or ethnicity) may be able to use that information to deduce damaging or private information about that participant. Breaches of confidentiality can cause many forms of harm to research participants, their community, the researchers, and others. Thus, procedures for rendering data anonymous or for ensuring confidentiality of data are an important element of ethical planning (see chapter 5).

Choosing Qualitative Versus Quantitative Methods

Research participants who are unwilling to submit to formal structured methods, controlled testing, or observation may be pleased to participate in a study using less intrusive and more qualitative methods such as the case study, interview, or focus group. For example, certain populations may have concerns about privacy, trust, or saving face that cause them to resist research participation unless it is on their terms. If the researcher conducts the research in a highly structured or directive way (e.g., administers a structured interview or questionnaire), some populations will not respond candidly or at all. In a similar way, many organizations will not permit study of organizational functioning except on the organization's terms. The researcher should be open to use of alternative methods such as ethnography or case study analyses. It is the researcher's responsibility to ensure that, regardless of the scientific method selected, valid and reliable information can be gained from the research. If individual or organizational mandates preclude gaining useful information, even when a variety of methodologies are considered, the value of the research must be questioned by the researcher. Potential participants from the targeted populations may be a valuable source of advice in the planning stage of research. They can provide important information about the concerns of the target populations and thus enable the researcher to select methods that will maximize research participation and minimize potential risks particular to that population.

Choosing Experimental Versus Epidemiological or Quasi-Experimental Approaches

It is unethical to randomly assign participants to experimental treatments that have a presumably harmful, long-term effect (e.g., the long-term effect on intelligence of lead in drinking water, or of certain diets on health). An epidemiological or quasi-experimental design, in which the treatment effect is not experimentally induced, may be ethically required.

Assessing Validity

An invalid research design is not only scientifically inappropriate, but can also violate ethical norms, specifically fidelity to science. Research that satisfies criteria for validity, however, may be dangerous, unfeasible, or even impossible to conduct. For example, valid manipulations of levels of aggression in field settings may not be practically, safely, or ethically conducted. Another example, how would one manipulate variables and protect research participants in a study of gang conflicts? Laboratory analogs are sometimes acceptable, but they can also be problematic because they lack external validity.

In other cases, there is no substitute for studying behavior in the natural setting, where problems of sampling and generalizability may be unresolvable and should simply be minimized to the degree possible and acknowledged in the reporting of the research. For example, a community-based study of effects of various prevention programs on teenage driving under the influence of alcohol (a) cannot assume that all extraneous variables are held constant or that there is no contamination between different experimental groups, (b) may not involve a pure control group because people cannot ethically be discouraged from using available prevention strategies on their own, and (c) cannot randomly sample from an adequate sample frame because none exists for teenagers who abuse alcohol (as is the case with any groups engaged in illegal or stigmatized behavior).

After considering the variety of research methods available to the researcher, and after designing the best research possible under the existing constraints, the researcher needs to then consider whether the project is worth doing or whether too much has been compromised. When design compromises need to be made, the principle of fidelity to science underscores the importance of stating the limitations of the research to research consumers.

Choosing Control-Group Conditions

The researcher should learn the probable effects of a proposed treatment and nontreatment from the literature and from specialists in the field. If there is genuine uncertainty about the effectiveness of the treatment, a control group is most often ethically and scientifically required to determine treatment effects. But the use of control groups can pose risks in certain circumstances. For example, in clinical studies, the control-group condition that is provided no treatment or a placebo may actually pose a risk when treatment with known effectiveness is available. In those cases, the researcher should consider using the modified control condition in which participants are given a treatment of known effectiveness rather than no treatment.

Placebos are often significant. It is important to consider study designs for which placebo conditions are *not* nontreatment or do-nothing conditions, but rather are treatment conditions that lack the essential characteristics assumed to underlie the proposed treatment effects.

Once an intervention is under way, frequent monitoring of outcomes can enable the researcher to avoid unnecessary risks of harm. For example, a purportedly valuable treatment may produce worse effects than no treatment (e.g., Canner, Berge, & Klint, 1973). Monitoring findings allows the researcher to remove the harmful intervention, quickly and ethically. Monitoring also may allow researchers to identify highly effective treatments before the planned research would have ended. Such data can justify terminating the research and providing all people with the beneficial treatment. For a more detailed examination of control-group considerations, monitoring, and alternative research designs, see Kazdin (1998) and Fisher, Hoagwood, and Jensen (1996).

Assessing Research Settings

Each kind of research setting brings with it various potential risks as well as benefits. Research conducted in an institutional setting (such as a school, hospital, workplace, or church) may pose special problems. For example,

- Members may feel coerced by the institution to participate.
- Participants may give the responses that they wish the institu-

tional gatekeepers to hear (rather than candid responses) if they do not believe the researcher's promises of confidentiality.

- Institutional gatekeepers may impose rigorous or unacceptable demands on the researcher with the intention of protecting themselves or their members. At the outset of planning, the researcher should become familiar with the institution's approval requirements and processes. In some cases, the institutional requirements are those of self-appointed gatekeepers (e.g., a drug dealer who provides a social psychologist access to a "shooting gallery" to interview drug addicts) who may have requirements every bit as exacting as those of formal gatekeepers (e.g., the research administrators and IRB of a hospital's drug abuse clinic).

- The researcher may disturb the institution's legitimate relationship with its members. For example, a researcher who is permitted to interview outpatients at a clinic would not want to harm the clinic's reputation for respecting and protecting the privacy of its patients. However, after entering into confidentiality agreements with participants, the researcher may later find himself or herself morally or legally bound to report to the participant institutional practices that might breach the promised confidentiality (see chapter 5).

- The institution may require ownership and control of the data, and it may conduct internal review and editing of any report that results from the research. Any such arrangement should be evaluated at the outset for its ethical implications.

Research conducted in a field setting (e.g., home or family, community or street) may invade privacy and pose special ethical risks. Whether researching families at home, homeless people, prostitutes, or members of a baseball team, the researcher is entering a group network in which people are curious about one another and can affect one another's lives. For example,

- Group members may learn information that the participant intended only for the researcher.
- Private information may be revealed about persons who did not agree to participate in the research.
- The researcher may learn about behavior such as child abuse, which he or she may be required by law to report.
- The researcher may be subject to evolving freedom-of-information laws that legally compromise the confidentiality of the participant from the other members of the group. Participants may need special assurances from the research institution or from trusted people in their own community that the researcher is bona fide and trustworthy.
- The safety of the individuals conducting the research may be at risk. Appropriate precautions should be developed before the re-

search begins (e.g., working in pairs; having a predetermined route known to the principal investigator; interviewing homeless people only in public places such as in a shelter or a restaurant, with prior permission of the owner).

Assessing Implications of Funding

It is important to determine whether funding restrictions or requirements may negatively affect the validity or ethicality of the research. For example, proprietary research (e.g., supported by a private sponsor who has a vested interest in the findings) may result in suppression of unfavorable results or misrepresentation of results. These issues of control and ownership of data and publication rights are discussed at length in chapter 7. In addition, inadequate funding or resources may lead to shortcuts that could compromise the validity or safety of the research.

Planning Dissemination of Research Findings

Research on sensitive issues is frequently open to misinterpretation by those who see political opportunities in denigrating both social science and the populations it seeks to serve (Sieber, 1993). The misinterpretation may then be recycled and amplified by irresponsible reporting in the popular media. It is sometimes difficult for researchers to predict which research will evoke such sensitivities. Some areas likely to be threatening or socially sensitive are

- research that intrudes into private or personal aspects of lives
- studies concerned with deviance and social control
- research involving political or religious topics
- research that touches on the vested interests of powerful persons.

Socially sensitive research can offend or upset persons not connected directly with the study. Hence, researchers need to give careful consideration to the way that they interpret and report findings. Yet, even the most thoughtful presentations of the research can backfire. For example, consider the following abstract from a study of adolescent drug use reported in the literature:

> The relation between psychological characteristics and drug use was investigated in subjects studied longitudinally from preschool through age 18. Adolescents who had engaged in some drug experimentation (primarily with marijuana) were the best adjusted in the sample. Adolescents who used drugs frequently were maladjusted, showing a distinct personality syndrome marked by interpersonal alienation, poor impulse control, and manifest emotional distress. Adolescents who, by age 18, had never experimented with any drug were relatively anxious, emotionally constricted, and lacking in social skills.

> Psychological differences between frequent drug users, experimenters, and abstainers could be traced to the earliest years of childhood and related to the quality of parenting received. The findings indicate that (a) problem drug use is a symptom, not a cause, of personal and social maladjustment, and (b) the meaning of drug use can be understood only in the context of an individual's personality structure and developmental history. It is suggested that current efforts at drug prevention are misguided to the extent that they focus on symptoms, rather than on the psychological syndrome underlying drug use. (Shedler & Block, 1990, p. 612)

Shedler and Block closed their article with the following admonition:

> In presenting research on a topic as emotionally charged as drug use, there is always the danger that findings may be misinterpreted or misrepresented. Specifically, we are concerned that some segments of the popular media may misrepresent our findings as indicating that drug use might somehow improve an adolescent's psychological health. Although the incorrectness of such an interpretation should be obvious to anyone who has actually read this article, our concern about media misrepresentation requires us to state categorically that our findings do not support such a view, nor should anything we have said remotely encourage such an interpretation. (p. 628)

Despite this admonition, headlines in the *San Francisco Chronicle* read "Furor Over Report on Teenage Drug Use: Researchers Said Those Who Experimented Were Healthier Than Abstainers or Abusers" (1990, p. A-10). The *Chronicle* went on to report that drug counselors were outraged and made to feel foolish. "What does this do to the kids who made a commitment to be abstinent? Now they're being told they're a bunch of dorks and geeks," said Dr. Gary Levine, director of Marin General Hospital's adolescent recovery center. "You can imagine how much more peer pressure is going to be put on them." Drug counselors were quoted as saying that Shedler and Block had harmed society by broadcasting their destructive ideas.

Certainly, researchers should not bow to the threats of those who wish to prevent valuable scientific activity, nor should they ignore threats by those who have the power to do harm. Researchers who recognize that their intended research may arouse sensitivities might carefully consider the ways that their work can be misrepresented and take appropriate steps to minimize possible harm. It may also be useful to seek advice from sources, such as a department chair, colleagues, dean, legal counsel, and IRB. Although public attack or misrepresentation of a researcher's work cannot be prevented, steps can be taken to anticipate and minimize harm to research participants, members of the community, the researcher and institution, and society.

Some of society's most pressing problems require sensitive research. Ignoring the ethical or methodological challenges of researching sensitive topics is irresponsible, as is avoidance of such topics of research. Rather, the researcher who studies sensitive topics needs to have effective skills for communicating findings to research participants, their community, elected officials, the media, and other special-interest groups. There is now an emerging literature on the conduct of socially sensitive research (e.g., Lee & Renzetti, 1993b, 1993c).

Seeking Consultation

In this chapter, emphasis has been placed on the development of alternative perspectives for resolving scientific and ethical problems that arise in research. Seeking ethical consultation may help develop such perspectives and answer questions such as "What aspects of the research are likely to have a real or perceived positive or negative impact on participants, their communities, or other stakeholders?" Sometimes it is difficult for the researcher alone to recognize the full ethical implications of his or her work without consultation. For example, risks and benefits can be evaluated from the perspective of the research participants, the target population, their community, the research institution, and society. Consultation with potential participants from the target population to be studied, the literature, the IRB, and knowledgeable colleagues can be particularly helpful in identifying and understanding these diverse perspectives. The preparation of the IRB protocol can be especially helpful in promoting a systematic review of ethical concerns.

Focus groups or ethnographic studies of members of the target population can help the researcher identify the perceptions and risks relevant to that population. Surrogate research participants may be introduced to the research procedure and asked to evaluate it with respect to their perception of risk, their overall evaluation of the procedure, and the kinds of benefits that they would like to receive for participating.

Unfortunately, however, consultation may result in an array of contradictory and sometimes impractical advice. Not all advice can necessarily be followed, of course, but there are many advantages to listening to the views of diverse stakeholders and advisors. For example, some advice will provide vital ideas for improving the research. Some will warn of potential public misunderstanding of the research—misunderstandings that are at least partially correctable via any information released about the project. And some will reveal the informal social networks among participants, their community, or elsewhere, and suggest ways to communicate effectively via that network.

Developing and Reviewing Agreements

Research projects may involve many agreements with the various stakeholders in the research. These agreements can raise ethical concerns regarding autonomy and fidelity to science. The researcher needs to keep track of the promises that are made and understand their ramifications.

Typically, there are agreements with the gatekeepers and administrators who enable the research to be conducted and with students who are involved as research assistants. There are also agreements concerning authorship, ownership of the data, and publication rights (see chapter 7). If the research is to be funded, the research proposal in some cases will contain a set of promises of work to be done or products to be delivered. Some funding agencies now require, as a condition of funding, that the investigator be willing to document and share the data that are gathered. These conditions should be carefully examined to determine what documentation and record keeping is required and to ensure that the agreement to share data can be fulfilled. When risks of sharing anonymous data can be identified, the informed consent agreement should mention that the anonymous data may be shared with other qualified scientists (see chapter 7).

Informal agreements regarding data sharing between an individual or an entity that has a data set and a researcher who wants to analyze those data are becoming increasingly common. It is advisable to have agreements about shared data formally approved by the IRBs of the cooperating institutions (Sieber, 1989). Informal agreements often lead to misunderstanding, misgivings, failure to provide needed clarification about the data, withdrawal of the privilege of using the data or publishing the results, and violation of participants' autonomy. Formal agreements typically include agreement not to share the data with a third party without permission of the donor, clarification of how the data will be used, agreement by the donor to provide adequate documentation and to provide (for an appropriate consulting fee) any advice or assistance needed by the secondary analyst, and agreement between donor and recipient on how confidentiality is to be ensured and deductive disclosure is to be prevented. The agreement should state what rights of review the data donor may have prior to publication of the secondary analysis.

Conclusion

Each research context presents new potential ethical conflicts, challenges, and opportunities to create innovative solutions. Being ethical in the way one conducts research is somewhat like being ethical in everyday life. There is no prescription—no simple rule—that suffices. Rather, being ethical is part of a process of intelligent and sensitive planning, trying, and evaluating, in which the researcher seeks to maximize good outcomes and minimize risk or harm. In many situations, this process is quite a challenge because there may be no way to pursue a given praiseworthy objective without some risk. Conventional assumptions and procedures may fail to take account of particular contexts and interests of particular stakeholders. An ethical research product, however, may be obtained through careful assessment of possible risks and benefits from the perspective of the stakeholders and through the development of procedures and methods that give these factors due consideration.

References

Canner, P. L., Berge, K. G., & Klint, C. R. (1973). *The coronary drug project* [Monograph 38]. New York: American Heart Association.

Doris, J. (1982). Social science and advocacy. *American Behavioral Scientist, 26,* 199–234.

Fisher, C. B., Hoagwood, K., & Jensen, P. S. (1996). Casebook on ethical issues in research with children and adolescents with mental disorders. In K. Hoagwood, P. S. Jensen, & C. B. Fisher (Eds.), *Ethical issues in mental health research with children and adolescents* (pp.133–266). Mahway, NJ: Erlbaum.

"Furor over report on teenager drug use." (1990, May 14). *San Francisco Chronicle,* p. A-10.

Kazdin, A. E. (1998). *Research design in clinical psychology.* New York: Allyn & Bacon.

Lee, R. M., & Renzetti, C. M. (1993a). Overview and introduction. In R. M. Lee & C. M Renzetti (Eds.), *Researching sensitive topics* (pp. 1–13). Newbury Park, CA: Sage Publications.

Lee, R. M., & Renzetti, C. M. (Eds.). (1993b). *Researching sensitive topics.* Newbury Park, CA: Sage Publications.

Lee, R. M., & Renzetti, C. M. (1993c). *Socially sensitive research.* Newbury Park, CA: Sage Publications.

Shedler, J., & Block, J. (1990). Adolescent drug use and psychological health: A longitudinal study. *American Psychologist, 45*(5), 612–630.

Sieber, J. E. (1989). Sharing scientific data I: New problems for IRBs to solve. *IRB: A Review of Human Subjects Research, 11*(6), 4–7.

Sieber, J. E. (1992). *Planning ethically responsible research: A guide for students and Internal Review Boards.* Newbury Park, CA: Sage Publications.

Sieber, J. E. (1993). The ethics and politics of sensitive research. In R. M. Lee & C. M. Renzetti (Eds.), *Researching sensitive topics* (pp. 14–26). Newbury Park, CA: Sage Publications.

3

Recruitment of Research Participants

Diane Scott-Jones

Researchers have ethical responsibilities in the recruitment of research participants. Throughout the recruitment process, researchers should be honest and forthright about the goals and requirements of the research and should respect the rights of individuals to decline to participate in the research. Researchers should not use coercive recruitment strategies and should not exploit individuals or social groups. Potential participants should be screened carefully to exclude those who might be harmed by their participation. Individuals representing a broad range of various social categories, such as ethnicity, socioeconomic status, and gender, should be recruited unless there is a compelling scientific or practical justification for a restricted or homogeneous sample.

Despite widespread agreement on the desirability of the above-noted goals, decisions regarding the ethical recruitment of research participants can be difficult. Researchers may experience competing demands. Their goal of recruiting a representative sample may conflict with participants' rights to decide whether to participate. Voluntary participation, however, is a hallmark of ethical research. Researchers need to strike a balance between concern for scientific fidelity and regard for the autonomy of potential participants.

In addition to the principle of autonomy and respect for persons, researchers are guided by the principle of beneficence in their efforts to screen carefully and exclude those who might be harmed by participation. Beneficence requires that researchers minimize possible harms and maximize possible benefits from research. The principle of justice underlies the researchers' obligation to recruit broadly, as long as the attempt at broad recruitment does not undermine the scientific integrity of the study. Justice requires that the benefits as well as the burdens of research be shared equally among various segments of the general population.

This chapter reviews aspects of the process of recruiting research participants and discusses ethical considerations that may arise as researchers recruit participants for their studies. Special attention is given to coercion, exploitation, and vulnerable populations.

Advertising

The researchers' initial contact with potential participants may be through advertisements for the research project. The advertisement may take several forms such as letters; newspaper advertisements; presentations to groups; or notices posted in public areas at schools, universities, institutions, or doctors' offices. These forms of outreach to potential participants should provide clear preliminary information about the research. Through this initial contact, the researcher can begin to establish an open line of communication between the research staff and research participants.

The advertisement ought to make clear that responding at this point does not constitute agreement to participate in the research. Potential participants who respond to an advertisement by calling or by providing their names and telephone numbers have not given consent. The purpose of contact during this phase of the research project is to give potential participants additional information so they can make informed decisions about participation. In research with children, the advertising is directed to parents. The researcher should provide clear information about procedures that the child will experience.

Researchers should submit their advertising plans, along with copies of any written materials to be used, as part of their application to the institutional review board (IRB). Usually the advertisement includes the name and address of the researcher, purpose of the research, eligibility criteria, incentives for participation, time and effort required for participation, location of the project, and name of the contact person.

Recruiting Through Archival Databases or Secondary Sources

In some cases, secondary analysis of existing datasets does not involve identification of the participants and thus does not constitute research with human participants. In other cases, however, ethical problems can arise when participants are recruited through archived data or secondary sources. For example, a researcher may want to identify potential participants by reviewing medical records or other documents that are not public. The privacy of individuals may be violated as these documents are reviewed. The research staff may see the records of many individuals not eligible for the study. Those eligible for the study may be offended to learn that a researcher obtained their names, addresses, telephone numbers, and other private information. These privacy concerns may be minimized, although not eliminated, by using automated record-keeping systems or by asking for consent for research at the time an individual enters the health care system. Another alternative is that persons with access to the data may ask individuals whether the researcher may contact them regarding participation in research. The researcher would contact only the individuals who respond affirmatively.

Offering Inducements for Participation

Researchers should not exploit potential participants' personal circumstances in order to recruit a research sample. When researchers offer inducements or compensation for participation, they must consider carefully the issues of coercion and exploitation. Because of the complexities surrounding issues of inducements, coercion, and exploitation, firm and simple standards cannot be established. Researchers should weigh these issues carefully and, if questions arise, seek the assistance of colleagues, IRBs, representatives of the community of participants, and other stakeholders. The inducements offered for research participation should be reviewed as part of the application to the IRB, to make sure potential participants are offered fair compensation but are not pressured to enroll in the study.

Coercion exists if individuals cannot refuse to participate in research, if refusal causes a substantial loss to the individual, or if individuals *believe* that participation is not truly voluntary. In addition, inducements that may be ethical in some circumstances can be coercive if the value of the inducement substantially diminishes the potential participant's freedom of choice. The provision of health care or psychotherapy, like money, may be an inducement that prevents potential participants from carefully evaluating the risks and potential benefits of participation. A person feeling in great need of some service such as psychotherapy might be willing to take greater risks and to sustain greater costs to obtain this help than would a person without such a felt need. Another example is research in which drugs are provided to individuals who abuse them. Although the drugs are given as an essential part of the study, the potential participants' desire for the drug may overshadow their consideration of the merits of the research and the appropriateness of their participation. Researchers need to exercise special caution in the recruitment process in such research.

Deciding whether a given inducement is excessive can be difficult. This decision may need to be based on considerations such as local standards, characteristics of the population, and magnitude of the potential harm of research participation. Potential participants must be free to decide whether a particular study has merit and whether their involvement in the study is appropriate. Their decisions must not be unduly constrained by concerns about personal losses and gains that are independent of the value and quality of the research.

Researchers also should be concerned about the costs of participation to individuals. Individual participants give their time to participate in research and may incur costs such as transportation to the research site. Researchers should consider compensating participants for such investments. Without some compensation, research participants may be exploited or may perceive themselves to be exploited by researchers. Participants may legitimately receive tangible rewards, such as money, as a fair payment for their participation in research. Participants also may be given personal help (such as discussing a personal health problem during an interview) or information (such as an explanation of the current state of knowledge in the field of study) as part of their compensation for participation. Finally, participants may perceive a personal benefit from helping to advance science or helping to solve a social problem (see also chapter 4).

Coercion might readily occur in some vulnerable populations, including prisoners, military personnel, patients, employees, children, and students. In these populations, those who participate in research may receive special benefits that are not available to nonparticipants. Individuals who do not participate may be penalized in some way or may be viewed less favorably by persons in positions of authority. In addition to the possibility of actual penalties for nonparticipation and rewards for participation, individuals in these populations may believe that participation is not genuinely voluntary. Individuals may believe that not participating will be held against them and that they will receive some special benefit from participating. Researchers studying these populations must strike a balance between active recruitment and explicit communication of the voluntary nature of participation.

Special provisions for prisoners (persons involuntarily confined in penal institutions) are described in the Code of Federal Regulations (Title 45, Part 46.301–306; Office for Protection from Research Risks, 1991). In research with prisoners, any possible advantages "when compared to the general living conditions, medical care, quality of food, amenities, and opportunity for earnings in prison" should not be of such a magnitude that the prisoners' "ability to weigh the risks of the research against the value of such advantages in the limited choice environment is impaired." Further, the recruitment strategy must be fair to all prisoners and "immune from arbitrary intervention by prison authorities or prisoners." Prisoners serving in control groups must be randomly selected from those prisoners having the characteristics needed for the research project. In addition, when recruiting prisoners for a study, the researcher must make clear that participation will have no effect on the possibility of parole.

In some special populations, a desirable safeguard is to have the researcher recruit only when there is no direct relationship with the potential participant. For example, physicians would not recruit their own patients, and professors would not recruit their own students. Potential participants might then be less likely to experience coercion that could result from recruitment by researchers who have authority over them or direct responsibility for their well-being. In addition, researchers must be sensitive to inducements that involve moral appeals, appeals to friendship, anticipated benefits to the potential participants' major reference groups, or the special needs of the researcher, because these appeals may be coercive for some participants.

Although providing children with rewards for participation is typically legitimate, researchers should not use the promise of rewards to arouse children's interest in participation prior to obtaining parental consent. The researchers' recruitment strategy should also take into account the requirement of soliciting assent, in addition to parental consent, from children who, because of their age, level of maturity, and psychological state, are capable of assenting (see chapter 4). For children who are wards of the state or another agency, an advocate is appointed who acts in the best interests of the child (45 CFR 46.609; see also chapter 4).

Researchers in most instances direct their recruitment strategies toward parents when children are the potential participants. In some contexts, however, the researchers' initial contact may be with the children themselves. In these instances, the researcher should take special care not to convey through words, tone of voice, or inducements that the requirement of parental consent is bypassed or diminished by appealing directly to the child. In many instances, the contact with the child is in a classroom at school. The researcher should not promote the idea that the study is part of the regular classroom activities or is an enhancement of regular activities.

The following example illustrates a recruitment strategy involving a minor and acceptable variation from the general expectation that recruitment strategies are directed toward parents and not children and that inducements are not offered to children prior to obtaining parental consent.

> In an attempt to increase response rate, a researcher planned to offer elementary school children a decorative pencil as a reward for returning a signed parental permission form. The researcher devised this strategy because the school did not give permission to mail forms directly to parents; instead, the school requested that forms be sent home with the children. The researcher emphasized that all children who returned a signed form would receive the pencil, including those children whose parents declined to participate as well as those whose parents agreed. At its initial review, the IRB objected to the pencil as an inducement, asserting that such a reward was coercive. On appeal, however, the IRB reversed its decision, acknowledging that the magnitude of this reward was modest and was unlikely to be coercive. In addition, the reward was given to children for returning the signed permission form, regardless of parents' decision to agree or decline to participate.

Using Student Participant Pools

Of the populations vulnerable to coercion and exploitation, student participant pools are a special concern. Students are widely used participants in university research because they provide convenient samples for researchers and greatly reduce the task of recruitment. Because students' receipt of passing grades in a course may be tied to research participation, the possibility of coercion or the perception of coercion requires careful consideration. The goals of the research requirement and its relationship to the pedagogical purposes of the course are critical in the ethical analysis. Participation in the research should have clear educational value for the student. The major justification for student participant pools is that being a participant in research helps students learn firsthand how research is conducted. Without some choice about participation, however, it is difficult to construe the student involvement as a voluntary act. Whether the research requirement is tied to the students' grade or provides extra credit toward the grade, students should be able to select from a variety of research projects. Students also should be provided research-related activities, such as reading and summarizing a journal article or attending a lecture on psychological research, as alternatives to research participation.

Concern for student autonomy also suggests that the course advertisement and course syllabus presented in class inform the students of the research requirement, the rationale for the requirement, and the alternative ways in which students can satisfy the requirement. Students would be aware of the research requirement before enrolling in a course. At the beginning of the course, students should be given details regarding the expectation of research participation along with the discussion of other course requirements. Student participants should be able to discontinue their participation at any point, without penalty. As in any research project, participation should be voluntary, even after involvement has begun. The student participant is not obligated to continue a procedure to completion; the student who wants to end participation should be allowed to choose one of the alternative activities to earn course credit.

Components of students' course grades cannot be determined solely by participation in research. The most easily justified position is that grades not be tied to research participation but to the completion of a research requirement that involves alternatives to serving as a participant in a study. If research participation is one of several options, such as reading and summarizing journal articles, the alternatives should not be more difficult or time-consuming than research participation. The alternatives offered should be equivalent to research participation in the effort required of the students and in educational value if these activities affect students' grades.

Screening

In recruiting, researchers should take care to eliminate potential participants who might be harmed psychologically or physically by the research. Researchers will need to address issues of confidentiality in acquiring information for screening (see chapter 5). Researchers should submit the basis for participant selection and specific exclusion and inclusion criteria as part of the application to the IRB for review and approval.

Recruiting a Representative Sample

The exclusion of various underrepresented groups, such as those defined by ethnic background, gender, age, sexual preference, or other social categories, has led to significant gaps in psychological knowledge. Exclusion is an ethical issue because these groups do not benefit from psychological research as much as do other groups. In addition, findings from studies using restricted samples may not be generalizable to those excluded from participation. In some instances, inappropriate generalization may result in harm to excluded groups.

In research sponsored by the National Institutes of Health (NIH), gender and ethnicity must be adequately represented in all studies with human participants unless there are compelling scientific or practical reasons for a restricted sample. NIH guidelines for including females and members of ethnic minority groups in research are presented in the *Federal Register* (NIH, 1994). Under these guidelines, researchers are expected to provide information about the inclusion of females and ethnic minorities and, if necessary, to provide a strong justification for their exclusion.

In some instances, a given study may not include both genders or a range of ethnic groups. Such exclusion may be appropriate in the particular study; collectively, however, such decisions lead to an imbalance in research in the field. It is this overall imbalance, rather than a single study, that clearly violates the principle of justice. Researchers have a responsibility to uphold the principle of justice, not only as they undertake their own research projects, but also in their other influential roles, as in the review of proposed research and in the editorial review process. In these latter roles, researchers influence the overall direction of research and should consider whether the benefits and costs of research are distributed equally across various social categories.

Outreach efforts in recruiting may be necessary to obtain samples that include women and members of ethnic minority groups. Researchers "are urged to develop appropriate and culturally sensitive outreach programs and activities commensurate with the goals of the study" (NIH, 1994, p. 14510). The NIH guidelines also encourage researchers to establish a relationship with the communities or populations of interest such that there is mutual benefit for the participants and researchers, to take care to minimize the possibility of coercion or undue influence in offering rewards during recruitment, and to address retention as well as recruitment in the outreach efforts.

Conclusion

Researchers should pay close attention to ethical issues when recruiting research participants. The principles of autonomy, respect for persons, beneficence, and justice undergird the thoughtful researcher's behavior in the recruitment process. The possibility of coercion, or even the appearance of coercion, should be considered when researchers seek the cooperation of potential participants. Researchers should avoid potentially coercive inducements to participate but, at the same time, should offer fair compensation for participants' time and costs, such as transportation to the research site. Some categories of participants are especially vulnerable to coercion and may be wary of research participation. Special provisions should be observed in the case of vulnerable groups such as college students who participate as part of course requirements, persons who are patients of the researcher, imprisoned persons, and persons with mental disabilities. Recruitment of children as research participants should be accomplished through the parents or others entitled to consent for a child. The researcher should not appeal to the child for participation prior to contacting the parents or guardians.

Unless there are strong scientific reasons for limited or specialized samples, recruitment should result in samples that represent both genders and the range of ethnic groups. Although an exclusive sample may be warranted in a particular study, collectively studies should provide information that benefits persons across a broad range of social categories. In the recruitment process, as in other aspects of research with human participants, researchers should seek the advice of their peers, IRBs, and stakeholders in the research. The researcher, however, remains responsible for the implementation of laws, professional standards, and ethical principles in the recruitment of participants.

References

National Institutes of Health. (1994). Guidelines on the inclusion of women and minorities as subjects in clinical research. *Federal Register, 59,* 14508–14513.

Office for Protection from Research Risks, Protection of Human Subjects. (1991, June 18). Protection of human subjects: Title 45, Code of Federal Regulations, Part 46 (GPO 1992 O-307-551). *OPRR Reports,* pp. 4–17.

4

Informed Consent

Marian W. Fischman

Psychologists should have concern for the rights, dignity, and welfare of their research participants. As a part of that concern, they should be careful to inform potential research participants about the studies for which they are volunteering. Except in a few instances in which consent is not required, informed consent is a formal process. Although such a formal process may have the reverse effect of raising suspicions of the participant, this formality is necessary to ensure that the participant is informed to the greatest extent possible and that, consequently, participation is voluntary.

Informed consent includes a clear statement of the purposes, procedures, risks, and benefits of the research project, as well as the obligations and commitments of both the participants and the researchers. The resulting explicit agreement is in most cases documented through the use of a written consent form, which should be clear, fair, and not exploitative. This chapter reviews the ethical and legal dimensions involved in informed consent, focusing on those elements required in the documentation of informed consent, the administration of this material, and the barriers to informed consent.

Ethical Obligation of Researchers

The ethical principle on which the requirement for informed consent is based is the principle of autonomy and respect for persons. This has been interpreted as including "at least two ethical convictions: first, that individuals should be treated as autonomous agents, and second, that persons with diminished autonomy are entitled to protection" (Office for Protection from Research Risks [OPRR], 1979, p. 4). Treating individuals as autonomous agents means that researchers do not interfere with their choices or encroach on their privacy unless the individuals agree that the researchers may do so. The researcher's obligation is to enhance the participants' capacity to be self-determining, insofar as that is possible. For cases in which individuals are not capable of self-determination, respect for such persons obliges us to protect them from harm.

It is clear that those individuals who are not fully autonomous should be protected from the potential harms associated with participation in a research protocol. However, those who are fully autonomous can make an informed decision only after being acquainted with any risks of research participation as well as the potential benefits of such participation. A researcher should design research protocols that minimize potential risks and maximize the benefits of research participation. However, participation in a research protocol generally carries with it burdens that can range from those that are inconvenient to those including psychological, physical, social, and economic risks. These can be at either the individual or the social level (Levine, 1986). It is incumbent on the researcher to inform all volunteers about the full range of such potential harms, including estimates of the likelihood, magnitude, and duration of the harm or the benefit. Potential benefits are often stated in terms of anticipated benefits to society, although there are also frequently benefits to be accrued at the organizational and individual levels (see chapters 2 and 3). It is not always possible to make a decision about the ethics of carrying out a research protocol based on weighing the potential benefits of that protocol against the potential harm related to participation, because all of the potential harms and benefits cannot be anticipated. This judgment is the responsibility of the researcher and should be made independently of the IRB reviewing that protocol.

Consent should be (a) voluntary, (b) informed, (c) and given by a competent individual. It is the responsibility of the researcher to guarantee that such consent has been obtained prior to allowing a volunteer to participate in a research protocol (see chapter 6 for other responsibilities to participants).

Legal Obligation of Researchers

In addition to a researcher's ethical obligation to inform potential volunteers for a research project, there is, under most conditions, a legal obligation for researchers carrying out research under federal funding (OPRR, 1991) to obtain a signed consent form documenting that each participant has provided informed consent prior to research participation, with some provisions for IRB waivers. There are situations in which documented consent is not required. "An IRB may waive the requirement for the researcher to obtain a signed consent form if . . . the only record linking the subject and the research would be the consent document and the principal risk would be potential harm resulting from a breach of confidentiality . . . or that the research presents no more than minimal risk of harm to subjects and involves no procedures for which written consent is normally required outside of the research context" (OPRR, 1991, 45 CFR 46.117(c), p. 10). Procedures deemed of minimal risk (e.g., questionnaires with no sensitive information being collected) do not require documentation of informed consent. It is, however, appropriate for researchers to provide a brief description of the procedures and purpose of the study for which they are inviting participation. It is important for researchers to keep in mind that a waiver of the need for a signed consent form does not mean that participants should not be informed. Researchers should proceed with the informing process whether or not it includes obtaining a signature on a form.

Many institutions have extended the obligation for documented informed consent from federally funded research only to include all publicly and privately funded research with human participants. In this way, the institution can be assured that all research with human volunteers is being monitored and that the interests of the institution are being protected. The consent form is thus a document designed to protect the interests of the participants as well as the interests of researchers and their institutions.

Before beginning a research project, researchers submit written protocols to their IRBs. The written submission includes a full discussion of the consent process and, in most cases, the actual consent forms necessary for the study. A consent form is not to be used as part of the informed consent process until the IRB has approved it. Submitting consent forms to the IRB can involve a process in which the IRB requests more information or changes in the consent process. Researchers can use opportunities in which IRBs have questions about their research to educate (in a collegial manner) the IRB in issues related to psychological research.

Obtaining Consent

Obtaining consent is more than simply having a potential research participant sign a consent form; it is a process by which necessary information is communicated to the participant by the researcher. To do this, the researcher should first assess prospective participants' mental (e.g., limited decision-making capacity) and legal ability to provide informed consent. If they have the ability to consent, the researcher should then assess their ability to comprehend the information that the researcher intends to communicate. Based on these determinations, information can be communicated and the appropriate informed consent obtained. Individuals with limited autonomy (e.g., children, prisoners, psychiatric patients) are special populations in which specific safeguards are required. Some of these safeguards are discussed in chapter 3, whereas issues related to the informing process are discussed in the context of participants with limited autonomy in the section that follows.

The Consent Form

The consent form is a written document attesting to the fact that participants are informed about the study for which they are volunteering. It is not intended to substitute for the informing process, which should occur first. In this process, researchers should make an effort to be as comprehensive as possible, giving participants repeated opportunities to ask questions, request clarification, and think about what is being presented.

According to federal regulations (OPRR, 1991, 45 CFR 46.116), the consent document can take two forms. It can be a relatively short written document, stating that the elements of informed consent have been orally presented to the participant. Under these conditions, a summary of that presentation must be approved by the IRB and signed by both the researcher and the participant, as well as a witness to the procedure. Levine (1986) pointed out that there is no advantage to the short form because nothing can be omitted from the summary and that there also is the added disadvantage of requiring a witness to the presentation of the summary, who is then present in a potentially confidential discussion. The alternative document, and the one that is generally used, is the longer form that includes the elements of informed consent described in the section that follows. After the participant signs the form, the researcher is responsible for retaining the signed consent form, assuring the participant of confidentiality as appropriate. A copy of the consent form should be provided to each participant as a continuing source of information about the study (see OPRR, 1991, 45 CFR 46.117). There are situations, however, when it might not be appropriate for participants to be given copies of the consent form. For example, if a consent form details illegal behavior that the participant previously engaged in, and the participant does not have a private place in which to keep the document, a signed form admitting to these illegal behaviors might become available to the people with whom the participant is living, thereby violating privacy.

The following is a listing of many of the areas to be addressed in ensuring informed consent on the part of a prospective research participant. In some cases, there are U.S. Department of Health and Human Services (DHHS) requirements that areas be addressed in a formal consent form. The topics required by DHHS are indicated by the section of the federal regulation in which they appear. In other cases, no formal requirement exists. Although it is not necessary to cover all of the areas listed below in order to inform a potential research participant, it is important to include what is appropriate for the study being carried out. In addition, if new issues emerge that might affect participants' willingness to continue in the research, the consent form should be re-reviewed and discussed with participants.

Invitation to Participate

An invitation to participate makes it clear that the participant is volunteering for the role of research participant.

Purpose of the Research

The purpose includes the overall reason for the research, including research goals at the individual and group level when appropriate (see OPRR, 1991, 45 CFR 46.116(a)(1)).

Selection Basis

A clear statement of the reasons why the participant is appropriate for the study has the added advantage of allowing prospective participants to exclude themselves if they do not believe that they meet the criteria for inclusion. If participants have to go through a screening process in order to meet inclusion and exclusion criteria, they should be informed about that process and about the study for which they will be appropriate if they pass the screening. If they are excluded, it is appropriate to tell them why they do not meet the criteria, unless the researcher has a good reason for not informing them. For example, if a specific behavioral or drug history is required for participation, informing potential volunteers about that requirement might encourage them to engage in the necessary behavior (e.g., smoking marijuana) in order to qualify for the research. In such instances, the researcher may choose not to inform the potential participant of that particular criterion.

Study Procedures

The study's procedures should be clearly described to prospective study participants (OPRR, 1991, 45 CFR 46.116(a)(1)). Some of the issues to be addressed include where the study will take place; who will be involved; how long it will last; what kind of work output will be required; and what kind of therapeutic intervention will be involved, if any. If there is a therapeutic element to the research, the treatment and research aspects of the study should be clearly delineated (OPRR, 1991, 45 CFR 46.116(a)(4)). When possible, an effective way of providing sufficient information is to invite the prospective participant to visit the research site and observe firsthand what the study requires.

Description of Risks and Discomforts

Volunteers are unable to make informed decisions about whether to participate in a research study if they are not adequately informed. Yet it is often difficult to present just the right amount of information—not so much detail as to be confusing and overwhelming, but not so little as to inadequately inform. For example, it would be possible in a drug study to provide such detailed information about potential side effects of the drug without information about the likelihood of their occurrence that all potential volunteers would be dissuaded from participating. This consequence was demonstrated in a study evaluating the effects of aspirin (Epstein & Lasagna, 1969). Groups of participants were shown a list of all possible side effects of that medication, varying in amount of detail, with no indication as to the likelihood of those effects. Many refused to participate based on the unedited list of potential effects. When queried, virtually all of those refusing were users of aspirin and believed aspirin to be a safe drug. The abundance of detail without any instructions about how to weigh the risks clearly was not informative. Researchers should include all "reasonably" anticipated risks and a statement that there may also be unforeseeable risks (OPRR, 1991, 45 CFR 46.116(a)(2)). Although IRBs are given the responsibility for determining the minimum standards for disclosure of risk, this does not absolve the researcher from making this determination separately. Often there are ways to reduce risk of participation in a study, and these should be clearly stated so that the participant can actively minimize the potential for harm. If more than minimal risk is involved, a statement describing availability of medical treatment and compensation should be included (U.S. Department of Health, Education, and Welfare, 1977). The consent form must not contain any clauses through which there is an attempt to have the participant's legal rights waived or to limit the researcher's liability for negligence (OPRR, 1991, 45 CFR 46.116). It may be appropriate to suggest to potential participants that they discuss their research participation with others who are knowledgeable in this research area. This discussion is most appropriate when the decision to participate is difficult or when specialized knowledge would be useful in the decision-making process.

Description of Benefits

In general, benefits can be summarized under the general category of anticipated additions to a systematic body of knowledge. In addition, occasionally there are potential benefits to the individual, to the subpopulation of which that individual is a member, or to society at large, which can be listed as well (OPRR, 1991, 45 CFR 46.116(a)(3)); (see chapters 2 and 3).

Available Alternatives

The requirement to provide information about available alternatives is primarily for therapeutic studies in which nonvalidated interventions are being studied. For such studies, the researcher should present alternatives to the experimental intervention (OPRR, 1991, 45 CFR 46.116(a)(4)).

Assurance of Confidentiality

Issues related to confidentiality are discussed elsewhere in this volume (see chapter 5). Because it is impossible to guarantee absolute confidentiality, the extent and limits to that guarantee should be described as part of the informed consent process. For example, issues related to data coding, disposal, sharing, and archiving might all be addressed as appropriate. For all federally funded research, universities are understood to own the data (see chapter 7). Therefore, if concern exists about the ability or likelihood of the university to maintain confidentiality, such information might be a part of the consent form. In addition, if a certificate of confidentiality is held (see chapter 5), that should be stated. There are conditions under which confidentiality must be broken, and those most likely to occur should be described (e.g., federal and state reporting requirements, Internal Revenue Service (IRS) reports, Food and Drug Administration (FDA) or pharmaceutical industry inspection in drug studies) (see OPRR, 1991, 45 CFR 46.116(a)(5)). Sometimes participants are paid by check, and records of payment are sent to the IRS via an institutional office. In other cases, research sponsors see raw data, or data that are entered in a medical record. Such information should be communicated to potential participants so that they may make an independent assessment of the level of confidentiality that can be maintained. Video data are also covered by any confidentiality assurance.

Financial Considerations

Any costs of participating in the research should be clearly described (OPRR, 1991, 45 CFR 46.116(b)(3)). Although federal regulations do not require listing any material inducements to research participation, it would be appropriate to list them as well. Economic advantages can include money, merchandise vouchers, food, access to improved facilities, therapy, physical exams, and subsidized transportation. In addition, it is appropriate to detail any bonuses for completion of the work or partial payments for early termination. There are fine lines between exploitation, paying for services, and coercion through excessive payment (see chapter 3). It is clear that different populations will respond to economic inducements differently, and careful evaluation of the potential volunteer population, with an eye to decreasing the likelihood that potential participants will feel coerced by the material inducements, is a part of the process of deciding on the level of these inducements. For example, Sieber (1992) has argued persuasively that most marginal populations (e.g., homeless people, runaways) will participate only if given money, and many advocates for poor and marginal populations argue that they should receive significant financial incentives if their participation is desired by scientists. Arguably such inducements are coercive, but they probably cause no greater risk than the risk that exists in the daily lives of those individuals, and they may even be of some benefit.

Offer to Answer Questions

It is important for participants to know whom to contact for answers to any questions they might have, any problems they might encounter as participants, and any injury they might incur while participating. Participants should be informed about how to redress any problems that might arise (OPRR, 1991, 45 CFR 46.116(a)(7)).

Noncoercive Disclaimer

Participation in research should be voluntary, and a decision not to participate or to discontinue participation should not result in any penalty or loss of benefits to the participant (OPRR, 1991, 45 CFR 46.116(a)(5)). This stipulation is particularly relevant when the researcher and participant have a relationship (e.g., teacher–student). Although researchers should make it clear that participants are free to withdraw from a study at any time, it is appropriate to have noncoercive inducements for study completion. A statement of the consequences for early withdrawal (e.g., a monetary bonus for study completion will not be paid) should be made (OPRR, 1991, 45 CFR 46.116(b)(2)) and, when appropriate, the statement should also include a discussion of the circumstances under which the researcher might terminate the participant's involvement in the study without his or her consent (e.g., health reasons, inadequate cooperation, the study is ending early); (see OPRR, 1991, 45 CFR 46.116(b)(2)). Research participants should also be informed that they are free to withdraw their data from the study, stating time constraints for that data withdrawal. If none are stated, it is understood that participants are free to withdraw their data at any time, including after their participation has ended. Of course, in some cases (e.g., anonymous surveys, interactive Internet data), the identity of the individual participant is not coded with the data, so it would be impossible for a participant to withdraw his or her data following data collection.

Incomplete Disclosure

Although the researcher should provide sufficient information for each volunteer to make an informed decision about whether to participate in a specific protocol, there are times when some information may be withheld. Although generally not the first choice of researchers (see chapter 6), it is sometimes necessary to omit information in order to protect the validity of the data collected. To the extent possible, information necessary to make an informed decision should be presented and, if possible, a statement in the consent form that some information is being withheld is a reasonable approach to this issue. Nonetheless, researchers who need to withhold the purpose of a study should be able to describe the tasks and procedures to study volunteers. For example, researchers studying conformity may not be able to disclose that the point of the study is to observe the extent to which each individual tailors his or her judgment to the judgments of the other group members, but the researchers could readily explain that the study requires each participant to make judgments within a group context. A promise to disclose all of the information at the termination of the study is generally desirable, although an assessment should be made of whether or not such a disclosure would do more harm than good (see Sieber, 1994). The decision to refrain from disclosing the nature of the study should not be taken lightly and should be made only when the alternative would cause greater harm than not informing the participants.

Additional Elements

When appropriate, the source of funding, who is conducting the study, how the data will be used, and so on, can be discussed (OPRR, 1991, 45 CFR 46.116(b)). The issue of continuing disclosure might also be relevant. The researcher should state that if new findings that could provide important information about continuing participation should become available, this information will be provided (OPRR, 1991, 45 CFR 46.116(b)(5)). Finally, at the end of the consent form, lines should be provided for signatures and dates. The following persons might sign:

- the consenter (with a statement of the relationship of the consenter to the participant if they are not the same individual)
- the participant (if not the consenter)
- the person who negotiated the consent (researcher, outside impartial professional, etc.)
- the person assessing capacity to consent (if different from the person negotiating consent)
- any other person present
- a witness to the participant's signature if the procedure carries more than minimal risk or the participant is not fully autonomous.

Significance of the Consent Form

The consent form is an agreement between the research participant and the researcher that describes expectations of the participant as well as the researcher. For example, the participant might be expected to refrain from drinking alcohol for 12 hours prior to a session, or to concentrate on the performance tasks being presented, or to answer questions as truthfully as possible. The researcher would be expected to carry out the study as described during the informing process, to maintain confidentiality, to pay what was promised, to be supportive during the study, and so on. In addition, the consent form is a legal document, required by federal regulations (OPRR, 1991, 45 CFR 46.117), which lists the elements to be included in the document. Researchers should make consent truly informed, and give participants the opportunity to ask questions and consider all of their options relative to research participation. Participants should also be informed of their right to refuse participation or withdraw data.

Barriers to Informed Consent

Although researchers should make every effort to institute an informed consent process that continues throughout the period of study participation, there are issues that can make this process more difficult. Under some conditions, it may be difficult to be sure that the material is actually being communicated. This possibility can often be evaluated by requesting volunteers to explain the study in their own words. Alternatively, some individuals may not be competent to provide informed consent, and there are procedures available to evaluate this possibility. Occasionally, available data, collected for other purposes (e.g., archived) might be useful to answer an important question, but the individuals from whom the data were collected are not available to provide their consent. As the subsequent discussion details, it is often possible to develop procedures for dealing with these and other potential barriers to informed consent.

Comprehension

Signing a comprehensive consent form does not guarantee that participants are informed about the study for which they are volunteering. It is clear that the language in which the information is presented and the reading ability of the participant will play a part in comprehension of the consent. For example, some participants may need to have the consent form read to them. In addition, it should be remembered that no single process works for all participants. Generally, consent forms with tables and increased white space have been found to be easier to comprehend (Peterson, Clancy, Champion, & McLarty, 1992). Other effective communication aids include using the active voice, informal prose, frequently used words, and short sentences. Researchers should be especially wary about technical vocabulary that may be familiar to specialists but not to participants. Some researchers, particularly when protocol participation is complicated, have volunteers participate in a simulation of the experimental procedure or in portions of the protocol. Regardless of the form of presentation, however, the researcher might build a procedure into the consent process for ensuring that participants understand the explanation they are given. Such procedures include requiring volunteers to explain the study in their own words or to answer objective questions about the study, thus providing behavioral evidence for their informed consent.

Limited Competence

The previous discussion is based on the assumption that those volunteering for research participation are fully competent in a legal sense. "When some or all of the subjects are likely to be vulnerable to coercion or undue influence, such as children, prisoners, pregnant women, mentally disabled persons, or economically disadvantaged persons, additional safeguards . . . [must be] included in the study to protect the right and welfare of these subjects" (OPRR, 1991, 45 CFR 46.111(b), p. 9). It is clear that some research may need to be carried out with those who are unable to provide voluntary consent (e.g., infants). Therefore, for those potential participants who lack the legal capacity to consent, a proxy consent can be obtained from a parent, guardian, or legally authorized representative (see chapter 3). The researcher should obtain informed consent from potential participants when they are legally competent to do so. When their competence limits their ability to provide consent, the researcher should obtain these individuals' assent to participate and the consent for their participation from their guardians.

Research with minors will be discussed as an example of the issues involved in dealing with research participants with limited autonomy. Federal regulations require that parents "permit" or "deny" permission for a child to participate in a research protocol. These regulations give minors the right to assent or refuse to participate (see Grisso, 1992). If permission is granted, it should be coupled with the agreement of the child. Therefore, to the extent possible, the assent of children is solicited along with the consent of a parent or guardian for children participating in a research protocol (OPRR, 1991, 45 CFR 46.408). Providing consent for participation is thus viewed as a shared decision. The assent for the child is presented at an age-appropriate level, with the goal of involving the child in the process (see Tymchuk, 1992, for a discussion of procedures for ensuring that assent is informed). Requiring the child's assent may be waived if the research is important for the health or well-being of the child or if the child cannot "reasonably be consulted" (e.g., if the child has moderate to severe mental retardation). Parents who do not actively refuse to consent cannot be presumed to have consented: "Passive consent" on the part of the parent or legal guardian is not consent.

There are also constraints on prisoner participation, related to the constitution of prison IRBs, advantages accruing to participants, fairness of participant selection, and kinds of research that may be carried out (OPRR, 1991, 45 CFR 46.3). However, once those regulations have been met, the consent elements listed previously are all relevant.

Insufficient Time

Potential research participants should be allowed adequate time to hear and consider all of the relevant information required to provide informed consent. This may include time to discuss the research with others and to seek advice if appropriate. Researchers should inform volunteers that such time is available and encourage seeking outside advice as needed.

Studies in Which Full Information Would Confound the Study Design

Under some research conditions, fully informing research participants before beginning the study could change the behavior being studied. For example, in drug versus placebo studies, informing a participant that he or she is in the placebo group would dramatically change the expectations and perhaps the effects of the substance being delivered. Studies of conformity or antisocial behaviors would also be very difficult if participants knew what was being studied. Major social issues could not be addressed unless it was possible for information to be withheld under some conditions. Because of this, researchers cannot always reveal the exact purpose of the research as part of the informed consent process (see chapter 6). However, the integrity of the consent process can be better preserved if it omits rather than misrepresents information.

Archived Data

In general, consent is obtained and data are collected for a specific purpose. The data are then retained by the researcher and in some cases, several years later, either that researcher or another finds those data useful to answer a different question, or archived hospital records become a potentially major data source for a new project. In neither case did the researcher have participants' consent for the information to be used for the purpose now required. It would be difficult, and in some cases impossible, to acquire consent for the new use of these data. In many cases, if the later use of the data were only for secondary analyses not requiring consideration of individual data (e.g., reanalysis of correlation matrices), consent may not be required. However, for cases in which individual participants' data would be used, it is important to assess the risk it poses to the participants. Researchers subject to IRB approval should make an application to their IRB for permission to use the data (see the earlier section on confidentiality).

Longitudinal Studies

In the course of a long-term study, many conditions can change; developmental changes occur, life circumstances evolve, and historical events can occur that can affect a study—and all can make necessary a reassessment of the agreement between the participant and the researcher. That is why it is important to remember that consent is an ongoing process. For example, in a study involving patients with Alzheimer's disease and their caregivers, as the patients age and the severity of the disease escalates, caregivers may find the burdens of care too great and may withdraw from the study. Or they may withdraw because they are no longer the primary caregiver. In another example, an adolescent who agreed to participate in a family study, given the information available about the study at that time, may need more information before making the decision to continue now that he or she is married and has a family of his or her own. It is often useful for these long-term studies to structure the formal signing of a consent form at set time points (e.g., 5 years) after the initial consent process. If formal consenting does not occur repeatedly during longitudinal studies, participants should be reminded of study procedures a short time before they are about to occur to refresh their memories about the study in which they have agreed to participate.

Debriefing

One benefit to participants in research protocols is an educational one, especially with college students participating as part of a psychology course requirement (see chapter 8). Researchers generally take the opportunity at the conclusion of a study to inform participants about why this study was conducted and how it fits in with what is already known. In addition, if incomplete information about the research was provided at the beginning of the study, this is often the time for a more complete transfer of information (a full discussion can be found in chapter 6). The debriefing session continues the informing process begun at the first contact between researcher and participant and it also provides the opportunity for researchers to obtain additional information from participants in their studies. For example, formal data collection may not focus on all aspects of the results of an experimental manipulation. Participants in a drug study might talk about changes in eating or sleeping, and participants in a learning study might point out sporadic changes in the environment that were intrusive and caused them to lose their concentration, or stimuli that were difficult to see. Such information could be useful in future experimental designs.

Community-Based Research

Researchers should take the opportunity to design an informed consent process that is sensitive to cultural mores. Sometimes it helps in accomplishing this objective to work with community leaders, knowledgeable people from the community, or other representatives who can educate the researcher about the culture of the community and help him or her gain entry. This is more than simply a research design issue because it allows the researcher to design a consent process that engages the population of interest and communicates effectively the scientific problem. In addition to providing entry into the community, these gatekeepers inform the researcher about the community and its needs relevant to the research being proposed. Although community leaders do not have the legal or ethical standing to either provide consent for individuals in the community they represent or to stop researchers from carrying out their studies, working with such people has the added advantage of educating the researcher about aspects of the research protocol that are not necessarily obvious. However, it is important for the researcher to ensure that the use of gatekeepers does not place undue pressure or coercion for members of the gatekeeper's community group to participate.

Conclusion

The consent process is a negotiation between the researcher and each potential participant or the entity or person having the right to consent for the potential participant. It requires clear and appropriate communication by researchers, coupled with respect for the autonomy of the individual or entity considering research participation. Individuals have the right to make a choice about research participation, but they can do so only after being fully informed about all relevant aspects of the study, with the exceptions noted above. It is the obligation of researchers to provide that information. Although there are legal requirements about documentation of consent (i.e., the consent form), that documentation is only one aspect of the consent process, and it should not be undertaken until the volunteer's level of comprehension and level of autonomy have been ascertained. Where the researcher's organization requires IRB approval, the IRB must approve both the consent process and the consent form. However, the primary responsibility for obtaining consent to participate remains with the researcher. Researchers have an obligation to take this responsibility seriously.

References

Epstein, L. C., & Lasagna, L. (1969). Obtaining informed consent: Form or substance? *Archives of Internal Medicine, 123,* 682–688.

Grisso, T. (1992). Minors assent to behavioral research without parental consent. In B. Stanley & J. E. Sieber (Eds.), *Social research on children and adolescents: Ethical issues* (pp. 109–127). Newbury Park, CA: Sage Publications.

Levine, R. J. (1986). *Ethics and regulations of clinical research.* Baltimore: Urban & Schwarzenberg.

Office for Protection From Research Risks, Protection of Human Subjects, National Commission for the Protection of Human Subjects of Biomedical and Behavioral Research. (1979). *The Belmont Report: Ethical principles and guidelines for the protection of human subjects of research* (GPO 887-809). Washington, DC: U.S. Government Printing Office.

Office for Protection From Research Risks, Protection of Human Subjects. (1991, June 18). Protection of human subjects: Title 45, Code of Federal Regulations, Part 46 (GPO 1992 0-307-551). *OPPR Reports,* pp. 4–17.

Peterson, B. T., Clancy, S. J., Champion, K., & McLarty, J. W. (1992). Improving readability of consent forms: What the computers may not tell you. *IRB: A Review of Human Subjects Research, 14*(6), 6–8.

Sieber, J. E. (1992). *Planning ethically responsible research: A guide for students and internal review boards.* Newbury Park, CA: Sage Publications.

Sieber, J. E. (1994). Will the new code help researchers be more ethical? *Professional Psychology: Research and Practice, 25,* 369–375.

Tymchuk, A. J. (1992). Assent processes. In B. Stanley & J. E. Sieber (Eds.), *Social research on children and adolescents: Ethical issues* (pp. 128–139). Newbury Park, CA: Sage Publications.

U.S. Department of Health, Education, and Welfare. (1977). *Education and welfare: Secretary's task force on the compensation of injured research subjects: Report* (DHEW Publication No. OS 77-003, Appendix A; DHEW Publication No. OS 77-004, Appendix B; DHEW Publication No. OS 7-005). Washington, DC: Author.

5

Privacy and Confidentiality

Susan Folkman

Respect for privacy and confidentiality is at the heart of the conduct of ethical research with human participants. Privacy and confidentiality derive from the respect for the autonomy of persons, the desire to do good (beneficence), and the principle of trust (see chapter 1). Whereas *privacy* refers to a person's interest in controlling other people's access to information about himself or herself (Sieber, 1992), *confidentiality* refers to the right to maintain private information divulged in the course of a professional relationship with a researcher.

Privacy

The concept of privacy is important to understand not only because the primary purpose of confidentiality is to protect privacy, but also because researchers who do not have a full understanding of privacy issues are likely to have difficulty conducting a study. Perceived threats to participants' privacy may result in biased sampling, evasive and false responses, and attrition. Participants who perceive a threat to privacy, but nonetheless answer questions honestly, may worry about the consequences of their actions.

Privacy has two major aspects. The first has to do with the person's freedom to pick and choose the time and circumstances under which facts about the person and, most importantly, the extent to which his or her attitudes, beliefs, behavior, and opinions are to be shared with or withheld from others (Kelman, 1972). The second has to do with the person's right not to be given information he or she does not want (Sieber, 1992).

The boundaries between wanted and unwanted information can be defined by sociocultural values. Some participants, for example, might be offended by information they regard as pornographic, or they might not want information about sexual behavior, the sharing of which may be part of a research protocol. Participants might also prefer not to hear feedback that might distress them; for example, they may not want to learn that they performed below a certain standard on a behavioral task, or that they scored above norms on measures of hostility or willingness to cheat.

The provision of unwanted information is a particularly sensitive issue in the case of research that involves HIV antibody testing. When HIV antibody testing is conducted or supported by the U.S. Public Health Service (PHS), individuals whose test results are associated with personal identifiers are not given the option "not to know"; they must be informed of their own test results and provided with the opportunity to receive appropriate counseling (Avins & Lo, 1989). Therefore, it is important that this information be included in the consent agreement.

Concerns about privacy can stem from many sources, including sociocultural values, characteristics of the physical environment, and characteristics of the political environment. Consider the following examples:

- "A researcher interviews poor Chicano families in Los Angeles about their attitudes concerning AIDS. Unknown to the researcher, these people consider it immoral, and sacrilegious, to even talk about homosexuality or AIDS. Most pretend not to understand his questions" (Sieber, 1992, p. 45).
- "A researcher decides to use telephone interviews to learn about the health history of lower-class older people, as the phone typically offers greater privacy than the face-to-face interview. She fails to recognize however that poor elderly people rarely live alone or have privacy from their families when they use the phone, and many keep health secrets from their family" (Sieber, 1992, p. 46).
- A researcher wants to conduct a study in California to establish the ethnic validity of a measure among Mexican Americans, some of whom are illegal aliens. State proposition 187, which prohibits publicly funded health care facilities from providing care to illegal immigrants and requires the reporting of suspected illegal aliens to government officials, had just been endorsed by nearly two-thirds of the voters. Potential participants are unwilling to participate in the research, even if anonymity is assured, because they are afraid that their status will become known to government personnel and that they and their families will suffer adverse consequences.

Researchers must be sensitive to privacy issues, many of which may be idiosyncratic to the research population. The researcher should consult with community leaders or others familiar with the research population to identify potential privacy issues and address them appropriately. Helpful sources include teachers and parents regarding privacy interests of children, child psychotherapists regarding abused minors, social workers with expertise regarding elderly or house-bound individuals, leaders and members of community-based organizations regarding various special or underserved populations, and other researchers who have worked with the population of interest.

Constitutional and federal laws say little about privacy in the context of social and behavioral research (Sieber, 1992). The few laws on this issue focus on the protection of children's privacy. For example, the Buckley Amendment (1985) to the Family Educational Rights and Privacy Act of 1974 (FERPA) prohibits access to children's school records without parental consent. The Goals 2000: Education Act (1994) prohibits asking children questions about religion, sex, or family life without parental permission. The National Research Act (1974) requires parental permission for research on children.

Privacy within the context of sociobehavioral research can best be protected through informed consent and, in the case of children, through informed parental consent (see chapter 4). The right to refuse to participate in research or to answer questions is central to protecting privacy and is an essential component of informed consent (see chapter 4). Anonymity provides excellent protection of privacy. Anonymity means that a participant's identity is not attached to the data and can never be inferred from the data through, for example, social security numbers, addresses, or combinations of occupational and other types of information that could be used to identify a given individual.

Research participants can take action against a researcher alleged to have invaded privacy under tort law by filing a suit against a researcher for "invasion of privacy." Such suits are likely to be dismissed if the research is socially important and validly designed, if the researcher has taken reasonable precautions to respect the privacy needs of typical participants and others associated with the research, and if the study has been approved by an institutional review board (Sieber, 1992).

Confidentiality

Confidentiality refers to agreements with persons about what may be done with their data (Sieber, 1992, p. 52). A researcher is expected to refrain from sharing private information with others that a participant shared with him or her when the sharing is done without the participant's authorization or some other justification (Levine, 1986). Authorization is obtained through the informed consent process (see chapter 4). An effective and appropriate informed consent requires language about accepted exceptions to confidentiality, potential threats to confidentiality, and ways of safeguarding confidentiality.

A breach of confidentiality can be particularly harmful in special populations. For example, information divulged to an employer that an individual is HIV-positive can affect his or her career, information about an illegal behavior by an individual who is on parole that is divulged can result in his reincarceration, a child's observations about a parent that are revealed to the parent can result in negative consequences for the child, and information about an individual's illegal alien status that is revealed to authorities could jeopardize the individual's rights or even his or her residence in this country. Although great care always needs to be taken to ensure confidentiality, researchers need to be especially vigilant about what they promise in the informed consent and the procedures that they implement to ensure confidentiality when their work involves vulnerable populations.

Exceptions to Confidentiality

The 1992 ethics code of the American Psychological Association (APA) allows psychologists who provide health care services to disclose confidential information without consent in order to protect patients, clients, or others from harm (see 5.05a(3)). Thus, confidentiality can be breached by practitioners to protect third parties. In California, a 1976 Supreme Court ruling in *Tarasoff v. Board of Regents of the University of California* (1976) mandated that therapists who know or should know of patients' dangerousness to identifiable third persons have an obligation to take all reasonable steps necessary to protect the potential victims. The principles of *Tarasoff* have been embraced by an increasing number of state and federal jurisdictions.

Individuals who conduct behavioral research, however, are not necessarily clinically trained. Such a researcher may inadvertently misinterpret a participant's verbal or behavioral communications. A serious violation of confidentiality could occur if the researcher inappropriately warns a third party of a potential threat. For example, a participant in a study of psychological stress who is asked to describe a recent stressful event might exclaim in a serious tone, "I am so angry at my boss I want to kill him!" It would be inappropriate for the researcher to call the supervisor. Instead, the researcher should consult immediately with a trained clinician or the institution's risk management department to determine the appropriate response. Researchers who collect data from samples that may be at risk for harming themselves or others, such as some patients with a mental or terminal illness, should make arrangements to have access to a licensed psychologist in advance of the study.

All states have mandatory reporting of child abuse or neglect, and many states also have mandatory reporting of elder abuse or neglect. Some states require mandatory reporting of a positive tuberculosis test, in which case partner tracing is required. Researchers should familiarize themselves with relevant requirements regarding mandatory reporting in their jurisdiction, and when statutes are relevant to a study, researchers should use language that indicates these requirements in the consent agreement (see chapter 4).

Threats and Safeguards to Confidentiality

Confidentiality is becoming increasingly hard to maintain. Simply stripping data of the participant's name does not always guarantee privacy. Confidentiality can be threatened in many ways—through legal actions, government statutes, the use of new technologies, access by third parties to data, data sharing, technical lapses in security, and breaches during presentation of data.

The best safeguard against threats to confidentiality is for the researcher to be well-informed about the law, to understand clearly the limits to confidentiality, and to use language in the consent agreement that reflects this knowledge as it pertains to a given study. The researcher also needs to be familiar with techniques that protect data and preserve the participant's anonymity and privacy.

Subpoenas

In general, research records that are essential to the resolution of an issue can be subpoenaed by the court to be turned over to the party who wants them. However, the courts have been uniformly willing to protect the identities of participants who had been promised confidentiality as a condition of participation in the study (Holder, 1993). Thus, research data can be subpoenaed as long as participants' rights to privacy are protected. These principles protect the privacy of the research participant but not the researcher's identity or data that are stripped of participant identifiers.

Cases in which research data are subpoenaed are rare because ordinarily the requested data do not bear directly on issues central to the litigation or because the information is available elsewhere (Cecil & Boruch, 1988). However, researchers whose data are subpoenaed have options. The researcher may try to convince the court that the burdens of disclosure, including the disruption of the research, outweigh the benefits of disclosure. "Honest brokers" can be used to respond to concerns about research data that have been raised in the context of litigation. Professional associations can serve in this capacity (Cecil & Boruch, 1988).

Another approach to safeguarding data from subpoena is to obtain a certificate of confidentiality, which provides immunity from the requirement to reveal names or identifying information in legal proceedings. Two federal agencies have the authority to grant them. Confidentiality certificates can be requested from the U.S. Department of Health and Human Services (DHHS; see 42 CFR Part 2a.6 (1997); see also NIH web site: http://grants.nih.gov/grants/oprr/humansubjects/guidance/certconpriv.htm [12/28/98]) for more information. Applicants need not be recipients of DHHS funds. The U.S. Department of Justice (DOJ), under the provisions of the Controlled Substances Act (21 CFR 1316.21), issues grants of confidentiality that authorize researchers to withhold the names and other identifying characteristics of participants of research that involves drugs or other substances subject to control. Researchers need not be funded by the DOJ to be eligible, but their research must be of a nature that the department is authorized to conduct.

Certificates should be renewed prior to expiration as long as new participants are being entered in the protocol, and new staff should be added to the certificates if they are to have any contact with participants or confidential data. If new staff are not added, they are not covered by legal provisions relating to the participants.

Access by Other Third Parties

Employers, school administrators or faculty, private funding sponsors such as drug companies or foundations, and insurance companies may ask for information about research participants who are in or are served by their institutions. These organizations often initiate and support the research, and their representatives may feel they have a right to the information. The situation may be particularly difficult for a researcher who is associated with the organization making the request.

Certain types of information can be requested under federal and state freedom-of-information laws and search-and-seizure laws. Law enforcement officers, attorneys, and other litigants acting under these statutes may try to search and seize research data.

Confidentiality can sometimes be breached inadvertently by access through third parties. For example, participants in a particular study were assessed over several days. Many participants traveled quite a distance to participate, and they stayed at a local hotel during their assessment period. Their hotel bills were charged to the university through the study's grant fund number. A reporter who was doing a story on research at this particular university requested and received records from the accounting department that included these hotel bills. The reporter was able to identify who participated in the study by linking the names on the hotel bills to the study's grant fund number.

As of this writing, the Internal Revenue Service (IRS) requires that payments of $600 or more be reported, which involves disclosure of the name and social security number of participants who meet this criterion. This procedure is generally handled through the institution's comptroller's office, because that is the only way the institution can assure the IRS that the regulations are being complied with. This procedure protects the privacy of the participant's data, although people who handle this procedure will know the names of study participants.

Disclosure of information that the researcher has promised not to disclose is forbidden without the individual's permission unless participants and the organization had an explicit agreement allowing disclosure in advance of data collection. Courts tend to protect the confidentiality of data in cases where such information is sought without the participant's permission. The risk of inadvertent breaches of confidentiality caused by requests from third parties, such as in the case of hotel bills, can be reduced by educating staff about the importance of confidentiality of research data, potential threats to confidentiality in their work, and safeguards to protect confidentiality.

Use of New Technologies

In recent years, the Internet (e-mail and interactive web sites) is increasingly being used to gather data for research purposes. The use of this medium for data collection is likely to increase in the future, as the technology becomes more sophisticated and refined. Researchers using the Internet to collect data should be sensitive to the difficulty in safeguarding the privacy and confidentiality of research participants. Although some security procedures designed to protect confidentiality are available, the changing nature of the technology, and the threats to confidentiality inherent in its use make security very difficult, if not impossible. Researchers should carefully consult with technology experts before using these techniques. They should make every effort to use these techniques only when security measures are available to ensure confidentiality of participants' responses. They should also try not to use these methods of data collection when breaks in confidentiality would have serious consequences for the participants involved. (For further discussions on issues related to conducting research via the Internet, consult Childress & Asamen, 1998; Libutti, 1999; Michalak, 1998.)

Data Sharing

The sharing of data is common. Problems arise when data sharing involves confidential, private, or potentially damaging information about research participants. Agreements to share data should consider, among other matters, who owns the data, who has access to the data, and what mechanisms are available for protecting confidentiality (see Sieber, 1988; chapter 7 in this volume).

Whenever data sharing is a possibility, the researcher should include this in the informed consent, noting whether the data would be anonymous. Techniques for protecting privacy in quantified data that are being shared include the introduction of a small amount of random error into a data archive that is insufficient to limit its research usefulness seriously but adequate to "denature" it for legal purposes. Other techniques include coding data to hide the identity of participants, scrambling computer data through data encryption, and using electronic security. Boruch and Cecil (1979, 1983), Fox and Tracy (1986), and Bongar (1988) provide overviews of this topic.

Mailed Questionnaires

Researchers who conduct cross-sectional research by mail often need to know who has responded in order to determine whether there is bias in the sample or so that they can follow up with nonresponders. Longitudinal studies pose additional challenges in that researchers often need to link research records on persons (exact matching) or on persons who are similar on some attributes (statistical matching).

With respect to cross-sectional research that is conducted by mail, respondents can be asked to mail the survey anonymously in one envelope and separately send a postcard with their name on it indicating that they have responded. For some studies, it is necessary to determine that only appropriate persons have responded and that their responses are complete. In such cases, a list of ID numbers that are linked to individuals' names can be created. The questionnaire contains only the ID number. Once the ID numbers from the returned questionnaires have been checked against the list, the names are destroyed, as is done at polling places.

With respect to longitudinal research, unique identifiers that are not associated with the participant's name can be used, such as the last four numbers of the individual's social security number or some combination of numbers from the individual's birth date and a parent's birth date. Care must be taken to devise unique identifiers that the participant can recall reliably from occasion to occasion. This system provides a link from questionnaire to questionnaire but no link to the individual's identity.

Publication or Presentation of Data

Most quantified data are presented in aggregate forms that protect research participants' privacy. However, other types of data, including case material, photographs, e-mail records, and video and audio recordings, can threaten privacy and confidentiality, especially if the individual involved is well known.

The most important safeguard is to inform participants in advance of the research about what will or might be done with the data and secure consent to the proposed uses. Case material and audio recordings should be stripped of identifiers, including names and possibly geographic markers and the dates of national or local historical events. Videotapes can be edited to obscure faces, but this procedure can be costly, and in some cases the facial expressions are the data and cannot be obscured without damaging the study. Care needs to be taken that videotapes are stored securely and that access to them is restricted and guarded.

Conclusion

Respect for research participants' privacy is achieved through a confidentiality agreement between the researcher and the participant. The researcher and the participant discuss this agreement during the process of informed consent (see chapter 4). The agreement needs to satisfy participants' needs for privacy and at the same time allow researchers to conduct their scientific investigations. Researchers should understand that violations of confidentiality could have serious repercussions for participants. Researchers should safeguard against threats to confidentiality as much as possible by becoming familiar with relevant local, state, and federal regulations and through careful planning (see chapter 2) and training of research staff (see chapter 8).

References

American Psychological Association. (1992). Ethical principles of psychologists and code of conduct. *American Psychologist, 47*(12), 1597–1611.

Avins, A., & Lo, B. (1989). To tell or not to tell: The ethical dilemmas of HIV test notification in epidemiologic research. *American Journal of Public Health, 79*, 1544–1548.

Bongar, B. (1988). Clinicians, microcomputers, and confidentiality. *Professional Psychology: Research and Practice, 19*, 286–289.

Boruch, R. F., & Cecil, J. S. (1979). *Assuring the confidentiality of social research data.* Philadelphia: University of Pennsylvania Press.

Boruch, R. F., & Cecil, J. S. (1983). *Solutions to ethical and legal problems in social research.* New York: Academy Press.

Cecil, J. S., & Boruch, R. (1988). Compelled disclosure of research data. *Law and Human Behavior, 12,* 181–189.

Childress, C. A., & Asamen, J. K. (1998). The emerging relationship of psychology and the Internet: Proposed guidelines for conducting Internet intervention research. *Ethics & Behavior, 8,* 19–35.

Controlled Substances Act, P.L. 91-513, 84 Stat. 1242 (1970).

Family Educational Rights and Privacy Act of 1974 (P.L. 94-63), Buckley Amendment. (1985). 20 U.S.C.A. Section 1232 et seq.; accompanying regulations, 34 CFR pt. 99.

Fox, J. A., & Tracy, P. E. (1986). *Randomized response: A method for sensitive surveys.* Beverly Hills, CA: Sage Publications.

Goals 2000: Education Act, P. L. 103-227, 108 Stat. 125 (1994).

Holder, A. R. (1993). Research records and subpoenas: A continuing issue. *IRB: A Review of Human Subjects Research, 15*(1), 6–7.

Kelman, H. (1972). The rights of the subject in social research: An analysis in terms of relative power and legitimacy. *American Psychologist, 27,* 989–1016.

Levine, R. J. (1986). *Ethics and regulation of clinical research.* Baltimore: Urban & Schwarzenberg.

Libutti, P. O. (1999). The Internet and qualitative research: Opportunities and constraints on analysis of cyberspace discourse. In M. Kopala & L. A. Suzuki (Eds.), *Using qualitative methods in psychology* (pp. 77–88) Thousand Oaks, CA: Sage Publications.

Michalak, E. E. (1998). The use of the Internet as a research tool: The nature and characteristics of seasonal affective disorder (SAD) amongst a population of users. *Interacting With Computers, 9,* 349–365.

National Research Act, P.L. 93-348, 88 Stat. 342 (1974).

Sieber, J. E. (1988). Data sharing. *Law and Human Behavior, 12,* 199–206.

Sieber, J. E. (1992). *Planning ethically responsible research.* Newbury Park, CA: Sage Publications.

Tarasoff v. Board of Regents of the University of California. (1976). 17 Cal. 3d 425, 131 Cal. Rptr. 14, 551 p 2d 334.

Part II

Ethical Concerns Within the Research Community

6

Other Responsibilities to Participants

Lorraine D. Eyde

Concerns about the rights and dignity of research participants are not satisfied when the consent process described in chapter 4 is successfully concluded. These concerns pervade every aspect of the research process and include establishing and maintaining participants' trust, continuously monitoring their safety, ensuring appropriate and effective debriefing, and attending to the special needs and vulnerabilities of certain research populations.

Maintaining Trust

The trusting relationship between the researcher and the participants, established during the informed consent process, should be maintained as the research process unfolds. The research team should continue to maintain trust by treating research participants and research assistants as respected partners in the research. The participants' contribution to the research effort is a gift of time and thoughts. The participants do the researchers an immense favor and deserve to be treated politely and with respect in all interactions. For example, respect should be communicated in the ways staff members greet participants and make appointments and in the dialogue that occurs during data collection. Further, staff members should not quote or make fun of participants during lunch-hour conversations or speak of them in hallways or restrooms.

The senior researcher who designs the study but who has the data collection carried out by collaborators, associates, students, or employees is as responsible for the humane treatment of the participants as if she or he collected the data. A principal investigator should supervise assistants and students to ensure that the participants are being treated well. The fact that the principal investigator or teacher retains responsibility for the humane treatment of the participants, however, does not relieve the assistant or student of equal responsibility to the participant. The student

The opinions expressed are those of the author and do not necessarily reflect the official policy of the U.S. Office of Personnel Management.

or assistant should be as sensitive to and solicitous of the welfare of participants, as if the research project were solely the student's or assistant's own. Thus, it is not acceptable to engage in unethical practices, even if ordered to perform such actions by an employer or teacher. If students or assistants feel a moral reluctance to carry out a research procedure, the supervisor should not pressure them to perform the procedure, even though the procedure might seem completely harmless to the researcher.

In addition to the trust that is established and maintained between the research team and the participants, trust needs to be established and maintained with many others who have a stake in the research. Other such persons may include families, guardians, research sponsors, unions, and employer groups.

Maintaining the Safety of Participants

The federal regulations for the protection of human participants require that "When appropriate, the research plan makes adequate provision for monitoring the data collected to ensure the safety of subjects" (OPRR, 1991, 45 CFR 46.111(a)(6)). During the research process, the researcher needs to monitor harms. Actual or potential harms for participants might change from those discussed in the original informed consent agreement. As the data accumulate or new knowledge becomes available, there may be a need to alert participants to a change in risks of harms. The following sections illustrate various types of harm that can occur and suggest how researchers might respond.

When the Risks of Harm Change

Although researchers do not intend harm to their participants, unintended harms can occur during the course of the research or as a consequence of it. Ongoing monitoring of study data may show that harm to participants is greater than expected. For example,

> A longitudinal study of pediatric AIDS that sought to evaluate several therapies showed that unexpected high rates of adverse side effects occurred in one of the treatment groups. As a consequence, the arm of the study in which this particular therapy was given was stopped ahead of schedule. The children and their parents or legal guardians in this group were offered the possibility of switching to one of the other treatment groups. (Fackelmann, 1995, p. 100)

The case for terminating a study treatment was quite clear in the above example. Less clear situations also arise. Research participants can experience adverse reactions such as shame, embarrassment, or anxiety as the result of a performance task; or they may experience an intense affective response to a mood induction; or they can experience actual pain and discomfort in response to a physical stressor. The researchers need to determine the implications of these adverse reactions. If the risk of harm is greater than expected, the researcher is responsible for correcting observed detrimental effects and for taking reasonable measures to remove those effects. One response to such potential occurrences is to debrief participants at the conclusion of the study, providing them with appropriate reassurance and information about normal reactions. The researcher should also train the research staff so that they know which kinds of responses to be alert to and how to respond.

Cross-cultural research may present special risks when the participant and researcher do not attach the same meaning and value to research or even speak the same language. Misunderstandings can easily arise in such situations. Participants may not have understood the full nature and consequences of the research or may expect a reward where there is none. The researcher can help reduce the risk of this type of harm by making an effort to understand the participant's culture and values during the planning phase. This awareness can also help make the debriefing process beneficial rather than harmful.

One special form of harm can occur from researcher errors. For example,

> In a longitudinal study of the effects of stress on the physical health of HIV-positive men, a systematic laboratory error resulted in CD4 reports 10% lower than they should have been. CD4 cell counts are used as one indicator of HIV disease progression. As HIV infection progresses, the CD4 count declines. A report of lower CD4 cell counts could therefore lead to considerable anxiety or encourage participation in alternative medical therapies for HIV disease or more aggressive traditional therapies. (Susan Folkman, personal communication, n.d.)

In deciding how to respond to such dilemmas, the researcher should consider a range of questions:

- Would the mistake cause physical or psychological harm to the participants?
- Is the error outside the normal range of fluctuation?
- Would the error be meaningful to the participants?

If any of the above questions are answered in the affirmative, the researcher should consider taking appropriate steps to protect the interests of the participants. For example, the researcher could send a letter explaining the mistake that had been made and providing a record of the old (incorrect) values and the new (corrected) ones. The researchers can also consider inviting participants to contact the project director if they have any questions or concerns. Finally, the researcher should make preparations for referrals for psychological care, if needed. As a general rule, participants need to be informed of errors and provided with corrected data when inaccuracies may be detrimental to their well-being, such as when mistakes lead to increased anxiety, depression, or medical compromise.

One of the most difficult ethical issues concerns studies in which participants receive something they value as part of the research protocol. What are the ethical implications of terminating the provision of this benefit when the research concludes? For example, consider children receiving special education interventions as part of a research procedure. Although the participants are left in their initial condition, or even benefited by the temporary enrichment involved in the research participation, termination of the benefits at the end of the research can be construed as harmful. Researchers, in weighing whether they ethically can undertake the study, should try to anticipate the development of participant expectations or dependencies (e.g., on the treatment protocol used as the research intervention), assess whether these can be satisfied after the research is terminated and, if not, whether the potential harm to participants of terminating the study outweighs the benefits of the research.

Right to Withdraw From the Study

Occasionally participants wish to withdraw from a study, raising complex issues because of competing ethical interests. On the one hand, the principle of autonomy suggests participants should have the right to withdraw their data. On the other hand, the principle of fidelity to science argues against such withdrawal. Most researchers balance these interests by concluding that it is unethical to coerce participants to stay in a study against their will. Therefore, participants should be given opportunities to express their desire to withdraw, and the researcher should guard against expressing subtle pressures to the participant to remain in the study. Researchers should try to relieve participants who wish to withdraw of any negative feelings or self-doubts about their decision. Researchers should be especially sensitive to signs that participants may not wish to continue in studies that involve physically or psychologically stressful procedures. In such cases, the researcher should take steps to make clear to the participant that termination is possible at any time during the procedure.

Whenever possible, the researcher should learn from participants why they wish to withdraw. This information is important because it might reveal a problem in a research procedure that needs to be addressed. The information is important also for the scientific purpose of documenting and analyzing attrition. Sometimes these conversations reveal that a participant's wish to withdraw is for a reason that the researcher can address. In such cases, the participant may choose to remain in the research.

Requests to withdraw data are a special form of requests to withdraw from a study. These requests should be given special consideration when, for sufficient reasons, the researcher has found it necessary to withhold or distort information during informed consent. For example, researchers customarily ask participants if they wish to withdraw their data when they are secretly videotaped and only told about this procedure after the conclusion of the research. (See below for further discussion of deception research.)

Updating IRB Protocols

Because of the possibility of changes in the risks associated with the study during the course of research, researchers should routinely review their IRB protocol to see if it needs to be modified. The regulations for the protection of human participants require "prompt reporting to the IRB of proposed changes in a research activity ... [which] may not be initiated without IRB review and approval except when necessary to eliminate apparent immediate hazards to the subject" (OPRR, 1991, 45 CFR 46.103(b)(4)(iii)). Researchers may need to have their protocol reevaluated when they

- modify their design
- find that an event has occurred that would change the risks for some participants
- wish to change the consent agreement.

Debriefing

Researchers customarily debrief participants on a timely basis, preferably right after their participation in the study or as soon as appropriate according to the nature of the research. Debriefing should be a two-way educational process between the researcher and the research participant. This process provides participants with information about the nature of the research and available results. It also facilitates their understanding of the educational or therapeutic value of their experience (Sieber, 1992). Researchers may learn how the research tasks were perceived by the participants or about their unstated assumptions about the research (Stewart, 1992). Thus, researchers may gain insight into the research results and identify questions for future research (Blanck, Bellack, Rosnow, Rotheram-Borus, & Schooler, 1992).

Although debriefing is widely considered to provide one of the benefits of participation in research, it is also a way of managing harm. Researchers should use the debriefing process to correct misperceptions that participants might hold. It is especially important that participants not be placed in a position in which they might take action that could affect their future on the basis of misinformation that they received during the research. (The special case of debriefing in the context of deception research is discussed below.)

On occasion, the debriefing itself may do more harm than good. The researcher may discover things about participants that could be psychologically damaging. For example, a participant may have performed very poorly at a task and may regard such performance as important. Assuming that the researcher knows the identity of the participant, should the researcher disclose unwelcome findings even when they might be only incidental to the main purpose of the research and when the participant does not inquire about them or appear to be aware that information of this nature has been obtained? In such cases, the researcher becomes involved in an ethical conflict between the obligation to inform the participant fully on the one hand and the desire to avoid harming the participant in any way on the other. If important information that could affect the participant (e.g., physical or personality problems) is uncovered, the researcher might consider informing the participant. Consultations with appropriate health care professionals might help the researcher reach a decision. Psychological assessment necessary to diagnose mental or physical health problems, more likely than not, requires much more information than may be provided in results obtained in a research protocol. Researchers should be cautious of sharing such information with the participant. More harm than good could occur given the possibility of false alarms due to the limited nature of the information gathered in the course of the research study. Any decision to provide such information to a participant must consider the legal and ethical implications of possible distress to the participant caused by acquiring this information. If the researcher does decide to inform the participant and suggest referral to a health professional, the information should be imparted together with a qualified professional, unless the researcher is qualified to handle the resultant distress and make appropriate referrals.

Recognizing Special Populations

In evaluating the continuing conduct of research, researchers need to recognize the special vulnerabilities of participants. These individuals include persons who are

- incompetent (e.g., people who are intellectually impaired or otherwise legally incompetent)
- lack resources (e.g., homeless individuals)
- are stigmatized (e.g., gay men and lesbians)
- are institutional residents (e.g., some people with mental disorders and prisoners).

Continuing recognition of vulnerabilities of special populations is important for the continued protection of participants' well-being. For example, effective researcher–participant relationships are especially important in such populations. Achieving such relationships may entail researchers spending more time listening to participants, answering their questions, and responding to their concerns through the research process (Prentice, Reitemeier, Antonson, Kelso, & Jameton, 1993). In addition, research teams can profit from having members who are from the populations being studied so that they may incorporate the perspectives of these populations accurately into the research planning and process (Scott-Jones, 1994).

Children are a special group for a number of reasons. Their cognitive skill levels and maturity vary according to their developmental stage, and they lack social power and the legal right to consent (Thompson, 1992; also see chapter 4 in this volume). In longitudinal studies, in particular, researchers need to be aware that risks may change as a result of changes in the children's developmental level. Thus, researchers need to be alert for behavioral signs in children who might wish to withdraw from the study but who do not articulate this wish. This concern is salient for children or adolescents who are stigmatized—for example, gay and lesbian adolescents and delinquents. When, in the course of research, researchers discover information that might jeopardize a child's well-being, they should consider discussing the matter with the child's parents or guardians and with experts to make referrals when appropriate (Society for Research in Child Development, 1993).

Some participants who have impaired judgment or distorted understanding of the nature of the research and its risk may forget that they are in a study even though they gave informed consent (DeRenzo, 1994). Periodically, especially in longitudinal studies, research teams need to review the risks of the research with such participants.

Moreover, whenever participants have special vulnerabilities, the research team should be alert to signs that participants are distressed and recognize the need for referrals to health care professionals (Fisher, 1993). Researchers who are not clinically trained have the responsibility for obtaining qualified professional help, offering information about available mental health counseling, or making other referrals to help vulnerable persons who appear distressed. Because problems can arise when relatively untrained research assistants carry out the day-to-day functions of the research project, researchers should be diligent in monitoring the activities of their research assistants and interviewers. This ensures that the participants' emotional problems, if any, are handled competently.

Conducting Research Using Deceptive Procedures

The topic of deception in research merits special attention. The scientific community continues to raise questions about the advantages and disadvantages of conducting deception research in which participants are deliberately misled about the purpose of the research (Baumrind, 1979, 1985; Sieber, 1983a). Some psychologists believe that to obtain valid and generalizable data, it may be necessary that research participants be less than fully informed about the study or parts of it. Others have argued that deception has little place in psychological research (Kelman, 1967).

There are certain phenomena that may be difficult to study validly if participants are aware of the behavior being observed. For example, if participants are told that their conformity behavior or their visual interaction will be observed, pride or self-consciousness may alter their behavior.

Some researchers argue that, following debriefing, participants' reactions in response to research involving deception are so trivial compared to normal everyday experiences that research participants characteristically shrug them off as inconsequential. In support of this view, Christensen (1988) has summarized research on the reactions of participants to experiments in which there was deception:

> Milgram (1964), for example, found that only 1.3% of his subjects reported any negative feelings about their experiences within the experiment, and 84% were glad to have participated. These findings were supported by Ring, Wallston, and Corey's (1970) conceptual replication of Milgram's study. These researchers found that only 4% of their subjects regretted participating in the experiment. Clark and Ward (1974) found that 95% of the subjects participating in a "bystander intervention in an emergency" experiment reported considering the research valuable and 94% considered the deception unavoidable. Such results suggest that the deception employed in these studies did not have an adverse impact on the subjects' assessment of the experiment. (p. 666)

Despite these reactions, deception raises significant issues:

- What responsibilities does a researcher have when considering this kind of research?
- How might participants be harmed by the deceptive information about the nature of the experiment?
- Which populations are at the greatest risk for experiencing this harm?
- To what extent are self-reports of no adverse impact by the deception judged to be expected and desirable responses to the experimenter?
- What might researchers do to counteract potential negative consequences of deception?

Deception May Bring Unforeseeable Problems

For example, consider the following scenario. Students in a university study were given the opportunity to earn course credit through their participation in a study on anxiety:

> Participating students are told that their reactions will be observed and recorded in the context of a stressful situation. They are then given individual appointment times for meeting with the researcher. On entering the building, the participant is met by his or her professor, the researcher. The researcher explains that the study will be conducted by a graduate assistant and that he will escort the participant to the appropriate laboratory upstairs. The researcher secures an elevator but pretends to have left his briefcase in his office. "In the interest of time," he asks the participant to take the elevator alone, saying that he will call up to the laboratory and instruct the graduate assistant to meet the participant at the elevator. There is a confederate in the elevator, and the elevator subsequently "gets stuck" for 10 minutes. The confederate serves to create either of two conditions, panic or calm. Partici-

pants' responses are videotaped so that they can be coded, given anxiety ratings and, ultimately, so that a comparison can be made between response under conditions of panic and calm (Melton & Stanley, n.d.).

If a participant were phobic or nearly so in elevators or in enclosed spaces, this experiment could be traumatic. Researchers should recognize the vulnerabilities of potential participants in deception research and evaluate the harms, the likelihood that the debriefing processes will return participants to their pre-experimental status, or whether some other intervention is required. For example, in the above vignette, one approach researchers could use to avoid the possible harm is to screen for potentially claustrophobic persons during mass testing and exclude them from the participant pool. The important consideration is that the researchers not harm participants.

Research participants and researchers may differ in their judgments about whether harm is likely to occur or is occurring. The same experience may be perceived by some as destructive and by others as a valuable opportunity for the development of self-understanding. Thus, to assess the likelihood of harm, the researcher should consider seeking consultation, including from members of the participant pool where possible. Where harm is likely to result, the researcher should consider ameliorative strategies, including the use of an alternative approach to conducting the research. In some investigations, the potential for negative after effects seems especially great, and the possibility of reversing these effects seems low. Under such conditions, the investigation obviously should not be conducted.

Under most circumstances, deception involves misleading participants, but not lying to them. In addition, they should be debriefed about the research as soon as possible after they finish their participation and certainly no later than at the conclusion of the research. Sufficient time needs to be set aside for this step to allow participants to raise questions and have them answered.

Debriefing Can Mollify Negative Effects of Deception

The debriefing process for a deception study is likely to be more complex than in the case of a regular study (Aronson, Wilson, & Brewer, 1998; Sieber, 1983b). It usually begins with revealing the deception to the participants and explaining to them how they were misinformed (Sieber, 1992). For example, consider a synopsis of the well-known Milgram (1963) obedience study:

> In the study a research assistant—actor posed as the participant, and the participant thought himself or herself to be the research assistant. Typically, the research assistant carried out the researchers' instruction to deliver severe shock to the "participant." At the end of the session, the real participant (who thought he was the research assistant) was debriefed by being told that the ostensible participant was really a re-

> search assistant—actor who was pretending to be shocked. The partic-
> ipant and the assistant—actor met and chatted, and it was shown that
> the shock apparatus was not hooked up.

Getting research participants to understand the deception and its implications may not work in all situations, however. For example, barriers
to understanding may exist with preschool and young schoolchildren because of immature cognitive processes.

The researcher should also make an effort to eliminate the undesirable emotional, cognitive, or attitudinal consequences that can result from
the deception process. Participants may have revealed their secrets and
weaknesses and thus feel guilty and ashamed. To ensure that the planned
debriefing is likely to be effective, researchers may find it useful to go
through the debriefing process with a limited number of participants before conducting a full-scale investigation. When feasible, it may be desirable to measure the effectiveness of the debriefing process. For example,

> In a study designed to assess the effects of negative emotions on social
> interactions, participants were given false-negative feedback on a mea-
> sure of problem-solving ability. To enhance the mood induction, partic-
> ipants were shown a normal curve—presumably a normative distri-
> bution of scores—and asked to guess how well they performed on the
> test. In the negative-feedback condition, participants were then in-
> formed that they had scored a standard deviation below their estimate
> of their performance. (June Tangney, personal communication, n.d.)

In this case, the experimenter bears a heavy responsibility to alleviate
any long-lasting effects on participants' assessments of their abilities or
chances for later success in life. Thus, the experimenter provided extensive
debriefing immediately following the experiment. In an individual, face-
to-face debriefing interview, the experimenter carefully and sensitively explained in lay terms the true nature and purpose of the experiment and
the reasons some degree of deception was necessary to construct a valid
experiment. The experimenter explained that the "problem-solving text"
was a bogus test, constructed for the purposes of the experiment, and that
there was, in fact, no answer key. Rather, an assistant flipped a coin to
determine the condition (negative or neutral feedback) for the participant.
The experimenter showed the participant his or her unscored test, which
had a code at the bottom (e.g., heads—negative feedback) to emphasize
the point. The experimenter then apologized for misleading the participant
and indicated that it would have been his or her strong preference to
conduct the study without any deception, explaining how it would have
been impossible to obtain the participant's natural reactions without the
subterfuge.

With the new knowledge about the bogus nature of the test and the
randomly assigned feedback, the participant was asked to estimate how
he or she would score on a "real" measure of problem-solving ability if
such were available. The experimenter and participant then together compared the debriefing estimate to the estimate obtained just prior to the

negative feedback to ensure that there was no residual effect of the induction. Following the suggestions of Ross, Lepper, and Hubbard (1975), the experimenter then explained, again in lay terms, that there still might be the possibility that the effects of the negative feedback may persist. Thus, people may have a tendency to discount subsequent information presented during the debriefing that is inconsistent with the prior negative feedback. Awareness of this possibility is important in helping dispel this effect.

Throughout the debriefing procedure, the experimenter carefully monitored the participant's affective reactions and encouraged the participant to share his or her reactions with the experimenter. The experimenter reassured the participant that the psychology lab had done extensive pilot-testing to make sure that the deception was believable and that the participant's acceptance of the ruse was not a reflection of the participant's gullibility, but rather of the lab's care and skill in designing the procedures. The experimenter closed the debriefing interview by reiterating his or her apology for misleading the participant and by offering the participant a small token of apology (candy or pen adorned with bright ribbons). The participant was provided with the debriefer's telephone number and invited to call if he or she had any additional questions or concerns. Last, the debriefer asked if he or she could call the participant a week later, just to check that the participant was feeling all right about the experience. These calls were made to further ensure that there were no residual negative effects of the participant's experiences in the experiment.

The importance of appropriate debriefing cannot be overemphasized because "persons often maintain initial impressions even when they learn that the information on which the impressions were based was false" (Holmes, 1976, p. 862). For instance, in a marketing study (Misra, 1992), participants had been told that there was a rumor going around that a fast food chain supposedly used red-worm meat in its hamburgers. The group of participants who afterward received a conventional debriefing had a significantly less positive attitude toward the fast food chain, whereas the group that had undergone the explicit debriefing did not hold a statistically different attitude toward the chain than the control group, which was not told of the red-worm rumor.

Appropriate and effective debriefing involves skills that researchers should teach their research staff. Novice researchers may learn about debriefing by observing an expert debriefer go through the entire process with a group of participants (Mills, 1976).

Conclusion

Establishing and maintaining trust and monitoring the safety of research participants is an ongoing process throughout the course of research. Researchers should take steps to ensure that the privacy of participants is continuously protected, that the actual and potential harms are continuously monitored and acted on as necessary, that the unique vulnerabilities of research participants be given special attention, and that there be appropriate and effective debriefing procedures. Decisions to use deception should be carefully considered. If a decision is made to use deception, researchers should take steps to remove any possible residual negative effects. By doing so, researchers establish conditions conducive to the collection of valid research results in an ethical manner.

References

Aronson, E., Wilson, T. D., & Brewer, M. B. (1998). Experimentation in social psychology. In D. T. Gilbert & S. T. Fiske (Eds.), *The handbook of social psychology* (4th ed., Vol. 1, pp. 99–142). Boston: McGraw-Hill.

Baumrind, D. (1979). IRBs and social science research: The costs of deception. *IRB: A Review of Human Subject Research, 1*(6), 1–4.

Baumrind, D. (1985). Research using intentional deception: Ethical issues revisited. *American Psychologist, 40*(2), 165–174.

Blanck, P. D., Bellack, A. S., Rosnow, R. L., Rotheram-Borus, M. J., & Schooler, N. R. (1992). Scientific rewards and conflicts of ethical choices in human subjects research. *American Psychologist, 47*(7), 959–965.

Christensen, L. (1988). Deception in psychological research: When is its use justified? *Personality and Social Psychology Bulletin, 14,* 664–675.

Clark, R. G. III, & Ward, L. E. (1974). Where is the apathetic bystander? Situational characteristics of the emergency. *Journal of Personality and Social Psychology, 29,* 279–287.

DeRenzo, E. G. (1994). The ethics of involving psychiatrically impaired persons in research. *IRB: A Review of Human Subjects Research, 16*(6), 7–10.

Fackelmann, K. (1995, February 18). AZT falls short for kids with HIV. *Science News,* p. 100.

Fisher, C. B. (1993). Joining science and application: Ethical challenges for researchers and practitioners. *Professional Psychology: Research and Practice, 24*(3), 378–381.

Holmes, D. S. (1976). Debriefing after psychological experiments: I. Effectiveness of post-deception dehoaxing. *American Psychologist, 31*(12), 858–875.

Kelman, H. (1967). Human use of human subjects: The problem of deception in social psychological experiments. *Psychological Bulletin, 67,* 1–11.

Melton, G., & Stanley, B. (n.d.). *Draft research ethics casebook.* Unpublished manuscript, Law/Psychology Program, University of Nebraska–Lincoln.

Milgram, S. (1963). Behavioral study of obedience. *Journal of Abnormal and Social Psychology, 67,* 371–378.

Milgram, S. (1964). Issues in the study of obedience: A reply to Baumrind. *American Psychologist, 19,* 848–852.

Mills, J. (1976). A procedure for explaining experiments involving deception. *Personality and Social Psychology Bulletin, 2*(1), 3–13.

Misra, S. (1992). Is conventional debriefing adequate? An ethical issue in consumer research. *Journal of the Academy of Marketing Science, 20*(3), 269–273.

Office for Protection From Research Risks, Protection of Human Subjects. (1991, June 18). Protection of human subjects: Title 45, Code of Federal Regulations, Part 46 (GPO 1992 O-307-551). *OPRR Reports,* pp. 4–17.

Prentice, E. D., Reitemeier, P. J., Antonson, D. L., Kelso, T. K., & Jameton. A. (1993). Bill of rights for research subjects. *IRB: A Review of Human Subjects Research, 15*(2), 7–9.

Ring, K., Wallston, K., & Corey, M. (1970). Mode debriefing as a factor affecting subjective reaction to a Milgram-type obedience experiment: An ethical inquiry. *Representative Research in Social Psychology, 1,* 67–88.

Ross, L., Lepper, M. R., & Hubbard, M. (1975). Perseverance in self-perception and social perception: Biased attributional processes in the debriefing paradigm. *Journal of Personality and Social Psychology, 32*(5), 880–892.

Scott-Jones, D. (1994). Ethical issues in reporting and referring in research with low-income minority children. *Ethics and Behavior, 4*(2), 97–108.

Sieber, J. E. (1983a). Deception in social research II: Evaluating the potential for harm or wrong. *IRB: A Review of Human Subjects Research, 5*(1), 1–6.

Sieber, J. E. (1983b). Deception in social research III: The nature and limits of debriefing. *A Review of Human Subjects Research, 5*(3), 1–4.

Sieber, J. E. (1992). *Planning ethically responsible research: A guide for students and internal review boards* (Applied Social Research Methods Series Vol. 31). Newbury Park, CA: Sage Publications.

Society for Research in Child Development. (1993). Ethical standards for research with children. In *Directory of Membership* (pp. 337–339). Washington, DC: Author.

Stewart, L. P. (1992). Ethical issues in postexperimental and postexperiential debriefing. *Simulation and Gaming, 23*(2), 196–211.

Thompson, R. A. (1992). Developmental changes in research risk and benefit: A chaining calculus of concerns. In B. Stanley & J. E. Sieber, (Eds.), *Social research on children and adolescents: Ethical issues* (pp. 31–64). Newbury Park, CA: Sage Publications.

7

Authorship and Intellectual Property

Matthew McGue

It is easy to understand why no area of scientific practice holds a greater potential for conflict than the area of data ownership and publication. Scholarly status and career advancement depend largely on one's record of publication, and the ability to publish will depend largely on one's ability to gather or access research data. Researchers have increasingly become involved in collaborative research (Over, 1982) and are therefore more likely than ever before to become involved in disputes over authorship credit and data access. Often these disputes are a consequence of differing perspectives on the nature of scholarly contribution to a joint project and thus a result of differing views on the appropriate credit individual collaborators should receive for their efforts.

Two of the basic ethical principles discussed in chapter 1, justice and fidelity to science, are especially relevant to the discussion in this chapter. Decisions regarding the ethical assignment of research credit and access to research data are informed by the principle of justice. Thus, application of the principle of justice would lead us to consider not only whether researchers are given appropriate credit for their scholarly contributions (distributive justice), but also whether the relevant discipline, research institutions, and investigative teams have established explicit procedures for fairly deciding how scholarly credit should be assigned (procedural justice). It is ideal when all members of the research team agree on the procedure for assigning and determining order of authorship on publications resulting from the research. Application of the principle of fidelity leads us to consider the integrity of scientific communications and their evaluations. Are research findings being reported accurately and thoroughly? Are the editorial evaluations of research reports obtained in a manner that minimizes the potential for reviewer bias?

Although ethical principles can provide guidance in the resolution of disputes like these, it is unlikely that an appeal to ethical principles alone will provide unequivocal resolution when the dispute involves differing interpretations of the nature and significance of individual contributions. Consequently, one of the recommendations of this chapter is that individuals involved in collaborative research, including faculty–student collaborations, establish agreements on how research responsibilities will be apportioned and how research credit will be allocated prior to initiating a joint research project. In an ideal situation, these agreements would form the basis for ongoing discussions and reevaluation as the research process unfolds and as the responsibilities and contributions of individual researchers shift.

Authorship

For the researcher, authorship is perhaps the single most important recognition of scientific contribution. Authorship also serves to identify those who are willing to take public responsibility for a piece of research. It is essential, then, that authorship accurately reflects those individuals who contributed fundamentally to the research.

Function

Authorship is used to identify to the public who is responsible for the work. In addition, authorship provides a record of scholarly productivity. As such, it is used in making hiring decisions, determining salary, deciding promotion and tenure, and evaluating candidates for awards and honors. A record of publication is used by others in a less formal sense for judging individual expertise and thus may be weighed heavily by professional organizations and agencies in deciding appointments and committee memberships, by colleagues interested in identifying potential collaborators, by students in selecting training programs that match their professional interests, and by editors in the selection of reviewers.

Authorship not only provides professional benefits but also requires the researcher to assume professional responsibility for the integrity of the research reported. Improper assignment of authorship can advance the careers of unethical scientists and erodes the confidence of colleagues, students, and nonscientists in the integrity of scientific research. Given the central role of authorship in career advancement and academic prestige, it is little wonder that the assignment of authorship is a common area of ethical concern for researchers (Swazey, Anderson, & Seashore, 1993).

Criteria

Authors should have contributed substantially to the conceptualization, design, execution, analysis, or interpretation of the research reported (American Psychological Association [APA], 1994, p. 4). An author may have contributed by formulating the research idea, designing the research protocol, engaging in creative analysis of the data, drafting a version of the manuscript, or critically commenting on a manuscript draft in a way that leads to substantive revisions in its content. In general, contributions to the research that are primarily of a technical nature do not warrant authorship but can be acknowledged in a publication note. Thus, authorship is not generally justified for individuals whose contributions to the research are limited to collecting, coding, or keying the data; running standard statistical analysis under the supervision of others; or providing ed itorial commentary on the manuscript. The contributions of methodologists and statistical analysts to the research project often merit authorship; the partnership of substantive researcher with a methodologist or statistician is important for large-scale research.

Responsibilities

By accepting authorship, an individual indicates that he or she is in fundamental agreement with its conclusions and willing to publicly defend the research and its interpretation. Authors should ensure that, to the best of their knowledge, the research was conducted ethically, the findings are reported accurately, and that all individuals contributing to the research have been given appropriate authorship credit. In submitting a manuscript for editorial review, authors are indicating that to the best of their knowledge the research reported has not been previously published or accepted for publication, and is not currently being considered for publication in another journal or book.

Occasionally after publication of a research report, an author will learn of errors in the data or its analysis that when corrected produce changes in the published findings. In those cases in which the data correction changes the interpretation of the research findings or could lead to possible misinterpretation by others, responsible researchers promptly communicate those corrections to the relevant editor and, when deemed appropriate, arrange for publication of an erratum or notification of publication retraction. Trivial errors or errors that are not likely to lead the careful reader to change his or her interpretation of the research do not, however, require publication correction. Thus, corrections that, for example, change a significant p value in the third decimal point, produce minimal changes in reported statistics, or add another participant to the sample without altering the overall pattern of results would not normally require correction, whereas the detection of an error in a scoring algorithm that when corrected results in substantial changes in the scores reported or the detection of an error in the statistical analysis that resulted in a qualitative change in the pattern of reported results should lead to a published erratum. If the researcher is uncertain about the need for publication correction, editorial consultation should be sought.

Researchers are encouraged to cooperate with editorial staff and institutional review boards (IRBs) or other responsible institutional officials when legitimate questions about the authenticity of published research data or findings arise. To be able to answer such questions, researchers need to archive primary data and accompanying records (usually for a minimum of 5 years after publication) and submit their data to the appropriate reviewing committees for verification when legitimate questions about authenticity arise.

The author communicating the manuscript to the journal editor (the corresponding author, typically the primary author) carries additional responsibilities. This author informs co-authors that the manuscript is being submitted for publication and gives each co-author the opportunity to read the manuscript and comment on its content prior to submission. The corresponding author should normally be able to identify the unique contribution of each individual listed as an author on the research report and assumes responsibility for providing the publisher with information about any prior publication of the research and copyright permissions when needed. The corresponding author attempts to keep co-authors apprised of the status of the review process and agrees to handle technical communications after the manuscript has been published. He or she also normally assumes the primary responsibility for arranging for an archive of the primary research data and for providing access to those data after publication.

Honorary Authorship

Ex-officio authorship is never appropriate. For example, authorship would not be warranted for individuals whose contributions were limited to either facilitation of the research through their administrative action (e.g., by providing laboratory space) or through providing technical assistance for the securing of research funds.

Although there may be general consensus against making authorship a benefit of administrative status, it is less clear how to decide authorship in cases, such as a longitudinal research project, in which those who initially conceptualized and designed the study (and thus might be seen as meeting authorship criteria) may no longer be actively involved in the research. Similar concerns about authorship can arise in large-scale collaborative research programs in which a laboratory director or principal researcher has charted the overall scientific direction of the research program but may not have been involved directly in how those ideas became implemented in a specific research design or analysis. Another situation in which comparable problems may arise may be when the contribution of one member is limited to granting access to data he or she collected for purposes other than addressing the research question at hand. Although it is not possible to offer general prescriptions governing authorship in cases like these, several factors might be considered in deciding whether an individual warrants authorship. First, rarely is the simple establishment of a data archive sufficient justification for authorship. Second, it may be difficult for individuals no longer actively involved in a research project to accept the responsibilities that go along with being an author (e.g., public defense). In any case, the contribution of the laboratory director or individual initiating a longitudinal study to the specific research project being reported should have been sufficiently substantial to justify authorship.

Conventions on Order

In the behavioral sciences, there exists a long-standing convention of ordering authors in multi-authored publications according to their degree of contribution. Thus, according to this convention and in the absence of any indication to the contrary, it would be assumed that the first listed author made the most substantial contribution to the work, the second author the next most substantial contribution, and so on. Order of authorship conventions can vary considerably among disciplines, however, greatly confounding the interpretation of the significance of authorship order. Thus, for example, authorship in some fields may be decided alphabetically, whereas in other fields the most prestigious authorship position may be the last rather than the first.

The interpretation of authorship order is further complicated by the existence of a second widely recognized (if not accepted) convention. A senior researcher will sometimes grant first authorship to a junior colleague even when the latter's contribution is not unambiguously greater than that of the senior researcher. Such practice is meant to serve the legitimate function of increasing the junior colleague's professional visibility (e.g., through citation counts and name recognition; Marshall, 1995). Further ambiguity about the meaning of authorship order arises when first authorship is rotated among principal researchers in a large collaborative research project or when the relative degree of author contribution cannot be decided easily.

The multiple meanings associated with authorship order in the different scientific disciplines and the increasing use of interdisciplinary collaborators would seem to preclude any general statement on how authorship order should be decided ethically. Nonetheless, several guidelines can be given. First, all authors, no matter what their position in a multi-authored publication, should meet criteria for authorship. Second, in the behavioral and social sciences, first authorship is likely to continue to be interpreted as identifying that individual who was the primary contributor to the work reported and thus be regarded as the most prestigious authorship position. Third, however decided, it is essential that the order of authorship reflect a consensus among those involved in the research. In order to achieve a consensus, it is important that individuals involved in collaborative research initiate discussions on how authorship will be decided prior to their beginning a joint research project. Fourth, when it is important to communicate to readers how authorship order was decided, authors should make use of a publication note.

Disputes and Prior Agreements

Many of the ambiguities and disputes surrounding authorship and authorship order could be prevented by establishing agreements among research collaborators prior to undertaking or writing up a research project. Prior agreements could detail how research responsibilities, including the responsibility for drafting the report, will be apportioned and how credit, including authorship order, will be decided. To minimize the potential for later misunderstanding and conflict, it is advisable that these agreements be documented in written form. It is important to recognize, however, that the establishment of prior agreements is not likely to preclude all disputes. Individuals' contributions can shift over the course of a research project in ways that could not have been easily anticipated at the outset. It is therefore important that authorship agreements are flexible and that collaborators' research involvement is subject to continuous review and the reassignment of responsibilities and credit as needed.

There will of course be times when collaborators are unable to resolve differences about authorship, methods of analysis, or interpretation of data. Resolving author disputes through multiple publication of essentially the same empirical finding is inappropriate, and alternatives should be sought. In psychology, duplicate publication of the same findings is an ethical violation (APA, 1992, Section 6.24). Even "piecemeal" publication of a research study (i.e., using different publications to report small parts of a dataset) rather than a more integrative report of the entire study is discouraged. When authors hold different interpretations of the data, it may be possible to include more than one interpretation in the research write-up. Or, when authors cannot agree about authorship order, they might seek the opinion of a third party. Some research institutions have established policies for resolving authorship disputes (e.g., National Academy of Sciences, 1993), and researchers are encouraged to consult with their research institutions about the existence and nature of these policies.

Student Publications

The same principles that guide decisions surrounding authorship in collaborative research among senior researchers apply also when students are involved. Thus, faculty members are not entitled to authorship solely by virtue of their status as advisors, nor should students expect to be recognized as authors when their research contributions have been technical rather than scientific in nature. To earn authorship, both faculty and student should meet the standard of having made a substantial intellectual contribution to the research and be willing to accept professional responsibility for the research reported. Determination of authorship should be made independently of any other compensation a student receives for his or her research efforts. The receipt of a research assistantship stipend is neither a substitute for nor a guarantee of authorship credit.

It is important to recognize that special safeguards may be needed to ensure that students receive proper credit for their scientific contributions. Students require the support of their faculty advisors both to finish their graduate programs and to successfully initiate their professional careers. The existence of this dependency may, if nothing else, lead students to feel disadvantaged in deciding matters of authorship with their faculty advisors. Faculty advisors and graduate training programs can minimize student perception of disadvantage by fostering an intellectual atmosphere in which students are neither embarrassed nor threatened by raising legitimate questions about authorship and the assignment of scientific credit.

The establishment of a prior agreement is perhaps the best safeguard against faculty–student authorship disputes. Prior to initiating a collaborative research project, students and their faculty advisors are encouraged to discuss how research responsibilities will be allocated and agree on how professional credit, including authorship and presentations at professional meetings, will be decided. In this way, both student and faculty member might enter a research collaboration with full knowledge of their responsibilities and assurance that their scientific contributions will be appropriately recognized. As is the case with any collaboration, however, it is important to recognize that an individual's level of involvement may shift over the course of a project so that the faculty advisor and student may need to reconsider authorship determination. In cases in which the student and faculty advisor cannot resolve an authorship dispute, consultation with a third party might be sought. Indeed, given the frequency with which concerns about authorship arise in joint faculty–student publications (Fine & Kurdeck, 1993; Goodyear, Crego, & Johnston, 1992), graduate training programs might want to consider the establishment of procedures for resolving faculty–student authorship disputes.

Dissertation research constitutes a special case of student research, warranting specific discussion. In most graduate training programs, the doctoral dissertation is viewed ideally as an independent student-initiated research project. Thus, the student would be expected to formulate the problem, develop the design, gather and analyze the data, and write up the report with relatively little substantive input from the faculty advisor. From this perspective, the faculty advisor may not warrant authorship credit. In practice, however, students come to the dissertation with varying degrees of prior experience and expertise. Indeed, in some instances, the dissertation represents the student's first research project, thus requiring substantial faculty input, or involves the student using a pre-existing dataset of the faculty mentor. In such cases, the faculty advisor might reasonably expect to be an author should articles derived from the dissertation be submitted for publication. In any case, it is generally expected that the student would have the opportunity to be the principal author on any publication resulting from the dissertation.

It is also important to recognize that the majority of dissertation research is never submitted for publication by the student and that failure to publish the dissertation can create serious difficulties for the faculty advisor if the dissertation research is an integral part of a larger collaborative research effort or if a funding agency expects publication as documentation of research progress. Prior to the initiation of the dissertation research, the faculty advisor and student should explicitly discuss and reach an agreement on publication requirements, including the alternatives the faculty member might pursue should the student fail to submit the dissertation for publication. Nonetheless, even in those cases in which the student failed to abide by an agreement to publish the dissertation, it would be inappropriate for the faculty advisor to submit the dissertation research for publication without the student's knowledge or appropriate authorship credit.

Reporting Research Results

Scientific progress depends on scientists submitting their research hypotheses, methods, and findings to the critical scrutiny of their scientific peers. Public dissemination allows other scientists to critically evaluate the soundness of an investigation's methodology and provides scientists with the opportunity to replicate research results. Toward these ends, researchers should attempt to provide accurate and thorough research reports, making sure to give appropriate credit when using the intellectual contributions of others. Although the most serious threat to the integrity of the scientific record is data fabrication or falsification, the scientific record is also compromised by research reports that are written in subtle ways that mislead the reader.

Accuracy in Reporting

Fundamental to any code of scientific ethics is that scientists honestly report their research findings. It is never appropriate to fabricate or falsify data. There are some cases where data are altered legitimately, if the nature of these alterations is described in the research report. Thus, the altering of demographic data to protect participant confidentiality or the statistical imputation of missing data are both examples of legitimate alteration of the primary research data. Because legitimate questions about the authenticity of observations can arise, the responsible researcher takes care to document and archive data associated with a given publication so that these records are available if a review is necessary. The generally accepted scientific practice is to retain research data for at least 5 years after results have been published.

Researchers should attempt to report their methods and analyses in a manner that allows readers to draw reasonable conclusions about the validity and generalizability of research findings and in sufficient detail to allow a competent researcher to replicate the study's methodology. Key details of the research protocol should not be concealed, nor should the researcher fail to report additional data analyses simply because findings from those analyses do not support the conclusions offered in the manuscript (Chalmers, 1990). In cases in which editorial policy precludes detailed description of research methodology, it is the accepted practice for researchers to provide those details on request. Also, it is generally expected that researchers will identify the source of their research funding when reporting research findings.

It is of course unreasonable to expect and unnecessary to require researchers to report every detail of the experimental protocol or every finding to emerge from the analysis of the data. There is a clear need for judgment. A useful guide in deciding what should be included in a research report is to adopt the perspective of a knowledgeable and interested reader. If the reporting of some finding, observation, or experimental detail is likely to substantially change the conclusions reached, then that information ought to be included in the report.

For example, whenever possible, researchers should report information on participation rates, sampling biases, and psychometric properties of measures, particularly when the reporting of such information serves to highlight deficiencies in research design. Researchers should also not report results selectively when a more comprehensive reporting would likely lead the reader to question the reliability of findings. Thus, researchers should not overstate the significance of results by reporting only a subset of the analyses completed, nor should they fail to report how key variables may have been redefined in the analyses in order to achieve desired results. Moreover, if manipulations of the data resulted in deletion of observations (e.g., as might occur with outliers), researchers should take care to carefully describe those manipulations and their justification. Researchers provide a context for evaluating the significance of research findings by noting limitations in research methodology and generalizability in the research report. A frank discussion of research limitations can have the added benefit of reducing the likelihood that nonscientists (including members of the media) will draw unwarranted generalizations from a research report.

In reporting research findings, researchers should also strive to protect the anonymity of research participants. In those cases in which anonymity cannot be assured (e.g., case studies and single-participant designs) researchers should obtain explicit consent from research participants for publication of material that might reveal their identities (see chapter 4).

Plagiarism and the Attribution of Intellectual Credit

Plagiarism occurs when the words, ideas, or contributions of others are appropriated in writing or speech without proper citation or acknowledgment. Researchers acknowledge the priority of the contributions of others by providing appropriate citations in research reports, by placing the material in quotes, or by otherwise indicating (e.g., by indenting longer quotations) that material is drawn from another source. When longer quotes, tabular information, or figures are reproduced, researchers by federal copyright law must secure reprint release prior to publication. Researchers should also avoid extensively paraphrasing the work of others without proper attribution (Levin & Marshall, 1993). But even then, it is advisable to seek written permission from the copyright holder and to acknowledge the paraphrasing in a footnote.

It is important to recognize that the protected nature of scientific communication is not limited to published material. Scientists are made aware of the ideas of others through many different mechanisms, including manuscript and grant review, presentations at professional meetings, and informal conversations with colleagues and students. In cases of privileged communications, such as grant applications and manuscripts submitted for review, researchers should maintain confidentiality by neither distributing the document to others nor using the information contained in the document for personal gain. In the case of unpublished communications such as conference presentations and informal conversations, it is expected that researchers will recognize the intellectual priority of others by giving them appropriate credit for their ideas.

The proper attribution of intellectual credit requires not only that individuals be given credit for their ideas but also that the nature and significance of their work not be knowingly misrepresented in a secondary source. Inappropriate citation can give the reader the false impression that there is greater scientific support for the argument being made than actually exists. Thus, researchers should ensure that the sources cited in a manuscript actually support the claims being made.

A common area of concern for many researchers involves the appropriate use of one's own published work (self-plagiarism). Thus, for example, researchers may want to use what is essentially the same methods description in all publications resulting from a large-scale project. Several factors can guide researchers' decisions involving the appropriate use of their own published writings. First, copyright release may not be needed to reproduce small amounts of published material. Second, extensive paraphrasing of a published methods section would be considered acceptable scientific practice if accompanied by a note indicating that the material had been adapted from an earlier publication. Third, the reprinting of tables and figures typically requires copyright release, regardless of word count. Fourth, extensive paraphrasing of other sections of a manuscript would be permissible if proper citation of the earlier work is included in the publication, copyright release is obtained as needed, and the publisher of the second article is made aware of the original publication. In uncertain cases, it is advisable to consult the relevant publishers and editors.

Piecemeal and Duplicate Publication

Piecemeal publication can arise from pressure from funding agencies, employers, and colleagues to demonstrate research progress and productivity. It can also result from a desire to ensure that all principals in a collaborative effort are recognized through distinct first-authored publications. Piecemeal and duplicate publication can lead to overstatements of the contributions of a given research project or investigative team. Piecemeal publication can result from the demands of journal editors and journal editorial policies that restrict article length. In this situation, researchers cannot be ethically faulted for wanting to have their work appear in what may be a well-respected journal in the field. Ethical concerns occur, however, when researchers report the results of a large research project in a larger number of overlapping publications rather than a smaller number of integrative reports, and this decision is unrelated to the demands of journal editors or policies. The existence of overlapping publications can make it difficult for the reader to gain an overall appreciation of findings from a given project, can unduly complicate the task of a reviewer aiming to summarize research in a given area, can lead to a waste of journal space and the effort of those involved in the editorial process, and can prevent researchers from confronting internal inconsistencies in their data.

Several recommendations can help researchers avoid piecemeal publication. First, the maximization of number of publications is not considered sufficient justification for multiple small publications rather than a single major publication. Second, it would be inappropriate to attempt to avoid internal inconsistencies in the data through piecemeal publication. Third, when overlapping publications do legitimately result from the same project, researchers should acknowledge the single larger project and attempt to describe how the multiple reports interrelate. Thus, for example, if publication of preliminary findings is followed by publication of a final set of analyses, the latter report should describe how the samples in the two sets of analyses relate, whereas the former might emphasize the tentative nature of the findings being reported.

Duplicate publication occurs when essentially the same material or research is published in more than one venue. However, given the efficiency of current abstracting technology, multiple publication of the same findings is not needed to reach a broad and diverse audience. Researchers should avoid duplicate publication in the primary research literature. Not only are there problems with copyright of the material, the practice is also considered unethical in psychology. There are, however, exceptions to the general proscription against duplicate publication. Published articles may be reprinted in anthologies or translated into another language if

- the priority of the original publication is clearly indicated in the reprinted work
- permission has been obtained from the original copyright holder
- the editor or publisher of the reprinted work has been fully informed about the existence of a prior publication.

In a similar way, it is appropriate for researchers to report in book chapters, research they have previously published in journals so long as all authors involved are informed and appropriate citations are given. It is also standard and accepted practice to follow a brief report (as might be published in a conference proceedings) with a more comprehensive report of study methodology and findings. Some conference proceedings, however, are considered archival publications and involve publication of considerably more than a brief abstract. In this case, the researcher is encouraged to consult the journal editor about the possible perception of duplicate publication between the proceedings and the journal publication, if considering journal publication after having the work appear in such proceedings.

Nonpublished Material and Media Releases

Ethical guidelines concerning scientific fraud, accuracy in reporting, plagiarism, and the appropriation of intellectual property apply to unpublished as well as published scientific communications. Thus, the same principles that guide researchers when contributing to the permanent scientific record would also apply when presenting at a scientific conference, writing a technical report, or producing a grant application.

Because the level of oversight may be relatively low and the competitive stakes relatively high, particular care may be needed when writing a grant proposal or progress report for a funding agency. Researchers should not make extravagant claims about the importance of their research, nor should they knowingly overstate research progress. In attempting to obtain research funding, it is expected that researchers will not propose research that they know is not feasible, that they have no intention of undertaking even if the application were to be funded, or that they have already completed.

A special instance of the nonpublished release of scientific findings involves communications through the lay media. Although some scientists may be reluctant to have their work reported in the popular press, it is important to recognize that there are legitimate reasons to support the popular reporting of scientific research. Both the scientist and the nonscientific public stand to benefit when scientific research is disseminated broadly and accurately. The public has a right to be kept informed of scientific advances, particularly when those scientific advances are funded through their tax dollars or donations. Moreover, popular support for scientific efforts and the translation of scientific findings into sound public policy depends on the existence of a scientifically informed populace.

Nonetheless, scientists have legitimate concerns about how their research is represented in the media. In particular, lay reporters can vary greatly in their degree of scientific sophistication, and some may not be able to judge the scientific validity of a given piece of research. As a result, lay descriptions of scientific research may overstate the significance of findings and may fail to contain the cautionary statements that would typically accompany publication in the scientific literature. That is, there is a risk that the nonscientific public will be misinformed by lay accounts of scientific research, resulting ultimately in the erosion of public confidence in science and perhaps also in the implementation of unsound policy decisions.

Although in a free society there may be no way to prevent the lay misrepresentation of scientific research, the potential for public misunderstanding can be minimized when scientists publish in the scientific literature before releasing their research findings to the general public. The goal of peer review is to ensure that research meets the methodological standards of a field and can survive expert critical scrutiny before warranting publication. As a consequence, scientists prefer to publish their research findings first in the peer-reviewed literature. Although the existence of peer review clearly does not preclude the subsequent publication of misleading lay research summaries, it does provide fellow scientists with a primary research report that can be critiqued and that can form the basis of a scientifically informed response to a misleading lay report.

Not Reporting Publishable Findings

A researcher's decision not to publish can have as many ethical implications as the decision to publish. For example, some individuals agree to participate in a research investigation only because they believe doing so contributes to a larger societal good. Failure to publish denies them the opportunity to fulfill that intention. Most significant, censoring certain research findings has the effect of producing biases and distortions in the research record. Researchers should attempt to minimize the distorting effects of censorship on scientific publications.

There are several ways in which research findings might be censored. Self-censorship occurs when researchers decide not to publish otherwise noteworthy findings because the results are theoretically inconvenient. In general, researchers should not engage in self-censorship. Institutional censorship occurs when a researcher's employer prevents or constrains research publication. In general, researchers are bound by the terms of their employment, and institutional censorship can serve legitimate organizational goals, including the protection of trade secrets and the promotion of competitive advantage. Nonetheless, conflicts may arise between individuals' professional obligations to their employer and their ethical obligations to society and their profession, such that there may be times when individuals are ethically justified in breaking employer bans on publication (see chapter 9).

Editorial censorship occurs when manuscripts are rejected for publication because they deal with controversial ideas rather than because of limitation in methodology or lack of theoretical significance. Editors and reviewers should minimize the likelihood of such censorship.

A special, temporary form of censorship exists at some journals. In order to protect their interests, some journals impose a media embargo between the time a paper is accepted for publication and the time the journal is officially released to the press. Media embargoes do not represent an ethical dilemma for the researcher unless delaying publication is likely to jeopardize the health or well-being of others. However, in these latter cases, journals typically release researchers from media embargo requirements.

The Editorial Process

Manuscripts submitted for publication are privileged communications. Editors and reviewers should respect the confidentiality of the manuscripts they review and refrain from discussing with those not directly involved in the review process the status or content of a review. Editors and reviewers respect the authors' intellectual property; they do not appropriate the ideas contained in a manuscript or proposal under review, nor do they communicate those ideas to others.

Reviewers should always strive to provide impartial evaluations and not knowingly delay or impede publication of a specific research report in order to gain earlier publication, and thus intellectual priority, for themselves or others. Thus, it is important that reviewers and editors attempt to become aware of their own scientific biases and to minimize the influence of those biases on the review process. Reviewers should not accept for review material that they are not qualified to evaluate. There are cases, however, in which reviewers are asked to evaluate some aspect of the manuscript (e.g., statistical procedures) because of their particular expertise, even when they are not experts in the field of the research. Reviewers should strive to submit reviews in a timely fashion, and they should provide clear documentation for the basis of a negative evaluation. Reviewers should be willing to disqualify themselves not only in cases in which they have a financial or personal incentive in seeing a paper published (e.g., in test or book reviews), but also when their own preconceived notions preclude a fair review of manuscripts and proposals or when their personal or professional relationship to the authors represents a conflict of interest.

Editors attempt to minimize bias in the review process by using reviewers with a diversity of backgrounds and theoretical orientations. Editors should consider establishing explicit guidelines for processing and reviewing manuscripts and consistently follow those guidelines when evaluating submitted work. Editors should attempt to ensure that manuscripts are evaluated in terms of the adequacy of the research methodology and significance of the theoretical issues addressed. Manuscripts should not be rejected simply because they espouse currently unpopular scientific ideas. Editors should investigate credible allegations of scientific misconduct directed at papers published in or under consideration at their journals and be prepared to publish an erratum or retraction if necessary (Caelleigh, 1993).

Data Ownership, Access, and Retention

Research data can take many forms; entries in a laboratory notebook, responses on a mailed survey, videotapes of an experimental session, observational logs, or computerized recordings. The term *primary data* refers to the raw data directly produced by an experiment or survey and is to be distinguished from processed data and derived results (Weinberg, 1993). In the discussion that follows, the term *research data* refers to the primary research data (or a copy of those data) along with their documentation.

Many groups have an interest in research data: researchers to produce valid reports, research institutions to fulfill their oversight responsibilities and protect their institutional reputations, funding agencies to further research initiatives, and students to complete academic requirements. Moreover, the goals of science can be furthered when research data are widely and freely accessible, even to those not directly involved in the production of those data. Unfortunately, there is currently much uncertainty among researchers about their rights and obligations concerning data ownership, access, and sharing.

The ensuing discussion distinguishes among the three. *Data owner-*

ship, a legal matter, concerns individual and organizational proprietary rights over research data. It serves to identify who ultimately controls access, publication, and destruction of research data. *Data access* concerns whether and how data are made available to those involved in the research, including researchers, individuals at institutions responsible for research oversight, and funding agencies. Data access thus concerns how those who control research data fulfill their commitments, both legal and ethical, to those involved in the production of the research data. Finally, *data sharing* denotes the practice of making research data available to individuals or researchers who are not directly involved in the research.

Data Ownership

Under current federal regulations, the grantee university or research institution holds legal title to research data acquired as part of a federally funded research project, unless the institution explicitly relinquishes its legal rights to data ownership (Fishbein, 1991). Thus, research institutions have the right to limit access to and control the dissemination of all research data produced by their staffs as part of a federally funded research project. Moreover, the legal principle of "works-for-hire" could be interpreted to further extend institutional ownership rights to all data generated by employee research, regardless of whether that research was federally sponsored (Fishbein, 1991). Under the works-for-hire principle, an employer can claim title to all employee work products, which in the case of an academic researcher would include all intellectual products and research data.

Many universities and research institutions have formal policies governing intellectual property, and these policies can range from the assertion of proprietary interest over all employees' intellectual work products to the complete waiving of institutional ownership rights. Researchers are encouraged to become knowledgeable about their own institution's policies governing intellectual property. It is nonetheless important to recognize that the failure of many academic institutions to exercise their intellectual property rights does not necessarily result in the nullification of those rights. There may be times when, in order to protect their own interests, researchers might want to seek an institutional waiver of legal title over a specific set of research data or intellectual product. If so, such waivers are best negotiated prior to initiating a research project.

By tradition and default, many universities have left it entirely up to researchers to decide the disposition of the research data that they produce. Thus, not only do researchers have unlimited access to their research data, but they also typically determine whether and with whom that data will be shared, whether and how the data will be disseminated, and ultimately how and when the data will be destroyed. Despite having what appear to be many of the perquisites of legal title, however, the academic researcher is probably better characterized as a caretaker rather than as an owner of the research data that he or she produces (Fishbein, 1991). Uncertainty over data ownership can lead to problems especially when researchers change institutions or are involved in multiresearcher collaborations. Nonetheless, departing researchers and individual collaborators are almost always allowed to have access to a copy of the primary research data.

Although the ownership of data produced by faculty research appears relatively certain, the status of student-produced research data raises some additional issues. If a student produces his or her thesis data as part of the conditions of employment (e.g., as a research assistant), then the academic institution may be able to claim legal title over the thesis data. At the same time, the principal researcher of the research grant that funded the student would have a clear interest in the data. In the behavioral sciences, however, many students do not receive any direct financial support for their thesis research from either their institution or a funding agency. Indeed, in many cases students may use their own finances and efforts to offset the cost of their thesis research. In these cases, students would have legitimate reason to claim legal title to their thesis data. Nonetheless, even if direct financial support is not provided, institutions typically support student research indirectly by providing institutional facilities (e.g., laboratories and participant pools) and research support services (e.g., IRBs, faculty consultation) and by allowing the student to use the institution's reputation to facilitate his or her research (e.g., to recruit participants). Moreover, faculty advisors help the student design, analyze, and interpret thesis research. Thus, academic institutions and their faculty have a legitimate interest in the products of student research, and it is reasonable to expect that in order to protect that interest institutions and faculty advisors may claim the right to access and review student research data. Students, like faculty, are encouraged to consult institutional policies governing research data before initiating their research in order to clarify ownership issues.

Data Access

Data access concerns how data are made available to those individuals involved, either directly or indirectly, in a research project. In the absence of any formal institutional policy governing research data, it is typically left to individual researchers to decide data access issues. In deciding such issues, researchers should attempt to represent fairly the interests of their institutions while complying with relevant law. Several factors can help guide researchers in making these decisions.

First, individual researchers may require data access in order to fulfill their authorship responsibilities. Thus, a co-author should be allowed to review research data in order to verify its authenticity and confirm the accuracy of processed results. Second, by increasing the scrutiny of research data, open access can result in improved data quality and validity. Open access is especially important in training programs in which mentors are expected to give constructive feedback to apprentice researchers.

Third, many colleagues and students enter a joint research project with the expectation that their efforts will earn them access to the research data for purposes of publication. These expectations should be discussed prior to the initiation of the research project and should lead to an agreement on data access. Fourth, data access may become mandatory when legitimate questions concerning data authenticity arise. For the purposes of verification, researchers may be required to submit primary research data to editorial review boards, funding agencies, or institutional oversight committees.

There can also be disadvantages to open access, although these can often be addressed through careful planning. For example, although open access can foster a sense of cooperation in large-scale collaborative projects in which several individuals are working on the same dataset, it can also create the potential for conflict when two individuals unknowingly pursue overlapping research projects. In order to minimize the potential for research overlap and conflict, investigative teams and laboratories could develop policies for how research priority would be established. These policies might also include explicit guidelines for how a specific research project is proposed and approved, as well as for how competing interests between different researchers would be mediated.

A special concern with data access arises when an individual changes institutions or becomes dissociated from a multiresearcher collaboration. In most cases, the departing researcher would be entitled to at least a copy of the research data. Moreover, academic institutions, which are not prepared to establish and maintain a data archive, by default often allow researchers to take research data with them when they leave the institution. In the case of multiresearcher collaborations, it is advisable for the researchers to establish an agreement over data access rights prior to initiating their joint research project.

Data Sharing

Data sharing, providing copies of research data to individuals or groups not directly involved in the original research or its publication, can serve two functions (Weinberg, 1993). First, an individual may have legitimate questions about the validity of a published research report. Rather than make a formal inquiry through an editorial board or funding agency, where right to data access could be claimed, that individual might elect to contact directly the principal author of the research report. Although not constituting a formal charge of scientific misconduct, individual requests to verify data should be made after much consideration, as these requests are likely to be interpreted as challenges to the authors' integrity. Second, and more frequently, requests for copies of published data may come from individuals or groups who wish to use the data in their own research.

The decision to share data is consistent with long-standing scientific norms on the free exchange of information. The benefits of data sharing are readily apparent. Data sharing can lead to better science by opening up the scientific process to public scrutiny and, more significantly, by encouraging maximal use of a scarce commodity. Some funding agencies and scientific journals now require that researchers share their data with other qualified researchers as a condition of accepting grant support or manuscript publication (Marshall, 1990). In some cases, researchers are expected to deposit their data in a public access data archive sometime after data acquisition is completed.

In the behavioral sciences, requests to share data have increased with the growing use of meta-analytic methods of literature review. Sometimes these requests cover both published and unpublished findings. Because the meta-analyst requires a representative sampling of research findings in order to draw valid summary conclusions, individual researchers can facilitate the accurate synthesis of research data by complying with these requests.

Despite its many benefits, some researchers will have concerns about sharing their data. These concerns include questions about the costs of data sharing, loss of publication priority, the increased scrutiny that is likely to accompany data sharing, and threats to confidentiality. Researchers may also be concerned that data sharing will lead to added criticism of their work. Many of these concerns can often be easily addressed, however (Sieber, 1991). Thus, the individual requesting data should be prepared to cover the nominal costs associated with its duplication and transmission, and researchers would not be expected to share data that are unpublished or being actively worked on, so that there should be little threat to publication priority. Researchers should agree to requests to share data where it is solely for the purpose of checking the accuracy of the researchers' analyses and where confidentiality of participants is assured (cf. Camara & Schneider, 1995).

In contrast, the concern that data sharing might result in a breach of confidentiality might not be easy to address (see chapter 5). Sometimes the data are not anonymous (e.g., videotapes, some case studies), or the publicity surrounding a given study might allow other researchers to identify specific research participants (e.g., as might occur in the study of a small group of individuals who all experienced a rare traumatic event). In cases like these, the researcher would likely need to obtain consent from research participants before sharing that data with other researchers. Researchers are advised to consult with their IRBs in cases in which sharing data could in any way compromise the protection of confidentiality of the participants.

Additional concerns may arise when data are deposited in a public-access data archive. In many cases, such data would be totally anonymous as to the participants, and the data would be used only for secondary analysis. In these cases, further informed consent would be unnecessary. However, when necessary, the process of obtaining informed consent involves a description of research goals and procedures as well as information on who will have access to the data (see chapter 4). Therefore, research participants ought to be informed if the researcher intends to establish a public-access data archive in which participants' data either individually or as a part of identifiable groups would be part of the shared data. Researchers may be restricted in establishing a public-access data archive if the decision to do so came only after they had completed data collection. That is, some participants might not have wanted the information that they provided to be publicly available, even if making that information available would not constitute any threat to their confidentiality or privacy. Again, researchers are encouraged to consult with their IRBs on cases where issues of confidentiality or privacy are involved.

It is important to recognize that the individual or group requesting copies of research data are ethically bound to maintain the confidentiality of the research data that they receive. In requesting data, they should indicate how they intend to use the research data and agree not to make copies of the data for others unless they have been given explicit permission to do so by the original researchers. In publishing findings from shared data, researchers should clearly acknowledge the source of that data.

Recent legislation in the United States serves to illustrate both the level of public interest in the sharing of research data as well as the difficulties such sharing can create for the researcher. In 1998, Congress passed the 1999 Omnibus Appropriations Bill (P. L. 105-277), which included language directing the Office of Management and Budget (OMB) to amend procedures for the award of research grants or contracts "to require Federal awarding agencies to ensure that all data produced under an award will be made available to the public through procedures established under the Freedom of Information Act" (FOIA) (p 496). The legislation was a direct response to the refusal of researchers at Harvard University to release data from a research project funded by the U.S. Environmental Protection Agency and used in developing environmental regulations.

The OMB request for public comment on the proposed rule change resulted in a flood of more than 9,000 responses. Commentators in support of the legislation argued that the public has a right to research data acquired with federal funds, especially when that data is used to formulate federal policies or guidelines. Members of the scientific community who responded also supported the importance of open access to research data but raised serious reservations with the proposed rule change. In particular, concerns were raised about the need to protect the confidentiality of research participants, the possibility that nuisance requests for research data made under FOIA will be used to discourage scientists from pursuing controversial research projects, and the need to ensure that research data not be released for public scrutiny prior to publication and review by the scientific community. OMB heeded warnings from the scientific community by significantly limiting the scope of applicability of the new law (i.e., to only published research that is used in formulating federal regulations that have an impact of at least $100 million). Nonetheless, given public interest in and support of scientific research, it seems likely that there will be continued efforts to encourage if not mandate the sharing of research data.

Data Retention

In principle, the primary responsibility for retaining and disposing of research data would fall to its owner, in most cases, the employing institution. In practice, the responsibility for data retention is likely to reside with individual researchers. The failure of research institutions to develop clear policies on data retention and disposition does not absolve individual researchers from handling data in a responsible and ethical manner. Although there is no universally agreed-on standard, most researchers agree that the primary research data should be retained for at least 5 years following publication. Researchers should develop and institute procedures for retaining primary research data that preserve the integrity of the data, protect the confidentiality of research participants, and adequately document the nature of the data.

There is even less guidance on how or when research data should be destroyed. It would be prudent for the individual choosing to destroy primary research data to provide ample notification to the institutional owners of the data and to those involved in the production and analysis of the data. Once data have been destroyed, it can be very difficult to establish research authenticity.

Conclusion

In this chapter, the issues concerning the status of intellectual property were examined, including authorship, the writing and review of research reports, and the ownership of research data. For researchers, authorship is the primary mechanism by which they gain recognition for their scientific contributions. It is also a means for conveying to others that they are willing to take professional responsibility for a piece of research. Researchers should neither accept nor award authorship where it is not warranted. The authorship criteria reviewed in this chapter serve as a guide to researchers in determining when authorship is justified.

In addition, as scientific progress depends on the accurate reporting of research findings, researchers should strive to produce research reports that are thorough and honest. In particular, they should not try to hide or minimize research flaws when knowledge of those flaws is likely to affect the interpretation or judged significance of their research. Researchers should also strive to acknowledge the intellectual contributions of others through proper citation and quotation and attempt to evaluate the work of others free from personal or self-serving bias.

Finally, a distinction was made among data ownership, data access, and data sharing. Research institutions, including academic institutions, have a legitimate legal interest in data produced by their employees and may have thus established institutional policies on data ownership, access, and sharing. Researchers are strongly encouraged to become knowledgeable of their institutions' policies governing intellectual property.

Although the status of intellectual property holds great potential for conflict, there are steps that researchers, training programs, and research institutions can take to help minimize the possibility that problems will occur. Researchers can discuss with their collaborators expectations for how research responsibilities and credit will be allocated. In an ideal situation, these discussions would begin prior to research initiation, continue throughout the duration of the joint research project, and lead to some agreement among collaborators about how authorship and data access will be decided. Training programs can provide research trainees with information about researchers' rights and responsibilities in the area of intellectual property. Training programs can also strive to foster a research atmosphere in which trainees feel neither disadvantaged nor embarrassed in raising legitimate concerns regarding their intellectual property rights. Finally, research institutions can develop policies that provide researchers with clear guidance on the treatment of intellectual property.

References

American Psychological Association. (1992). Ethical principles of psychologists and code of conduct. *American Psychologist, 47*(12), 1597–1611.

American Psychological Association. (1994). *Publication manual of the American Psychological Association* (4th ed.). Washington, DC: Author.

Caelleigh, A. S. (1993). Role of the journal editor in sustaining integrity in research. *Academic Medicine, 68*[Suppl. 3], S23–S29.

Camara, W. J., & Schneider, D. L. (1995). Questions of construct breadth and openness of research in integrity testing. *American Psychologist, 50,* 459–460.

Chalmers, I. (1990). Underreporting research is scientific misconduct. *Journal of the American Medical Association, 263,* 1405–1408.

OMB Circular A-110 (1999). Uniform administrative requirements for grants and agreements with institutions of higher education, hospitals, and other non-profit organizations. *Federal Register, 64,* 54926–54930.

Fine, M. A., & Kurdek, L. A. (1993). Reflections on determining authorship credit and authorship order on faculty-student collaborations. *American Psychologist, 48,* 1141–1147.

Fishbein, E. A. (1991). Ownership of research data. *Academic Medicine, 66,* 129–133.

Goodyear, R. K., Crego, C. A., & Johnston, M. W. (1992). Ethical issues in the supervision of student research: A study of critical incidents. *Professional Psychology: Research and Practice, 23,* 203–210.

Levin, J. R., & Marshall, H. H. (1993). Publishing in the *Journal of Educational Psychology*: Reflections at midstream. *Journal of Educational Psychology, 85,* 3–6.

Marshall, E. (1990). Data sharing: A declining ethic? *Science, 248,* 952–957.

Marshall, E. (1995). Better relationships the Stadtman way. *Science, 268,* 1713.

National Academy of Sciences, Panel on Scientific Responsibility and the Conduct of Research. (1993). *Responsible science: Ensuring the integrity of the research process* (Vol. II). Washington, DC: National Academy Press.

Over, R. (1982). Collaborative research and publication in psychology. *American Psychologist, 37,* 996–1001.

Sieber, J. E. (1991). Openness in the social sciences: Sharing data. *Ethics and Behavior, 1,* 69–86.

Swazey, J. P., Anderson, M. S., & Seashore, K. S. (1993). Ethical problems in academic research. *American Scientist, 81,* 542–553.

Weinberg, R. A. (1993). Reflections on the current state of data and reagent exchange among biomedical researchers. In National Academy of Sciences, Panel on Scientific Responsibility and the Conduct of Research (Ed.), *Responsible science: Ensuring the integrity of the research process* (Vol. II, pp. 66–78). Washington, DC: National Academy Press.

8

Training

June Tangney

In the course of conducting research, researchers encounter numerous opportunities to educate and train others. These opportunities arise not only with students and research staff, but also with human research participants and with the public at large. In discussing ethical issues related to education and training in the context of research, this chapter draws on each of the five moral principles described in chapter 1. Of particular relevance are the moral principles of autonomy, beneficence and nonmaleficence, and fidelity.

Most researchers work to maximize the benefits of research by sharing new knowledge whenever feasible in a clear and accessible manner with students, participants, colleagues, policy makers, and society as a whole. To maximize the benefits and minimize the potential harm of research, researchers try to work closely with students and research staff and provide ample supervision. These activities include ensuring that research staff are adequately trained in procedures and issues relevant to the specific research project, that they have a working familiarity with ethical principles in general, and that there is sufficient opportunity to address unforeseen challenges as the research process unfolds. Such careful instruction and supervision of students and research staff have the advantage of promoting staff competence and the scientific integrity of the research. Equally important, careful supervision creates a climate that is most likely to minimize the potential harm to participants and maximize the benefits to human welfare. In their supervision of research staff, psychologists promote respect for human research participants, and they model such respect in their interactions with students and staff.

Educating Students and Staff on Ethics

Researchers are responsible for the ethical conduct of research conducted by them and by others under their supervision or control. Researcher–supervisors have a responsibility to ensure that research staff and students are familiar with ethical principles and standards relevant to research, and researcher–supervisors take an active role in helping students and staff learn to apply these principles and standards to research contexts.

Many research-training programs have required research ethics courses or workshops. These courses can provide a useful forum for discussion of ethics and ethical principles across the variety of expertise areas found in most graduate programs. National Institutes of Health–sponsored research training programs require that trainees (both predoctoral and postdoctoral) be formally trained in issues of research ethics.

However, more than formal training is needed. Ethical concerns that arise in the course of research can be subtle and unanticipated. Part of training students and research staff includes teaching them to recognize and frame ethical issues in the course of their day-to-day research activities. Researcher–supervisors may be in a special position to help bring to life abstract ethical principles in a way that formal course work may not; ethics training in the context of an ongoing research project has immediate relevance to students.

Moreover, as emphasized by Whitbeck (1995, 1996), such context-based training in ethics teaches students much about the process of ethical problem solving and decision-making (see chapter 9). Rather than being presented with preselected ethical dilemmas, students learn to identify potential ethical problems. Rather than being presented with a multiple-choice menu of prefabricated responses (of which one is typically "best" or "right"), students learn to formulate and refine alternative options. Most important, they do so in the context of real-life problems that are often subtle and complex. Consequently, students learn when to gather additional relevant information and where to turn for consultation and advice. In the process, they learn that new information can substantially transform the problem, resulting in the need for reevaluation and reformulation of possible solutions. In short, by learning about research ethics through hands-on experience, students can learn to become active ethical agents (Whitbeck, 1995).

To facilitate this learning, researchers are encouraged to include students and research staff in their consideration of ethical issues during the design phases of the work, as well as in the preparation of materials for the institutional review board (IRB). In this context, researchers can encourage students to review this volume and the *Ethical Principles* of the American Psychological Association (APA) found in appendix A (APA, 1992) as they are designing and reviewing the research plan. And they can provide more general information on the nature, purpose, and requirements of IRBs.

Because of IRB requirements, there is sometimes a tendency to overemphasize ethical issues during the formulation of research to the exclusion of ethical issues that arise during and after the research. Researchers can underscore that the ethical conduct of research is a process extending from initial design, to pilot testing, through data collection, through data reduction and analysis, and to the dissemination of findings and beyond by including students and staff in their own deliberations on ethical matters as they arise. Researchers are encouraged to alert students and staff to ethical problems and dilemmas that might be anticipated as this process unfolds. In addition, it is good practice to construct an ongoing training and supervision experience in such a way that students and staff are encouraged to raise ethical questions and concerns, as well as procedural questions, throughout the duration of the project. This may be done, for example, through regular meetings of the researcher–supervisors, students, and staff.

Regular research staff meetings are especially helpful during the initial phases of data collection when a research plan is put into action. As a research project comes to life, unanticipated challenges and issues are more the rule than the exception, and assistant errors are virtually inevitable. Students and staff on the front line of pilot testing and data collection are often best placed to notice the unexpected (e.g., unanticipated adverse reactions of participants, errors in implementing the research protocol). Their observations and input on the day-to-day realities of research procedures, as they are implemented, as well as the dialogue that arises from periodic discussions of ethical issues will almost certainly enhance the ethical integrity of the project.

Regular staff meetings can be indispensable even beyond the critical early phases of data collection. Once the kinks have been worked out of a research protocol, the initial excitement for a project may wane. As monotony sets in, research assistants' attention may drift, and care in implementing procedures may decline. It is helpful for researcher–supervisors to prepare students and research staff for this likelihood and to encourage continued vigilance. Regular research meetings and associated discussion can help focus research staff and infuse later stages of data collection with a renewed sense of purpose.

In summary, structured training and supervision can play an important role in helping researchers fulfill their primary responsibility—to monitor the conduct of students and research staff to ensure that the research project is conducted in a scientifically sound and ethical manner.

Ensuring Student and Staff Competence

Just as researchers should maintain high standards of competence in their own work, they should educate students and research staff to perform similarly. For example, when working with child research participants, it is good practice to provide research staff with adequate training and supervision on how to tailor the informed consent process and research procedures to the child's developmental level. When working with participants from culturally diverse backgrounds, it is good practice to provide research staff with adequate training and supervision so that research procedures are conducted in a culturally sensitive manner. When conducting interviews on personally relevant topics (e.g., episodes of stress or trauma, experiences of shame and guilt, the sequelae of divorce, and so forth), it is important to instruct research staff on the ethics of confidentiality and the potential problem of overstepping the bounds of their role as researchers by inappropriately offering advice or guidance. When conducting studies involving deception, research staff can typically make good use of training and supervision on how to sensitively and effectively debrief participants at the conclusion of the study (Ross, Lepper, & Hubbard, 1975).

As already noted, the training of students and staff is most effective when viewed as an ongoing process. Although a substantial period of training is typically necessary prior to the initial phase of data collection, ongoing supervision, and discussion (e.g., through regular meetings of the researcher–supervisor, students, and staff) can be indispensable throughout the duration of a project. Unanticipated questions and challenges are inevitable. Research assistants are bound to make an occasional error. And human research participants are, in a very real sense, active participants in a study, adding their own source of variability and surprise to the research process. Even with the best plan, situations will arise in which research assistants will not know what to do. It is important for researcher–supervisors to acknowledge that students and staff may encounter situations that they cannot and should not handle themselves without consultation. It is essential to provide staff with regular opportunities to raise questions and to solve problems on shared concerns. In so doing, students and research staff are more likely to feel valued and supported, they are better able to conduct the research at a high level of competence, and the data resulting from the project are ultimately enhanced.

In order to provide quality training and supervision, researchers do not supervise outside the bounds of their own competence. This issue can arise, for example, in the context of dissertation supervision, in which advanced students sometimes tackle independent research that is within a supervisor's central area of study. When aspects of a research project tread outside of the researcher's area of expertise (e.g., in terms of topic, statistics, or methods), the researcher may find it necessary to turn to knowledgeable colleagues for consultation and, when appropriate, assistance in supervision. As researchers develop and extend their research, they may find it necessary to seek continuing education through workshops, course work, individualized study, consultation with colleagues, and so on. And students and research staff can be an invaluable source of new knowledge and skills, too. At its best, research supervision is a shared enterprise in which researcher–supervisors share their knowledge and experience, while at the same time drawing on the special skills and expertise of those under their supervision.

Ensuring Student and Staff Familiarity With Legal Obligations

Researchers have a responsibility to ensure that students and research staff are familiar with the legal obligations and issues that may arise with regard to the research, including federal regulations regarding IRBs, informed consent, and limits of confidentiality. For example, when working with children or families in many contexts, research staff need to be made aware of the duty to report suspected child abuse and the mechanism for doing so. In this regard, it is important to provide research staff with clear instructions on how and when to alert the researcher–supervisors that a potential problem exists. In many cases, researchers and staff may not have sufficient clinical background to adequately identify and evaluate signs of potential child abuse. When necessary, researcher–supervisors should seek appropriate consultation to ensure that decisions to report are made competently, with sufficient grounds, and without biases related to ethnicity or socioeconomic status (Scott-Jones, 1994).

Ensuring Safety

In designing research procedures, researcher–supervisors take steps where necessary to ensure the safety of students and research staff in the course of the research. For example, when working with biological data such as blood samples, research staff are provided with training on universal precautions. In studies involving fieldwork (e.g., home visits), research procedures are designed with the safety of data gatherers in mind (e.g., conducting home interviews in pairs, providing staff with emergency pagers). Even in the case of minimal risk research, there is the possibility of emergencies unrelated to the research (e.g., heart attacks, epileptic seizures). Consequently, it is helpful to provide staff with information on resources for dealing with emergencies at the research site (e.g., telephone numbers should the need arise for counseling, medical care, or police assistance).

Avoiding Abusive or Exploitative Relationships

Researchers respect the rights of their students and staff to hold values, attitudes, and opinions that differ from their own. Researchers show respect for the fundamental rights, dignity, and worth of students and staff, as well as research participants. Researchers should be aware of the power they wield over the careers of their students and research employees. It is important that all members of the research team have opportunities for professional development and that their skills not be exploited for the sole benefit of the principal investigator. Researchers do not engage in abusive or exploitative relationships with students or research staff. They also do not engage in sexual relationships with students or research staff over whom they have evaluative or direct authority. They should instruct their students and research staff that it is inappropriate to become personally or sexually involved with research participants. Finally, researchers endeavor to be sensitive to the potential conflicts that may arise in cases in which they have essentially dual roles with student research assistants (e.g., when serving as both employer and faculty evaluator). Researchers should be aware that students may be reluctant to set appropriate limits in one role because of researchers' power in the second role (see chapter 9).

Clarifying the Nature of Supervision and Honoring Agreements

Supervision of students and research staff is enhanced by a clear understanding of the nature of supervision to be provided, by a mutual understanding of each party's responsibilities, and whenever possible by a working timetable for completion of those responsibilities. This is especially helpful in the context of thesis or dissertation work. Some students work well independently or under moderate supervision. Others may make excessive demands or have erroneous assumptions about the extent of supervision to be provided. Misunderstandings can be avoided by early candid discussion of the nature of the supervisory experience and the manner in which feedback is to be provided. Researcher–supervisors then honor their agreements to the best of their abilities, providing timely feedback.

Students and research staff may embark on a project with an expectation that the project will ultimately result in publication or formal presentation. Such "products" may be seen as especially important for individuals at the beginning stages of their careers. Researcher–supervisors can do much to avoid erroneous assumptions or later misunderstandings by explicitly discussing the long-term plans for a project, including plans for dissemination of results and issues of authorship (see chapter 7). In many instances, such agreements may need to be reevaluated and adjusted according to the performance of the parties involved. As projects progress, researcher–supervisors honor their agreements to the best of their abilities, avoiding, for example the "file drawer" problem (partially completed projects or manuscripts that end up in the file drawer). Such agreements help ensure that researchers produce quality work in good faith and in a timely manner.

Giving Publication Credit

Researchers ensure that principal authorship and other publication credits accurately reflect the relative scientific or professional contributions of the individuals involved, regardless of their relative status and regardless of whether individuals received monetary compensation for their work (see chapter 7). For example, some students may receive a research assistantship stipend for their work, but such payment does not preclude authorship. Determination of authorship should be independent of monetary awards and based solely on the substantive contributions of the assistant.

Novice researchers may have limited knowledge or mistaken assumptions about the basis for determining authorship. Researcher–supervisors can educate students and research staff about the norms for assignment of publication credit by explicitly discussing the basis for credit, as well as the question of data ownership, with those who are substantively involved in a project at the outset of the work. Recognizing that the nature of individuals' contributions may shift in the course of a project, researchers should attempt to clarify implications of their specific involvement as the research process unfolds (see chapter 7).

Questions frequently arise concerning the appropriateness of authorship credit for supervisors of theses or dissertations. In practice, students come to the dissertation with varying degrees of prior experience and expertise. In fact, in some instances, the dissertation represents the student's first research project. Thus, there is considerable variability in the degree to which faculty supervisors play a substantive role in the development and implementation of dissertation or thesis work (Goodyear, Crego, & Johnston, 1992). Throughout the dissertation process, researcher–supervisors are encouraged to discuss and evaluate together with the student the appropriateness, if any, of supervisor co-authorship, based on their relative contributions to the project. There is a presumption that the student will be listed as principal author on any multiple-authored article that is substantially based on the student's dissertation or thesis, unless there is a clear and compelling reason to do otherwise. Issues of authorship (with students and in general) are discussed in greater detail in chapter 7.

Educating Research Participants

In the course of conducting research, opportunities arise for educating research participants. As part of their commitment to contribute to the welfare of those with whom they interact professionally, researchers seek to maximize the benefits of participation to human research participants. Increased scientific knowledge is one of the most common benefits accrued by participants in psychological research. Thus, in conducting research, researchers are encouraged to make concerted efforts to structure debriefing procedures to be educational and informative. Good practice involves providing participants with a clear explanation (in language that is understandable to them) of the nature and purpose of the study, of existing scientific knowledge on which it is based, the manner in which it is intended to extend the scientific literature, and the importance of the research to society in general. In addition, researchers can provide research participants with an opportunity to subsequently obtain appropriate information about the results and conclusions of the research, in language that is understandable to them. For example, the researcher may maintain a mailing list of participants who are interested in a future summary of the study findings. The researcher may provide participants with a telephone number, inviting them to contact the researcher for an update on the study results at some specified later date. In the case of a longitudinal investigation, the researcher may routinely mail updates of the study's progress to research participants. When a promise is made to provide such information, researchers make every effort to honor these obligations. In practice, however, it is often difficult to reach former participants with updates, especially in nonlongitudinal studies. Moreover, because it typically takes months (sometimes many months) to code, enter, and analyze study data, such subsequent updates may be less meaningful to participants because the context of the research has been lost. In many respects, information provided during the initial debriefing (e.g., immediately at the end of the study) may be the most useful and informative to participants, although the actual results of the study are not yet known.

Researchers have a special responsibility when drawing on undergraduate participant pools, in which a key purpose of participation is education—that is, to provide students with firsthand experience with research and an increased understanding of how broad scientific principles and methods are applied to address specific questions. In effect, researchers are placed in a dual role as scientist and educator. They are encouraged to take special care to structure their feedback to students in a way that significantly enhances the students' understanding of science.

At the same time, researchers recognize that some participants may not be interested in the information and explanations that the researcher had intended to provide. Some participants might prefer, if given the choice, to forgo a detailed explanation. It is important to recognize and respect the participant's preference in such instances.

Educating the Public

The ultimate reward of psychological research is increased knowledge and understanding of human behavior—information that can often have substantial applied implications. As part of their commitment to contribute to the welfare of others, researchers are encouraged to communicate research findings to public policy makers and to the public at large in language understandable to lay audiences and to promote the use of those findings to benefit human welfare. In doing so, researchers make efforts to ensure that their findings are presented accurately and in such a way as to avoid misuse or misinterpretations and to increase appreciation of the importance of social and behavioral research (see chapter 7). Currently, most researchers in psychology and related disciplines receive little training in how to interact effectively with public policy makers and the media. The contributions of behavioral science research to society's welfare would be substantially enhanced by increased attention to these issues in graduate training programs and beyond.

Researchers may consider interacting with their institutional public relations offices to familiarize the officials with their research and to provide accurate and appropriate reporting of important research findings, especially when these findings have direct public-policy implications. Institutional public-relations colleagues can provide assistance in drafting accurate press releases and in helping researchers prepare for interviews by the media. Especially in the case of publicly funded research, researchers may thus fulfill their responsibility to share their research findings with the public. It is highly recommended that a peer-reviewed publication of the findings precede a report of the research results in the public media. Interactions with the press often result in better public appreciation of behavioral research than would be promoted by the scientific publication alone.

Conclusion

Educating and supervising research staff and students is an important component of conducting research in many contexts. This chapter reviewed a range of ethical issues that arise when training and supervising junior collaborators and research employees. Researchers have an ethical obligation to educate students and staff about legal and ethical issues relevant to a research project, to provide adequate training and supervision, and to monitor the research process as it unfolds. In doing so, researcher–supervisors treat their students and research staff with dignity and concern, taking steps to ensure staff safety, avoiding abusive or exploitative relationships, and establishing and honoring clear and equitable agreements with junior colleagues. This chapter also emphasized that opportunities to educate others extend beyond the confines of laboratory staff. Researchers can maximize the benefits and appreciation of behavioral research by sharing new knowledge with research participants and with the public at large, in this way promoting the use of research findings to benefit human welfare.

References

American Psychological Association. (1992). Ethical principles of psychologists and code of conduct. *American Psychologist, 47*(12), 1597–1611.

Goodyear, R. K., Crego, C. A., & Johnston, M. W. (1992). Ethical issues in the supervision of student research: A study of critical incidents. *American Psychologist, 23,* 203–210.

Ross, L., Lepper, M. R., & Hubbard, M. (1975). Perseverance in self-perception and social perception: Biased attributional processes in the debriefing paradigm. *Journal of Personality and Social Psychology, 32,* 880–892.

Scott-Jones, D. (1994). Ethical issues in reporting and referring in research with low-income minority children. *Ethics and Behavior, 4,* 97–108.

Whitbeck, C. (1995). Teaching ethics to scientists and engineers: Moral agents and moral problems. *Science and Engineering Ethics, 1,* 299–308.

Whitbeck, C. (1996, May–June). Ethics as design: Doing justice to moral problems. *Hastings Center Report,* pp. 9–16.

Part III

Methods for Ethical Decision-Making

9

Identifying Conflicts of Interest and Resolving Ethical Dilemmas

Bruce D. Sales and Michael Lavin

Before a researcher can resolve potential or actual conflicts of interest, he or she first needs to identify what the conflicts of interest are. Such conflicts are often described as those between the obligation to promote the public good and the obligation to promote self-interest. But this definition only partially addresses the types of conflicts of interest that can face researchers. Conflicts can also be created if the researcher occupies more than one role or applies multiple ethical and moral principles and standards. This chapter considers each of these potential sources of conflicts in some detail. It then presents heuristics for the resolution of the potential and actual conflicts of interest and ethical dilemmas, and discusses relevant considerations in applying them.

Sources of Conflicts of Interest

Conflicting Roles

The first step in identifying conflicts of interest is to notice that human beings occupy multiple roles, each of which has specific duties, interests, and goals. Although the duties, interests, and goals that adhere to any one role can be laudable and ethical, they can contribute to conflicts of interest when the individual occupies multiple roles. For example, consider a clinical researcher studying depression. As a researcher, his or her goal is to eliminate confounds in the experimental investigation of depression. But attaining this goal might lead to the short-changing of clinical goals connected with relieving a patient's suffering. In cases of conflicts arising from multiple roles, the problem is likely to involve deciding which moral duty carries the greatest weight; this point will be elaborated later.

Conflicts of interest are not limited to the case in which an individual occupies multiple roles; they can also arise within a given role. Consider a researcher's intermediate goal of pricing a scientific project to fit within the sponsor's requirement. Attaining this goal might lead the researcher to inappropriately modify the design of the study and thereby compromise the long-term goal of generalizability.

Conflicts produced by different roles, such as in the example of the clinical researcher, or conflicts faced within a single role, such as when fitting research within a budget predetermined by the sponsor, are real dilemmas. Whether designing a treatment study with real patients or in writing a proposal to a sponsor, researchers must deal with these conflicts in the context of competing goals.

Finally, concerns over conflicts of interest arise when a person has self-interests that create suspicions about his or her ability to meet the duties imposed by some role or roles. Most people grant that there is such a thing as their own best interest (self-interest). A person's self-interest, as ordinarily understood, will not always coincide with the requirements of morality. For example, suppose that a researcher has submitted a proposal for funding. Even if the researcher is of unimpeachable honesty and of unquestioned objectivity, most researchers reject the notion of letting the grant applicant serve on the committee that decides whether to fund the proposal.

Conflicts between morality and self-interest are of special concern because of the widespread belief that morality tends to take a back seat when self-interest is involved. This need not be because people are intentionally immoral, but because, whether recognized or not, motivational forces connected with a person's self-interest tend to be strong. Such self-bias may be unintentional but may still occur in some situations. People are more likely to need a reminder to give everybody a fair share than a reminder to take their fair share. Stated another way, when self-interest is involved there is a fear that the researcher has good reasons for compromising moral and ethical responsibilities.

Self-interest cannot be understood in isolation. Somebody, for example, who holds a substantial financial interest in a company that develops and produces psychological tests would, by virtue of that fact alone, have a potential conflict of interest if he or she agreed to review that company's products. In fact, the National Institutes of Health (NIH) requires members of review groups to disclose in writing all financial interests that could potentially produce conflicts of interest when making decisions about the merits of research proposals.

However, the appearance of a conflict does not translate automatically into an actual conflict. A researcher who uses his or her influence to attain for a former lover a position with another research group has a potential but not automatic conflict of interest. Judgment about whether the researcher acted ethically in making the recommendation cannot be made without knowing more of the facts. The past personal relationship may have nothing, something, or everything to do with the recommendation. And even if it had something or everything to do with the recommendation, it may not reflect a conflict of interest, but rather a knowledge of the applicant's skills and abilities that was acquired because of the personal relationship. These motives, however, are difficult to separate; hence, it is recommended that researchers avoid situations in which unintentional bias can influence decisions or in which others can attribute bias because of an acknowledged relationship. In the NIH case, if a recommendation is being made about a proposal involving an applicant for whom the reviewer has disclosed a financial relationship, the reviewer simply leaves the room while the proposal is being evaluated. Whether or not the reviewer would intentionally bias his or her decisions because of the relationship is not the issue. Situations in which even unintentional self-interest could potentially influence decisions are avoided whenever possible.

Sometimes role conflicts involving conflicting duties, interest, goals, and self-interest can easily be found in the following contexts that are familiar to all researchers and that are often difficult to avoid.

Researcher–teacher. Given the disparities of power between teachers and students and the related potential for abuse of this power (Blevins-Knabe, 1992), people who are researchers and teachers may either intentionally or unintentionally find themselves in situations of conflicting interests. For example, a researcher may use his or her role as a teacher to acquire participants without paying adequate attention to the educational needs of the student–participants. Moreover, researcher–teachers should be sensitive to preventing their interest in acquiring knowledge from leading them to exploit their students.

Researcher–clinician. The clinical situation itself can produce conflicts of interest (Cassel, 1988), partially because clinical researchers often occupy simultaneously the roles of therapist and scientist. As a scientist, the researcher's principal role-given duty is to make new discoveries, by conducting research in accordance with the best possible designs. As a therapist, the researcher's premiere role is to offer the best possible care to the participant. If therapist–researchers decide to ask clients to become participants in research, they should be cautious that they are not placing their roles as therapists and researchers in irremediable conflict because of a desire to achieve a research goal that may not be in the clients' best interest. The therapist–researcher can avoid this potential conflict by recruiting only when there is no direct relationship with the potential participant. Application of the moral principles of nonmaleficence and beneficence (Moral Principle II discussed in chapter 1) require this result.

Researcher–employee. As Pryor (1989) and Korenman (1993) have observed, the roles of scientist–employee can create potential or actual conflicts of interest. Although the researcher's chief moral allegiance is to the principle of fidelity to science, a researcher–employee has a duty to work as an agent of his or her company, with a subsidiary duty to further the interest of the company. For example, a tobacco company might hire a researcher to investigate the addictive properties of nicotine, with a plan of keeping any adverse findings a company secret. A company that designs statistical software programs might hire a researcher to investigate the accuracy of its software packages, with no intention of publicly announcing subtle flaws that are discovered. In these two cases, as well as in many others, the dual roles force researcher–employees to consider potential and actual conflicts of interest.

Researcher–funding recipient. Sometimes research is funded by a party with an interest in its outcome. In such cases, researcher–funding recipients should avoid letting their relationship to the funding organization skew either the research design or interpretation (Korenman, 1993). For example, continued funding from a religious organization might encourage a researcher–recipient to downplay research results showing that religious training bears no relation to a child's moral development. Researcher–funding recipients should guard against the possibility that the expectations of the funding agency and their role as recipient are creating conflicts of interest that compromise the scientific integrity of their work.

Researcher–program evaluator. Program evaluators, who perform evaluation research for an entity such as a university, a private company, a health maintenance organization, or a school, often face numerous moral difficulties (Morris & Cohn, 1993). They may face a conflict of interest because the entity being evaluated controls the funding that supports the research–program evaluator, and the entity wants the program evaluation design modified to achieve a particular outcome. In addition, other types of conflicts of interest may occur. For example, a researcher–program evaluator might encounter a promising program that would lose funding if honestly evaluated, thereby jeopardizing both a developing program that the researcher–program evaluator supports and the potential for future contracts for evaluation of the program. Sometimes researcher–program evaluators may find themselves asked to perform evaluations without adequate resources to do the research well, but they are tempted to proceed in order to provide continuing financial support for their graduate students. Thus, researcher–program evaluators should be cautious that their desire for financial support, their support for a program, or political considerations (e.g., their support for the goals of the program being evaluated) do not subvert their commitment to perform quality ethical research.

Researcher–member of society. Finally, all researchers occupy a role as a member of society and thus have the responsibilities that go with citizenship. In particular, researchers should weigh the social effects of their research because it can, in some circumstances, stigmatize other citizens or be misused to perpetuate unjust arrangements. This is not to argue that researchers should modify their otherwise ethical work to avoid unwelcome social findings. Rather, to the extent that the scientific goals are not violated, researchers should consider and minimize any negative impact of their research on participants and other persons.

Conclusion. Although the roles discussed previously are not the only ones that can produce conflicts of interest, the frequency of their co-occurrence makes it important for researchers to be conscious of the ethical dilemmas presented by the simultaneous occupancy of one or more of these roles. Discussing them gives researchers the opportunity to reflect on how their own occupancy of a role or roles can create conflicts of interest and makes it easier for researchers to identify what kinds of conflicts might arise.

It is important to stress that potential and actual conflicts of interest generated by a researcher occupying one or more roles do not inevitably lead to irresolvable ethical dilemmas or even undesirable dilemmas. In everyday life, people experience these conflicts of interest and often meet the associated moral challenges successfully. Being aware of these potential sources of conflicts of interest makes it easier to prevent adverse outcomes.

The emphasis so far in this chapter has been on identifying possible conflicts. Once these are identified, the researcher can take appropriate steps to rectify the situation. If possible, the researcher can avoid situations in which conflicts exists. For example, the researcher–program evaluator could recommend that a neutral party conduct the program evaluation. Or the researcher–teacher could recruit research participants from classes of other faculty and not involve his or her own students. In many cases, however, the conflict cannot be avoided. In these cases, it is important that the potential conflict be acknowledged and decisions be made with the potential conflict in mind.

Conflicting Applicable Moral Principles

Over time, a consensus has emerged on moral principles governing a researcher's behavior (see chapter 1). For example, most researchers acknowledge that their work should respect the self-determination or autonomy of participants. Also, most researchers recognize the importance of doing research that promotes well-being, prevents harm, is consistent with a just distribution of benefits and burdens, and advances human knowledge. One might say that researchers should conduct their work in a manner consistent with principles of autonomy, beneficence and nonmaleficence, justice, trust, and fidelity to science. Reflection on these principles has led to the formulation of the more specific guidelines contained in this volume.

Despite the consensus on the moral principles governing the conduct of research, conflicting interests can arise when attempting to apply the relevant principles in particular cases (Beauchamp & Childress, 1994). Consider research requiring the deception of a participant. The principle enjoining a researcher to pursue knowledge could conflict with the principle of self-determination. In Milgram's (1963) often-cited obedience experiments, he convinced the majority of participants to administer what they falsely believed to be dangerous shocks to an actor hired by Milgram. The participants were ordered to administer a shock whenever the actor responded incorrectly to a memory task. The actor feigned pain when shocked. The greater the shock, the more pain the actor pretended to experience. A substantial proportion of participants followed orders to continue administering what they thought were dangerous levels of electrical shock, even when the actor screamed that he could endure no more. The experimental protocol required that participants be deliberately misled about the experiment's goal, the identity of the actor, and the fictitiousness of the shocks. Milgram apparently decided that the potential importance of the study outweighed the importance of telling his participants about what they would in fact be doing. Thus, Milgram appeared to have assigned less weight to the moral principles of autonomy or beneficence than to the principle of fidelity to one's science. Once some of the participants had displayed emotional distress, another decision faced by Milgram was whether the experiment should be continued. As discussed earlier, often the researcher has to adjust the weightings of his or her decisions in the midst of the research. Once the effects of the deception were apparent, however, it could be argued that Milgram could have adjusted his weightings and either stopped or changed the experiment. It is important to understand the historical context of this study—that is, the experiment was conducted in the aftermath of World War II, and decisions today may be completely different from those made over 35 years ago.

To better understand Milgram's choice, it is helpful to distinguish between prima facie (self-evident) obligations and actual obligations (Beauchamp & Childress, 1994; Rawls, 1971; Ross, 1939). In Milgram's case, the moral principle of respecting the autonomy interests of the research participants created a prima facie obligation to tell them the truth about the research to enable them to decide whether they wished to participate. The moral principle of fidelity to science simultaneously created a prima facie obligation for Milgram to do the experiment in the most effective way possible. It was impossible for Milgram to satisfy both of these prima facie obligations, but that does not mean that it was impossible for him to satisfy his actual obligation. Milgram viewed his actual obligation as doing the best research possible, being sure to provide his participants with a thorough debriefing at the experiment's end. In retrospect, questions can be raised about the ethical decisions made in this experiment and whether the actual obligations were appropriately met. Whether Milgram reached the correct decisions, either in the design of the experiment or in continuing the experiment once the consequences of the design were known (i.e., the potential harm to the participants) depends on how the conflicting moral principles are weighted and how appropriate the behavioral strategy is for implementing that weighting decision.

In summary, there are conflicts that can arise from researchers occupying numerous roles. These are conflicts rooted in conflicting duties, goals, and interests. There are also conflicts that result from a researcher assigning different weights to the applicable moral principles. These are conflicts that can arise from honest differences in judgment or from the intrusion of inappropriate reasoning into decisions based on one of these three (i.e., duties, goals, and interests) conflicts. Finally, these conflicts can occur in combination.

Additional Aids for Identifying Conflicts of Interest

As described later in this chapter, moral principles are abstract and general and as a consequence are difficult to apply to particular cases. To provide more specific guidance, many professional organizations have derived specific ethical guidelines from these general moral principles to assist their members in identifying conflicts of interest. These guidelines cover aspects of research that working scientists are likely to encounter and represent the collective wisdom of a profession at a given point in time. As such, they are an important resource for researchers.

The *Ethical Principles of Psychologists and Code of Conduct* (APA, 1992) is such a document (see appendix A). The APA code is a statement of general aspirational principles and enforceable standards (rules) that can be used to guide the conduct of psychologists in all professional contexts.

Resolving Ethical Dilemmas

Researchers who identify a potential or actual ethical conflict or dilemma in connection with their work face the need of reaching an ethically defensible response. The identification of the dilemma or conflict is only a first step. The next step is to engage a defensible decision-making process for addressing and responding to the concern.

Some researchers believe that ethical problems are not susceptible to rational analysis in the way that scientific problems are, because ethical thinking is subjective (Rachels, 1993). Accordingly, researchers may be tempted to think that, as long as they act in good conscience, nobody has the right to blame them or to tell them that what they have decided to do is ethically wrong.

Ethical decision-making, however, can be both rational and informed. There are agreed-on ethical principles that can guide our decision-making process. There are moral principles as discussed in chapter 1 and referred to throughout the monograph. There are also specific codes of ethical conduct (e.g., see appendix A) that provide standards for ethical decisions made by scientists. In fact, throughout the history of ethics, ethicists have offered explicit models of ethical decision-making (e.g., Canter, Bennett, Jones, & Nagy, 1994; Sidgwick, 1907). Instead, this chapter discusses useful heuristics that can assist researchers find defensible solutions to the kinds of ethical dilemmas and conflicts that they are likely to encounter. These heuristics involve (a) using existing professional ethical standards, (b) following ethical and moral principles, (c) being aware of legal responsibilities, (d) applying professional standards, and (e) consulting with professional colleagues.

Decision Scheme for Resolving Ethical Dilemmas and Conflicts

To engage in ethical decision-making, researchers should first know if there are ethical standards applicable to their dilemma or conflict. For psychologists, these ethical standards are contained in the *Ethical Principles of Psychologists and Code of Conduct* (APA, 1992, see appendix A). If these standards do not resolve their concerns and provide them with guidance, they then should turn to the general ethical principles listed at the beginning of the APA code. If these aspirational ethical principles do not provide the needed guidance, they should then consider applicable moral principles (see chapter 1). Even if a researcher believes that an ethical resolution has been found at any of the prior stages, however, the researcher should still seek guidance on the legal ramifications of their proposed solution. Section 6.08 (Compliance With Law and Standards) of the APA code instructs researchers to consider both the law and professional standards that are applicable to their work. If, however, the laws or regulations are incompatible with ethical standards, researchers should make known their commitment to the ethics code and take whatever steps possible to resolve the conflict in a responsible manner (Section 1.02, Relationship of Ethics and Law). This may mean withdrawing from the research effort in order to obey the law and at the same time behave ethically.

Finally, researchers should consider consulting with colleagues who are knowledgeable about ethics prior to formulating their response to dilemmas. Let us consider these steps in greater detail.

Application of ethical standards. First, researchers should articulate as precisely as possible the nature of the conflict. Second, they should attempt to identify what factual information may be relevant to the conflict and its resolution. Researchers should then look to the standards listed in the APA code. Many of the ethical dilemmas or concerns that researchers face are addressed by standards that are both straightforward and easy to endorse. By design, considerable efforts have gone into including only values that enjoy overwhelming support within the scientific and professional community. Consider the following example:

> Dr. Jones was being pressured by her university administration to serve on an important committee. She already had a full load in terms of teaching and departmental service and was just getting under way the data collection on a NIH-funded grant. She considered hiring some graduate and undergraduate students to perform the current phase of her research project in order to free up critical time for herself. She was tempted to require the graduate students to master the procedures with minimal help from her and to let the graduate students train the undergraduates. After reviewing Section 6.07 (Responsibility), Dr. Jones realized that she had an ethical responsibility to ensure that the students were appropriately trained and supervised. Because data collection required the use of sophisticated instrumentation, she recognized her responsibility to appropriately train the students who work for her. Thus, she decided to look elsewhere in her busy schedule to find some activity that she could give up so that she could comfortably serve on the university committee. If this were not possible, she would decline the invitation to serve.

Or consider this situation:

> Dr. Smith was considering asking his graduate research assistant John
> to house sit while he attended a scientific conference in Europe where
> he was discussing their joint research. John had worked for Dr. Smith
> for several years as he progressed through graduate school toward his
> doctorate degree. During that time, John had co-authored four articles
> with Dr. Smith and was currently drafting a National Science Foun-
> dation postdoctoral application to continue this work. Dr. Smith was
> helping John with the proposal in order to have him stay in his labo-
> ratory at the university for several more years and continue their evolv-
> ing collaboration. Dr. Smith liked not only John's scientific skills, but
> also liked him as a person. Dr. Smith was concerned, however, that
> there may be ethical implications to his request, so he checked the code
> for guidance. Referring to Section 1.19 (Exploitative Relationships)
> helped Dr. Smith quickly and comfortably resolve his concerns. He
> would invite John to house sit, offer him fair compensation for his time,
> and make it clear that he would understand if John could not or did
> not want to do it. Dr. Smith's approach took care of any possibility that
> John could or would feel exploited by a person who held power over
> him.

Although searching the code after the dilemma has arisen can provide
guidance in many cases, it usually is more helpful for researchers to review the code periodically to refresh their recollection of their ethical obligations. Knowledge of the code can sensitize researchers to ethical obligations and potential ethical dilemmas that can arise from breaching those
obligations, so researchers can avoid these dilemmas.

> Dr. Rodgers, an applied researcher, worked for a for-profit consulting
> research organization. One of his clients needed psychometric instru-
> ments that could be used by its human resource management people.
> Although it was outside Dr. Rodgers's area of expertise to develop such
> instruments, he did so, did limited research on their reliability and
> validity, and submitted them to the client. Had Dr. Rodgers been fa-
> miliar with the code in advance of his "creative" leap into a new applied
> research direction, he would have been made aware of several sections
> that address competence to engage in research and require such com-
> petence prior to research initiation (Section 1.04, Boundaries of Com-
> petence). By not heeding the code, Dr. Rodgers could lead his client into
> inappropriate corporate decisions. Had he done so, he would have rec-
> ognized the desirability of consulting with colleagues who are compe-
> tent in the area of research in which he wanted to engage.

Finally, a careful reading of the code will inform researchers of their
obligation to be familiar with its guidance (Section 8.01, Familiarity With
Ethics Code).

Application of ethical principles. If the code provisions fail to suggest
a course of action that eliminates a conflict or identify an acceptable al-

ternative, the researcher should use the next heuristic of following ethical and moral principles. At this stage, the researcher needs to consult aspirational ethical principles in the code, which are more general than the specific enforceable standards of the code. Although these principles are neither specific nor enforceable, they can offer substantial guidance for addressing ethical concerns. Indeed, by applying the relevant aspirational ethical principles to the facts of the conflict situation, the researcher is likely to achieve a satisfactory resolution of the conflict, if one has not been reached through the application of the specific code standards.

> Dr. Barker is spending inadequate time preparing for her class because of the current demands of a research project. She is excited about her research, and merit increases at her university are heavily based on research performance. Even a regular reading of the standards would not alert Dr. Barker to the ethical dimensions of her decision to slight her teaching obligations, because the need to ethically balance the demands of teaching and research—and the methods by which this is possible—is not addressed by the standards of the code. By referring to the general ethical principles, however, Dr. Barker should conclude that an appropriate balance between research and teaching should be restored. This result is reached using Ethical Principles A, B, and E of the code. By applying these, Dr. Barker would realize that her professional responsibilities extended to both the classroom and the laboratory. She had ethical responsibilities and obligations to her students that could not be compromised by the competing demands of her research.

Application of moral principles. Accepting guidance from an ethics code does not excuse researchers from moral accountability for their decisions. If a researcher believes that the code has given a morally wrong answer, the researcher has an obligation not to implement the answer. However, in rejecting the guidance provided by the code, particularly if it is unequivocal, the researcher should seriously consider his or her own moral views. Ethics codes allow conscientious refusal of guidance, but the researcher should bear in mind that codes arose from a consensus of reasonable people. It may be that the researcher has a moral standard that shames the conventional moral wisdom captured by ethics codes, but it is also possible that some feature of the researcher's personal moral code has made him or her less morally responsible than other people.

To make this assessment, researchers should familiarize themselves with moral principles relevant to the research enterprise. For instance, most researchers are likely to accept the principles discussed in the introductory section of this document and in the Belmont Report (OPRR, 1979; see appendix C) or in the monograph *Protecting Human Subjects* (President's Commission for the Study of Ethical Problems in Medicine and Biomedical and Behavioral Research, 1981). Although a researcher might dissent on the reasoning offered on behalf of the principles, few researchers are likely to deny that autonomy, beneficence, nonmaleficence, justice, trust, and fidelity to science are important moral principles.

These moral principles, like the aspirational ethical principles adopted by the APA in 1992, can be particularly helpful in identifying and clarifying the competing interests and concerns of the parties involved in ethical dilemmas. Consider another example:

> Dr. Henly was invited to evaluate a services program for a private agency. The agency hinted to Dr. Henly that she could receive future evaluation contracts if her evaluation was positive and supported its renewal application to the funding agency. Dr. Henly's moral analysis considered fidelity to science, which required her to conduct an honest and unbiased evaluation. She then applied the moral principle of nonmaleficence, which also led her to conclude that the evaluation had to be performed honestly, without bias, and accurately. Not to do so, she reasoned, would harm both the funding agency and current and future recipients of services from the program. It would harm the funding agency because it would be relying on her evaluation in making a decision about whether to continue funding the project. It would harm current and future recipients of services from the program because they might be receiving inadequate care and would have no opportunity to be apprised of it and little hope that the agency would change its approach. Her decision thus became clear. Her evaluation would not be influenced by the inducement that the agency offered.

Application of legal standards. The law, in almost all cases, specifies obligations that are consistent with both moral interpretation and ethical requirements. But the law has a more important relationship to ethics, which is highlighted in Section 6.08 (Compliance With Law and Standards). A direct implication of this section is that noncompliance with the law is a violation of the code. This obligation places a substantial burden on the researcher because the law is not easy to find. It exists in federal and state constitutions; statutes; case law; and administrative rules, regulations, and decisions. For example, maintaining the confidentiality of research information can be addressed by all of the previously listed federal and state sources of law in any given circumstance. Constitutional law addresses the privacy of information; statutory and case law addresses confidentiality, privileged communications, search-and-seizure, and subpoena laws; administrative agency rules, regulations, and decisions may be relevant if the data are collected through a state or federally funded program (e.g., treatment research with drug abusers). Thus, it may take a complex search and interpretation of the laws to find out what the law is that controls the presenting dilemma (see e.g., Boruch & Cecil, 1983). As mentioned earlier, if existing laws conflict with ethical standards, the researcher should acknowledge his or her commitment to the code and take appropriate steps to resolve the conflict (Section 1.02, Relationship of Ethics and Law).

Section 6.09 (Institutional Approval) is also relevant in this regard. Because almost all research institutions comply with federal IRB regulations, Section 6.09 is indirectly requiring knowledge of and compliance with federal statutory and administrative law. It is a federal statute (P. L.

99-158, The Public Health Service Act as amended by the Health Research Extension Act of 1985) that authorized the U.S. Department of Health and Human Services to promulgate the federal regulations that specify rules and procedures for protecting human research subjects in federally funded institutions and programs (OPRR, 1991, 45 CFR Pt. 46). Although other federal laws apply, the point should be clear. The code requires compliance with the law in order to be ethical, and the law in many cases specifies what is the minimally acceptable behavior to be both ethical and within the bounds of the law.

Although it is often difficult for researchers to keep up with changing legal and regulatory rules, fortunately there are publications of learned societies that consider relevant laws, as do treatises (e.g., Sieber, 1992). In academic settings, researchers can also seek the advice of their research office, IRB, and the university's legal office to ensure that their research proposals are consistent with legal requirements. But ultimately, it is the researcher's ethical responsibility to know and comply with relevant legal mandates that affect the conduct of their work.

Application of professional standards. The cumulative, iterative nature of the research enterprise is such that, although knowledge is constantly expanding, there are stages at which researchers are able to come together and agree on a body of standards to guide future work in a particular area. Standards for test construction and evaluation provide one such example (American Educational Research Association, APA, & National Council on Measurement in Education, 1999). Section 6.08 (Compliance With Law and Standards) requires researchers to act in accordance with these standards.

For the code not to require this would indeed be strange. Section 1.05 (Maintaining Expertise) requires researchers to stay current with scientific information, and Section 1.06 (Basis for Scientific and Professional Judgments) further instructs psychologists to base their judgments and decisions on scientifically derived knowledge.

Researchers should stay abreast of these professional standards. However, there can be cases in which researchers ignore both their ethical and scientific obligation to do so, with a result not unlike the case of Dr. Rodger considered earlier.

Seeking consultation for resolving ethical conflicts. A formal decision scheme for resolving ethical dilemmas and conflicts has the advantage of forcing researchers to make their ethical thinking known to themselves and reconstructible for others. Sometimes, however, conflicts may present so many complications that researchers fear that they may have overlooked important elements of the situation. Thus, there are many cases and reasons why researchers should seek the advice of third parties (Section 8.02, Confronting Ethical Issues).

Researchers seeking a consultation about ethics should, of course, pay attention to the requirements of confidentiality, but once that is done, discussing the ethical dilemma with colleagues and other advisors can provide fresh perspectives on the problems at hand. It is also possible to make use of formal settings, such as the meeting of an IRB reviewing the research protocol or the ethics committee of a medical school. In the formal setting, the researcher might indicate what the concerns are in order to receive feedback and instruction from a group that has the benefit of having reviewed many proposals.

Despite the desirability of such a course of action, researchers should remember that advisors are fallible. Their recommendation is but one alternative response that would need to be run through the formal decision-making scheme to determine whether it can survive ethical scrutiny. Researchers can never evade their ethical responsibilities by letting somebody else decide for them what they should do.

Responding to Differing Fact Patterns

Although some ethical dilemmas will be simple to resolve using these heuristics, others, because of their fact patterns, may take substantial effort before an ethically defensible position is reached. To help the reader recognize the importance of understanding the facts and factual issues in the research situation, consider the following example.

> Sometimes researchers (R1) have gathered data for one set of studies that other researchers (R2) subsequently desire to use for a different study. For example, in studying the factors that make a person susceptible for acquiring HIV, R1 gathered information about this vulnerable population that would be invaluable for secondary analyses that test hypotheses different from the ones initially studied. What position should R1 take toward a request by R2 to share the data?

Although the specific facts in any case will determine which code standards are relevant, the following are plausible candidates for being relevant given the brevity of the facts presented: 1.01, Applicability of the Ethics Code; 1.02, Relationship of Ethics and Law; 1.07, Describing the Nature and Results of Psychological Services; 1.08, Human Differences; 1.09, Respecting Others; 1.14, Avoiding Harm; 1.15, Misuse of Psychologists' Influence; 1.16, Misuse of Psychologists' Work; 1.19, Exploitative Relationships; 1.24, Records and Data; 5.01, Discussing the Limits of Confidentiality; 5.02, Maintaining Confidentiality; 5.03, Minimizing Intrusions on Privacy; 5.04, Maintenance of Records; 5.05, Disclosures; 5.07, Confidential Information in Databases; 5.10, Ownership of Records and Data; 6.06, Planning Research; 6.07, Responsibility; 6.08, Compliance With Law and Standards; 6.09, Institutional Approval; 6.10, Research Responsibilities; 6.11, Informed Consent to Research; 6.12, Dispensing With Informed Consent; 6.15, Deception in Research; 6.16, Sharing and Utilizing Data; 6.19, Honoring Commitments; and 6.25, Sharing Data.

The sheer number of standards that are potentially relevant to a particular case may initially alarm researchers wishing to reach a quick ethical conclusion about what they should do. However, in most situations, as researchers begin to think about the situation, it will become apparent that a much smaller set applies.

As the decision-making heuristics presented in the previous section of this chapter show, researchers may also discover that ethical and moral principles may help them reach an ethical decision. For instance, most of the ethical principles enumerated in the code appear relevant to the issue at hand: Principle B, Integrity; Principle C, Professional and Scientific Responsibility; Principle D, Respect for People's Rights and Dignity; Principle E, Concern for the Others' Welfare; and Principle F, Social Responsibility.

And all of the moral principles apply: autonomy, beneficence and non-maleficence, justice, trust, and fidelity.

Finally, in the process of gathering the relevant materials to engage in an ethical analysis of the dilemma, R1 still should be alert to possible legal requirements and professional standards that apply in a given case. For didactic purposes, however, the legal questions presented by this case will not be considered. It will also be assumed that there are no relevant practice standards to guide the decision-making.

With this beginning level of analysis in mind, R2's request for R1's data can be used both to illustrate the use of the heuristics and to show how their application will vary with changes in case facts.

Resolution via ethical standards. Suppose R2 sought the data to learn what percentage of monozygotic and dizygotic twins, if any, were in the data and then to conduct secondary analyses on the disease progression within each type of twin. Also assume that the participants had signed consent forms that stated that they would agree to the release of information if it had no personal identifiers on it and if the release was to qualified researchers. In this case, the code permits the release of the information. The researchers had obtained informed consent, as required by Section 6.11 (Informed Consent to Research). Further, the consent specified that the researchers would release only information that had no identifiers on it. To refuse to release the information would violate Section 6.19 (Honoring Commitments). Finally, there are no countervailing facts, such as potential harms to participants, that could make it reasonable to believe that satisfying the request, to take one possible example, would violate Section 1.14 (Avoiding Harm).

Resolution via ethical principles. Matters are not always so simple. Suppose the initial research looked at personality types and behavior that led to the acquisition of HIV. Incidentally gathered data included information about the zip codes of the participants and the locations that may have been the sites (e.g., particular bars) for part of the chain of behaviors that could have led to the acquisition of HIV. R2 requests access to the previously analyzed location data for analysis in a study designed to develop and disseminate HIV prevention materials. The delivered data would have no identifiers on it. As before, the participants who provided the information signed a consent form that stipulated that data be shared with qualified researchers on request.

In this case, it is unlikely that the issue can be resolved at the level of code standards. The initial temptation might be to assume that the researcher had obtained permission to distribute this information in the process of obtaining an informed consent and that Standard 6.19 (Honoring Commitments) obligates the release of the data. This view neglects important facts, however. First, participants may have had different ideas about what they were consenting to be released. If they were told that the purpose of the initial study was to look at personality and HIV acquisition, they might reasonably have assumed that was the kind of data that would be released, not additional data regarding general area of residence or the category of places that might have had some involvement with their ultimately contracting HIV. Second, even if one ignored that difficulty, the researcher's duty toward research participants, as articulated in Section 1.14 (Avoiding Harm) and Section 1.16 (Misuse of Psychologists' Work), does not vanish just because participants signed a consent form. After all, one would also want to know that the participants did not consent as a result of a violation of Section 1.19 (Exploitative Relationships). In the present case, even if R2 has no intention of further stigmatizing people with HIV, R1 has an obligation to consider possible harmful consequences, relative to what is known at the time of the request for the release of the information. If, for example, it seemed reasonable, perhaps because of previous episodes, that the police or insurance companies would gain access to this data from R2 and would use this information to target people and places (e.g., increased rates for life and health insurance for people living in that geographic location; increased police scrutiny of particular establishments in the areas identified by the data), then issues relating to harm do arise. The resolution of the ethical dilemma requires the researcher to turn to the ethical principles.

Ethical Principles C, D, and E support the view that the researchers should refuse to share the data if the facts are as described. The participants would be likely to suffer foreseeable harms. In particular, Ethical Principle C requires psychologists to "serve the best interests of . . . recipients of their services." The case described is contrary to the best interests of the participants. Further, Ethical Principle D requires that "psychologists accord appropriate respect to the fundamental rights, dignity, and worth of all people. They respect the rights of individuals to privacy, confidentiality, self-determination, and autonomy. . . ." Given the harms threatening the participants, the researcher should question whether the participants actually intended to provide consent to release the data. Unless the potential harm that could reasonably occur was known to the participants when they signed the consent forms, the researcher should not assume that the consent for subsequent data release is valid. In addition, the requirement of Ethical Principle E to have concern for the welfare of others also supports withholding the data. Disclosure would be an act of indifference to the welfare of the participants. And even Ethical Principle F supports nondisclosure, because psychologists "make public their knowledge of psychology in order to contribute to human welfare." Relative to the facts at hand, disclosure would be contrary to the welfare of the participants without there being significantly countervailing gains to the public. There are, in different situations, reasons to think that data should be shared but not in the situation used here.

Resolution via moral principles. Suppose that participants face genuine risks of being stigmatized and that this risk exceeds what the research participants would have consented to had they understood the risk in advance. Also suppose that the research team requesting the data had significantly better resources and funding to analyze this dataset than did the original researcher. The countervailing factual considerations now favor disclosure, because the additional facts can lead to different interpretations of concern for the welfare of others, respecting dignity, or honoring one's social responsibilities. Thus, the ethical principles cannot be used to resolve the dilemma.

The researcher would need to turn to the moral principles of justice, beneficence and nonmaleficence, autonomy, trust, and fidelity to science. Nobody can pretend once the matter reaches this level, that all people would reach the same conclusion. What is important is that the researcher set out, as clearly as possible, his or her ethical analysis. For example, suppose the researcher decided to share the data. The researcher considers the potential harms to the participants, but concludes that fidelity to science, concern about advancing the welfare of all people, and perhaps even justice favor sharing the data. The researcher need not deny that the research participants may suffer as a result of the decision that he or she made, but the researcher can argue that the moral costs are worth it.

Resolution via consultation. The same situation might pose a different problem if the researcher has reason to believe that homophobic community members might harm the participants as a result of data sharing. Here the researcher may want to consult with knowledgeable people about likely outcomes of data sharing. This example also illustrates that getting ethical advice does not always consist in securing the "right" answer from an assumedly ultimate source, but often it can involve seeking the advice of people who are better positioned to have an accurate picture of the facts and the ethical implications of different courses of action.

Another reason for consultation is that the researcher's own moral beliefs may bias the ethical analysis. Perhaps sex with a person of the same gender goes against the researcher's own religious beliefs. This situation might lead the researcher to worry less about the participants than would people who do not share this belief. It is important for the researcher to note when he or she has moral beliefs that conflict with the code and moral principles. At a minimum, the researcher should recognize that he or she is dissenting from moral and ethical beliefs on which researchers, who have thought long and hard on these issues, have converged. Perhaps those people are not morally consistent, but it is worth considering whether one's own moral beliefs could survive the same level of scrutiny. Holding a moral belief that is inconsistent with the code might carry real social costs. The code, however, cannot force people to change their moral beliefs. It can only invite people to subject them to scrutiny and, in conjunction with the law, remind the dissenter of the potential costs of acting contrary to reflective, moral, and ethical opinion.

Reaching Different Decisions

In most cases, ethical decision-making would lead to clear resolution of conflict. For most ethical dilemmas, ethical standards, ethical principles, and moral principles are sufficient to lead researchers to the proper decision. It should already be clear, however, that the decision-making heuristics offered within this chapter do not guarantee a unique solution to every problem. Quite conceivably, two researchers thinking about the same ethical dilemma or conflict could reach different and even incompatible solutions. There are many reasons for this outcome (Hare, 1987; Sales & Shuman, 1993).

Factual disagreements. Even if two people rely on the same decision-making rules, they disagree sometimes about the facts. If two researchers, for example, have different beliefs about how dangerous an experiment is, they might reach different conclusions about its permissibility, even when they agree about everything else. Returning to the Milgram research cited earlier, although Milgram most likely concluded that research participation would not harm research participants, another researcher could easily conclude the opposite. What, in fact, were the consequences of participation in Milgram's experiment? Milgram believed that most of his participants felt that the deception and the resultant consequences were trivial. Others, looking at the emotional stress experienced by some of the participants, would reach an opposite conclusion. Without follow-up information to empirically determine consequences of participation, it may be impossible to determine which interpretation of the consequences of participation is accurate. Yet this fact, the consequence of harm to the participants, would be critical for determining whether Section 1.14 (Avoiding Harm) and Section 6.15(b) (Deception in Research) should apply to the research project in question.

Disagreements over the applicable standards and principles. Even when two people agree on the facts, they may disagree about the applicable standards and principles. For example, researchers studying how gifted children read may disagree about whether Standard 6.06(b) (Planning Research) is an important consideration in their work. It is obvious that if the research is likely to be used for policy making, this standard would take on heightened importance. However, it is not always clear, prior to the conduct of a study, how that research might be applied and how it might affect public policy.

Making ethical decisions across diverse research contexts. The diversity of research contexts sometimes makes it difficult to interpret and apply the code consistently. A decision in one research context may be very different from the decision made in another context. For example, Section 6.14(b) (Offering Inducements for Research Participants) states, "Psychologists do not offer excessive or inappropriate financial or other inducements to obtain research participants, particularly when it might tend to coerce participation." Yet what constitutes excessive or inappropriate, and when might the inducement pass over the imaginary threshold to become coercive? An offer of $10 may be coercive to a poor youth but not to a middle-aged businessperson. In this case, a decision about whether an inducement was coercive would depend on the research participants being solicited.

Or consider the researcher who seeks to study members of a particular Native American tribe. Within the Native American culture, tribal leaders are often gatekeepers to activities involving tribal members. For this reason, should the researcher first seek guidance and permission from the tribal leaders before seeking the approval of the individual participant? Section 6.07(a) (Responsibility) states, "Psychologists conduct research . . . with due concern for the dignity and welfare of the participants." Does the omission of seeking the approval of the tribal leaders violate the dignity or welfare of the research participants? Consultation with the ethical principles provides similar interpretative problems with this hypothetical case. Ethical Principle A (Competence) advises, "Psychologists make appropriate use of . . . technical, and administrative resources." Yet, are the tribal leaders a technical or administrative resource?

Ethical Principle B (Integrity) instructs, ". . . psychologists are honest, fair, and respectful of others." Is it disrespectful to avoid or ignore the tribal leaders? Ethical Principle C (Professional and Scientific Responsibility) notes, "Psychologists . . . adapt their methods to the needs of different populations." And Ethical Principle D (Respect for People's Rights and Dignity) instructs, ". . . Psychologists are aware of cultural, individual, and role differences, including those due to . . . race, ethnicity, national origin . . .." If the Indian Nation regarded it as essential that all outsiders receive the approval of the tribal leaders before engaging with members of the group, are Ethical Principles C and D violated if the researcher was not aware of this fact and did not seek tribal leader approval? These issues would not arise if a researcher were interested in studying residents of a single large city. The researcher would rarely consider seeking permission from the mayor of the city prior to soliciting participants for the research. In these examples, ethical standards and principles that may apply to conducting research in a Native American tribal community might be irrelevant to the conduct of the same study in an urban environment.

Ethical standards and principles, like law, are meant to apply to a broad array of situations; it is inevitable that questions about applicability, however, will occur in ethical analysis involving different research contexts.

Uncertainty as a result of the choice and application of decision-making heuristics. Disagreements among researchers about the ethical course of action in a specific situation could emerge because they disagree about how to reason about ethics. Disagreements can emerge if one researcher believes in following his or her "instincts" and another uses a formal decision-making model, or two researchers may use different formal decision-making rules. For example, the researcher who starts the analysis by reference to moral principles might conceivably reach a different result to an ethical dilemma than a researcher who starts with reference to the code standards. Researchers also may reach different conclusions in similar factual circumstances because they have failed to apply their decision rules consistently when identifying and resolving ethical dilemmas.

Conclusion

The first section of this chapter is designed to help researchers spot potential conflicts of interest. Thus, researchers should reflect on their multiple roles and duties, the potential conflict between interests and goals generated by different roles (Kimmel, 1991), the potential conflict generated from self-interest, and the potential conflict caused by the application of multiple moral and ethical principles and ethical standards. Another excellent way for researchers to identify potential and actual conflicts of interest is to describe their research goals and plans to colleagues, advisors, and friends. Whether because of objectivity from noninvolvement or because of their experience, others may be more perceptive about the dangers that researchers are too close to see in their planned research.

In the latter part of the chapter, actions that may be taken to resolve ethical conflicts and dilemmas in research were discussed. Using the heuristics proposed here, rational and ethical decisions may be reached. However, the sources of uncertainty discussed in this chapter can lead to disagreement about ethics. That these are genuine sources of disagreement does not mean that any disagreements resulting because of them are irresolvable. Researchers may honestly disagree about ethical courses of action called for in a particular situation. However, rational and productive discussion, and even consensus is possible using the various standards and principles discussed here.

References

American Educational Research Association, American Psychological Association, National Council on Measurement in Education. (1999). *Standards for educational and psychological testing.* Washington, DC: American Educational Research Association.

American Psychological Association. (1992). Ethical principles of psychologists and code of conduct. *American Psychologist, 47,* 1597–1611.

Beauchamp, T. L., & Childress, J. (1994). *Principles of biomedical ethics* (4th ed.). New York: Oxford University Press.

Blevins-Knabe, B. (1992). The ethics of dual relationships in higher education. *Ethics and Behavior, 2,* 151–163.

Boruch, R. F., & Cecil, J. S. (1983). *Solutions to ethical and legal problems in social research.* San Diego, CA: Academic Press.

Canter, M. L., Bennett, B. E., Jones, S. E., & Nagy, T. F. (1994). *Ethics for psychologists: A commentary on the APA Ethics Code.* Washington, DC: American Psychological Association.

Cassel, C. K. (1988). Ethical issues in the conduct of research in long term care. Special Issue: Autonomy and long term care. *Gerontologist, 28*[Suppl.], 90–96.

Hare, R. M. (1987). *Moral thinking.* Oxford, England: Clarendon Press.

Kimmel, A. (1991). Predictable biases in the ethical decision-making of American psychologists. *American Psychologist, 46,* 786–788.

Korenman, S. G. (1993). Conflicts of interest and the commercialization of research. *Academic Medicine, 68,* S18–S22.

Milgram, S. (1963). Behavioral study of obedience. *Journal of Abnormal and Social Psychology, 67,* 371–378.

Morris, M., & Cohn, R. (1993). Program evaluators and ethical challenges: A national survey. *Evaluation Review, 17,* 621–642.

President's Commission for the Study of Ethical Problems in Medicine and Biomedical and Behavioral Research. (1981). *Protecting human subjects.* Washington, DC: U.S. Government Printing Office.

Pryor, R. B. (1989). Conflicting responsibilities: A case study of an ethical dilemma for psychologists working in organizations. *Australian Psychologist, 24,* 293–305.

Office for Protection From Research Risks, Protection of Human Subjects, National Commission for the Protection of Human Subjects of Biomedical and Behavioral Research. (1979). *The Belmont Report: Ethical principles and guidelines for the protection of human subjects of research* (GPO 887-809). Washington, DC: U.S. Government Printing Office.

Office for Protection From Research Risks, Protection of Human Subjects. (1991, June 18). Protection of human subjects: Title 45, Code of Federal Regulations, Part 46 (GPO 1992 O-307-551). *OPRR Reports,* pp. 4–17.

Rachels, J. (1993). *The elements of moral philosophy* (2nd ed.). New York: McGraw-Hill.

Rawls, J. (1971). *A theory of justice.* Cambridge, MA: Harvard University Press.

Ross, W. D. (1939). *The foundations of ethics.* Oxford, England: Oxford University Press.

Sales, B. D., & Shuman, D. (1993). Reclaiming the integrity of science in expert witnessing. *Ethics & Behavior, 3,* 223–229.

Sidgwick, H. (1907). *The methods of ethics* (7th ed.). London: Macmillian.

Sieber, J. E. (1992). *Planning ethically responsible research: A guide for students and internal review boards* (Applied Social Research Methods Series Vol. 31). Newbury Park, CA: Sage Publications.

Appendix A: Ethical Principles of Psychologists and Code of Conduct

CONTENTS

INTRODUCTION

PREAMBLE

GENERAL PRINCIPLES

Principle A: Competence
Principle B: Integrity
Principle C: Professional and Scientific Responsibility
Principle D: Respect for People's Rights and Dignity
Principle E: Concern for Others' Welfare
Principle F: Social Responsibility

ETHICAL STANDARDS

1.   General Standards

1.01 Applicability of the Ethics Code
1.02 Relationship of Ethics and Law
1.03 Professional and Scientific Relationship
1.04 Boundaries of Competence
1.05 Maintaining Expertise
1.06 Basis for Scientific and Professional Judgments
1.07 Describing the Nature and Results of Psychological Services
1.08 Human Differences
1.09 Respecting Others
1.10 Nondiscrimination
1.11 Sexual Harassment
1.12 Other Harassment
1.13 Personal Problems and Conflicts
1.14 Avoiding Harm
1.15 Misuse of Psychologists' Influence
1.16 Misuse of Psychologists' Work
1.17 Multiple Relationships
1.18 Barter (With Patients or Clients)

1.19 Exploitative Relationships
1.20 Consultations and Referrals
1.21 Third-Party Requests for Services
1.22 Delegation to and Supervision of Subordinates
1.23 Documentation of Professional and Scientific Work
1.24 Records and Data
1.25 Fees and Financial Arrangements
1.26 Accuracy in Reports to Payors and Funding Sources
1.27 Referrals and Fees

2.   Evaluation, Assessment, or Intervention

2.01 Evaluation, Diagnosis, and Interventions in Professional Context
2.02 Competence and Appropriate Use of Assessments and Interventions
2.03 Test Construction
2.04 Use of Assessment in General and With Special Populations
2.05 Interpreting Assessment Results
2.06 Unqualified Persons
2.07 Obsolete Tests and Outdated Test Results
2.08 Test Scoring and Interpretation Services
2.09 Explaining Assessment Results
2.10 Maintaining Test Security

3.   Advertising and Other Public Statements

3.01 Definition of Public Statements
3.02 Statements by Others

3.03 Avoidance of False or Deceptive
     Statements
3.04 Media Presentations
3.05 Testimonials
3.06 In-Person Solicitation

4.   *Therapy*

4.01 Structuring the Relationship
4.02 Informed Consent to Therapy
4.03 Couple and Family Relationships
4.04 Providing Mental Health Services
     to Those Served by Others
4.05 Sexual Intimacies With Current
     Patients or Clients
4.06 Therapy With Former Sexual
     Partners
4.07 Sexual Intimacies With Former
     Therapy Patients
4.08 Interruption of Services
4.09 Terminating the Professional
     Relationship

5.   *Privacy and Confidentiality*

5.01 Discussing the Limits of
     Confidentiality
5.02 Maintaining Confidentiality
5.03 Minimizing Intrusions on Privacy
5.04 Maintenance of Records
5.05 Disclosures
5.06 Consultations
5.07 Confidential Information in
     Databases
5.08 Use of Confidential Information
     for Didactic or Other Purposes
5.09 Preserving Records and Data
5.10 Ownership of Records and Data
5.11 Withholding Records for
     Nonpayment

6.   *Teaching, Training Supervision,
     Research, and Publishing*

6.01 Design of Education and Training
     Programs
6.02 Descriptions of Education and
     Training Programs
6.03 Accuracy and Objectivity in
     Teaching
6.04 Limitation on Teaching
6.05 Assessing Student and Supervisee
     Performance

6.06 Planning Research
6.07 Responsibility
6.08 Compliance With Law and
     Standards
6.09 Institutional Approval
6.10 Research Responsibilities
6.11 Informed Consent to Research
6.12 Dispensing With Informed
     Consent
6.13 Informed Consent in Research
     Filming or Recording
6.14 Offering Inducements for
     Research Participants
6.15 Deception in Research
6.16 Sharing and Utilizing
     Data
6.17 Minimizing Invasiveness
6.18 Providing Participants With
     Information About the Study
6.19 Honoring Commitments
6.20 Care and Use of Animals in
     Research
6.21 Reporting of Results
6.22 Plagiarism
6.23 Publication Credit
6.24 Duplicate Publication of
     Data
6.25 Sharing Data
6.26 Professional Reviewers

7.   *Forensic Activities*

7.01 Professionalism
7.02 Forensic Assessments
7.03 Clarification of Role
7.04 Truthfulness and Candor
7.05 Prior Relationships
7.06 Compliance With Law and
     Rules

8.   *Resolving Ethical Issues*

8.01 Familiarity With Ethics
     Code
8.02 Confronting Ethical Issues
8.03 Conflicts Between Ethics and
     Organizational Demands
8.04 Informal Resolution of Ethical
     Violations
8.05 Reporting Ethical Violations
8.06 Cooperating With Ethics
     Committees
8.07 Improper Complaints

Introduction

The American Psychological Association's (APA's) Ethical Principles of Psychologists and Code of Conduct (hereinafter referred to as the Ethics Code) consists of an Introduction, a Preamble, six General Principles (A–F), and specific Ethical Standards. The Introduction discusses the intent, organization, procedural considerations, and scope of application of the Ethics Code. The Preamble and General Principles are *aspirational* goals to guide psychologists toward the highest ideals of psychology. Although the Preamble and General Principles are not themselves enforceable rules, they should be considered by psychologists in arriving at an ethical course of action and may be considered by ethics bodies in interpreting the Ethical Standards. The Ethical Standards set forth *enforceable* rules for conduct as psychologists. Most of the Ethical Standards are written broadly, in order to apply to psychologists in varied roles, although the application of an Ethical Standard may vary depending on the context. The Ethical Standards are not exhaustive. The fact that a given conduct

---

Reprinted from *American Psychologist*, Vol. 47, pp. 1597–1611. Copyright 1992 by the American Psychological Association.

This version of the APA Ethics Code was adopted by the American Psychological Association's Council of Representatives during its meeting, August 13 and 16, 1992, and is effective beginning December 1, 1992. Inquiries concerning the substance or interpretation of the APA Ethics Code should be addressed to the Director, Office of Ethics, American Psychological Association, 750 First Street, NE, Washington, DC 20002-4242.

This Code will be used to adjudicate complaints brought concerning alleged conduct occurring on or after the effective date. Complaints regarding conduct occurring prior to the effective date will be adjudicated on the basis of the version of the Code that was in effect at the time the conduct occurred, except that no provisions repealed in June 1989 will be enforced even if an earlier version contains the provision. The Ethics Code will undergo continuing review and study for future revisions; comments on the Code may be sent to the above address.

The APA has previously published its Ethical Standards as follows:

American Psychological Association. (1953). *Ethical standards of psychologists*. Washington, DC: Author.

American Psychological Association. (1958). Standards of ethical behavior for psychologists. *American Psychologist, 13*, 268–271.

American Psychological Association. (1963). Ethical standards of psychologists. *American Psychologist, 18*, 56–60.

American Psychological Association. (1968). Ethical standards of psychologists. *American Psychologist, 23*, 357–361.

American Psychological Association. (1977, March). Ethical standards of psychologists. *APA Monitor*, pp. 22–23.

American Psychological Association. (1979). *Ethical standards of psychologists*. Washington, DC: Author.

American Psychological Association. (1981). Ethical principles of psychologists. *American Psychologist, 36*, 633–638.

American Psychological Association. (1990). Ethical principles of psychologists (Amended June 2, 1989). *American Psychologist, 4*, 390–395.

Request copies of the APA's Ethical Principles of Psychologists and Code of Conduct from the APA Order Department, 750 First Street, NE, Washington, DC 20002-4242, or phone (202) 336-5510.

is not specifically addressed by the Ethics Code does not mean that it is necessarily either ethical or unethical.

Membership in the APA commits members to adhere to the APA Ethics Code and to the rules and procedures used to implement it. Psychologists and students, whether or not they are APA members, should be aware that the Ethics Code may be applied to them by state psychology boards, courts, or other public bodies.

This Ethics Code applies only to psychologists' work-related activities, that is, activities that are part of the psychologists' scientific and professional functions or that are psychological in nature. It includes the clinical or counseling practice of psychology, research, teaching, supervision of trainees, development of assessment instruments, conducting assessments, educational counseling, organizational consulting, social intervention, administration, and other activities as well. These work-related activities can be distinguished from the purely private conduct of a psychologist, which ordinarily is not within the purview of the Ethics Code.

The Ethics Code is intended to provide standards of professional conduct that can be applied by the APA and by other bodies that choose to adopt them. Whether or not a psychologist has violated the Ethics Code does not by itself determine whether he or she is legally liable in a court action, whether a contract is enforceable, or whether other legal consequences occur. These results are based on legal rather than ethical rules. However, compliance with or violation of the Ethics Code may be admissible as evidence in some legal proceedings, depending on the circumstances.

In the process of making decisions regarding their professional behavior, psychologists must consider this Ethics Code, in addition to applicable laws and psychology board regulations. If the Ethics Code establishes a higher standard of conduct than is required by law, psychologists must meet the higher ethical standard. If the Ethics Code standard appears to conflict with the requirements of law, then psychologists make known their commitment to the Ethics Code and take steps to resolve the conflict in a responsible manner. If neither law nor the Ethics Code resolves an issue, psychologists should consider other professional materials[1] and the dic-

---

[1]Professional materials that are most helpful in this regard are guidelines and standards that have been adopted or endorsed by professional psychological organizations. Such guidelines and standards, whether adopted by the American Psychological Association (APA) or its Divisions, are not enforceable as such by this Ethics Code, but are of educative value to psychologists, courts, and professional bodies. Such materials include, but are not limited to, the APA's *General Guidelines for Providers of Psychological Services* (1987), *Specialty Guidelines for the Delivery of Services by Clinical Psychologists, Counseling Psychologists, Industrial/Organizational Psychologists, and School Psychologists* (1981), *Guidelines for Computer Based Tests and Interpretations* (1987), *Standards for Educational and Psychological Testing* (1985), *Ethical Principles in the Conduct of Research With Human Participants* (1982), *Guidelines for Ethical Conduct in the Care and Use of Animals* (1986), *Guidelines for Providers of Psychological Services to Ethnic, Linguistic, and Culturally Diverse Populations* (1990), and *Publication Manual of the American Psychological Association* (3rd ed., 1983). Materials not adopted by APA as a whole include the APA Division 41 (Forensic Psychology)/American Psychology–Law Society's *Specialty Guidelines for Forensic Psychologists* (1991).

tates of their own conscience, as well as seek consultation with others within the field when this is practical.

The procedures for filing, investigating, and resolving complaints of unethical conduct are described in the current Rules and Procedures of the APA Ethics Committee. The actions that APA may take for violations of the Ethics Code include actions such as reprimand, censure, termination of APA membership, and referral of the matter to other bodies. Complainants who seek remedies such as monetary damages in alleging ethical violations by a psychologist must resort to private negotiation, administrative bodies, or the courts. Actions that violate the Ethics Code may lead to the imposition of sanctions on a psychologist by bodies other than APA, including state psychological associations, other professional groups, psychology boards, other state or federal agencies, and payors for health services. In addition to actions for violation of the Ethics Code, the APA Bylaws provide that APA may take action against a member after his or her conviction of a felony, expulsion or suspension from an affiliated state psychological association, or suspension or loss of licensure.

Preamble

Psychologists work to develop a valid and reliable body of scientific knowledge based on research. They may apply that knowledge to human behavior in a variety of contexts. In doing so, they perform many roles, such as researcher, educator, diagnostician, therapist, supervisor, consultant, administrator, social interventionist, and expert witness. Their goal is to broaden knowledge of behavior and, where appropriate, to apply it pragmatically to improve the condition of both the individual and society. Psychologists respect the central importance of freedom of inquiry and expression in research, teaching, and publication. They also strive to help the public in developing informed judgments and choices concerning human behavior. This Ethics Code provides a common set of values upon which psychologists build their professional and scientific work.

This Code is intended to provide both the general principles and the decision rules to cover most situations encountered by psychologists. It has as its primary goal the welfare and protection of the individuals and groups with whom psychologists work. It is the individual responsibility of each psychologist to aspire to the highest possible standards of conduct. Psychologists respect and protect human and civil rights, and do not knowingly participate in or condone unfair discriminatory practices.

The development of a dynamic set of ethical standards for a psychologist's work-related conduct requires a personal commitment to a lifelong effort to act ethically; to encourage ethical behavior by students, supervisees, employees, and colleagues, as appropriate; and to consult with others, as needed, concerning ethical problems. Each psychologist supplements, but does not violate, the Ethics Code's values and rules on the basis of guidance drawn from personal values, culture, and experience.

General Principles

Principle A: Competence

Psychologists strive to maintain high standards of competence in their work. They recognize the boundaries of their particular competencies and the limitations of their expertise. They provide only those services and use only those techniques for which they are qualified by education, training, or experience. Psychologists are cognizant of the fact that the competencies required in serving, teaching, and/or studying groups of people vary with the distinctive characteristics of those groups. In those areas in which recognized professional standards do not yet exist, psychologists exercise careful judgment and take appropriate precautions to protect the welfare of those with whom they work. They maintain knowledge of relevant scientific and professional information related to the services they render, and they recognize the need for ongoing education. Psychologists make appropriate use of scientific, professional, technical, and administrative resources.

Principle B: Integrity

Psychologists seek to promote integrity in the science, teaching, and practice of psychology. In these activities psychologists are honest, fair, and respectful of others. In describing or reporting their qualifications, services, products, fees, research, or teaching, they do not make statements that are false, misleading, or deceptive. Psychologists strive to be aware of their own belief systems, values, needs, and limitations and the effect of these on their work. To the extent feasible, they attempt to clarify for relevant parties the roles they are performing and to function appropriately in accordance with those roles. Psychologists avoid improper and potentially harmful dual relationships.

Principle C: Professional and Scientific Responsibility

Psychologists uphold professional standards of conduct, clarify their professional roles and obligations, accept appropriate responsibility for their behavior, and adapt their methods to the needs of different populations. Psychologists consult with, refer to, or cooperate with other professionals and institutions to the extent needed to serve the best interests of their patients, clients, or other recipients of their services. Psychologists' moral standards and conduct are personal matters to the same degree as is true for any other person, except as psychologists' conduct may compromise their professional responsibilities or reduce the public's trust in psychology and psychologists. Psychologists are concerned about the ethical compliance of their colleagues' scientific and professional conduct. When appropriate, they consult with colleagues in order to prevent or avoid unethical conduct.

Principle D: Respect for People's Rights and Dignity

Psychologists accord appropriate respect to the fundamental rights, dignity, and worth of all people. They respect the rights of individuals to privacy, confidentiality, self-determination, and autonomy, mindful that legal and other obligations may lead to inconsistency and conflict with the exercise of these rights. Psychologists are aware of cultural, individual, and role differences, including those due to age, gender, race, ethnicity, national origin, religion, sexual orientation, disability, language, and socioeconomic status. Psychologists try to eliminate the effect on their work of biases based on those factors, and they do not knowingly participate in or condone unfair discriminatory practices.

Principle E: Concern for Others' Welfare

Psychologists seek to contribute to the welfare of those with whom they interact professionally. In their professional actions, psychologists weigh the welfare and rights of their patients or clients, students, supervisees, human research participants, and other affected persons, and the welfare of animal subjects of research. When conflicts occur among psychologists' obligations or concerns, they attempt to resolve these conflicts and to perform their roles in a responsible fashion that avoids or minimizes harm. Psychologists are sensitive to real and ascribed differences in power between themselves and others, and they do not exploit or mislead other people during or after professional relationships.

Principle F: Social Responsibility

Psychologists are aware of their professional and scientific responsibilities to the community and the society in which they work and live. They apply and make public their knowledge of psychology in order to contribute to human welfare. Psychologists are concerned about and work to mitigate the causes of human suffering. When undertaking research, they strive to advance human welfare and the science of psychology. Psychologists try to avoid misuse of their work. Psychologists comply with the law and encourage the development of law and social policy that serve the interests of their patients and clients and the public. They are encouraged to contribute a portion of their professional time for little or no personal advantage.

Ethical Standards

1. General Standards

These General Standards are potentially applicable to the professional and scientific activities of all psychologists.

1.01 Applicability of the Ethics Code

The activity of a psychologist subject to the Ethics Code may be reviewed under these Ethical Standards only if the activity is part of his or her work-related functions or the activity is psychological in nature. Personal activities having no connection to or effect on psychological roles are not subject to the Ethics Code.

1.02 Relationship of Ethics and Law

If psychologists' ethical responsibilities conflict with law, psychologists make known their commitment to the Ethics Code and take steps to resolve the conflict in a responsible manner.

1.03 Professional and Scientific Relationship

Psychologists provide diagnostic, therapeutic, teaching, research, supervisory, consultative, or other psychological services only in the context of a defined professional or scientific relationship or role. (See also Standards 2.01, Evaluation, Diagnosis, and Interventions in Professional Context, and 7.02, Forensic Assessments.)

1.04 Boundaries of Competence

(a) Psychologists provide services, teach, and conduct research only within the boundaries of their competence, based on their education, training, supervised experience, or appropriate professional experience.

(b) Psychologists provide services, teach, or conduct research in new areas or involving new techniques only after first undertaking appropriate study, training, supervision, and/or consultation from persons who are competent in those areas or techniques.

(c) In those emerging areas in which generally recognized standards for preparatory training do not yet exist, psychologists nevertheless take reasonable steps to ensure the competence of their work and to protect patients, clients, students, research participants, and others from harm.

1.05 Maintaining Expertise

Psychologists who engage in assessment, therapy, teaching, research, organizational consulting, or other professional activities maintain a reasonable level of awareness of current scientific and professional information in their fields of activity, and undertake ongoing efforts to maintain competence in the skills they use.

1.06 Basis for Scientific and Professional Judgments

Psychologists rely on scientifically and professionally derived knowledge when making scientific or professional judgments or when engaging in scholarly or professional endeavors.

1.07 Describing the Nature and Results of Psychological Services

(a) When psychologists provide assessment, evaluation, treatment, counseling, supervision, teaching, consultation, research, or other psychological services to an individual, a group, or an organization, they provide, using language that is reasonably understandable to the recipient of those services, appropriate information beforehand about the nature of such services and appropriate information later about results and consultations. (See also Standard 2.09, Explaining Assessment Results.)

(b) If psychologists will be precluded by law or by organizational roles from providing such information to particular individuals or groups, they so inform those individuals or groups at the outset of the service.

1.08 Human Differences

Where differences of age, gender, race, ethnicity, national origin, religion, sexual orientation, disability, language, or socioeconomic status significantly affect psychologists' work concerning particular individuals or groups, psychologists obtain the training, experience, consultation, or supervision necessary to ensure the competence of their services, or they make appropriate referrals.

1.09 Respecting Others

In their work-related activities, psychologists respect the rights of others to hold values, attitudes, and opinions that differ from their own.

1.10 Nondiscrimination

In their work-related activities, psychologists do not engage in unfair discrimination based on age, gender, race, ethnicity, national origin, religion, sexual orientation, disability, socioeconomic status, or any basis proscribed by law.

1.11 Sexual Harassment

(a) Psychologists do not engage in sexual harassment. Sexual harassment is sexual solicitation, physical advances, or verbal or nonverbal conduct that is sexual in nature, that occurs in connection with the psychologist's activities or roles as a psychologist, and that either: (1) is unwelcome, is offensive, or creates a hostile workplace environment, and the psychologist knows or is told this; or (2) is sufficiently severe or intense to be abusive to a reasonable person in the context. Sexual harassment can consist of a single intense or severe act or of multiple persistent or pervasive acts.

(b) Psychologists accord sexual-harassment complaints and respondents dignity and respect. Psychologists do not participate in denying a person academic admittance or advancement, employment, tenure, or promotion, based solely upon their having made, or their being the subject of, sexual-harassment charges. This does not preclude taking action based upon the outcome of such proceedings or consideration of other appropriate information.

1.12 Other Harassment

Psychologists do not knowingly engage in behavior that is harassing or demeaning to persons with whom they interact in their work based on factors such as those persons' age, gender, race, ethnicity, national origin, religion, sexual orientation, disability, language, or socioeconomic status.

1.13 Personal Problems and Conflicts

(a) Psychologists recognize that their personal problems and conflicts may interfere with their effectiveness. Accordingly, they refrain from undertaking an activity when they know or should know that their personal problems are likely to lead to harm to a patient, client, colleague, student, research participant, or other person to whom they may owe a professional or scientific obligation.

(b) In addition, psychologists have an obligation to be alert to signs of, and to obtain assistance for, their personal problems at an early stage, in order to prevent significantly impaired performance.

(c) When psychologists become aware of personal problems that may interfere with their performing work-related duties adequately, they take appropriate measures, such as obtaining professional consultation or assistance, and determine whether they should limit, suspend, or terminate their work-related duties.

1.14 Avoiding Harm

Psychologists take reasonable steps to avoid harming their patients or clients, research participants, students, and others with whom they work, and to minimize harm where it is foreseeable and unavoidable.

1.15 Misuse of Psychologists' Influence

Because psychologists' scientific and professional judgments and actions may affect the lives of others, they are alert to and guard against personal, financial, social, organizational, or political factors that might lead to misuse of their influence.

1.16 Misuse of Psychologists' Work

(a) Psychologists do not participate in activities in which it appears likely that their skills or data will be misused by others, unless corrective mechanisms are available. (See also Standard 7.04, Truthfulness and Candor.)

(b) If psychologists learn of misuse or misrepresentation of their work, they take reasonable steps to correct or minimize the misuse or misrepresentation.

1.17 Multiple Relationships

(a) In many communities and situations, it may not be feasible or reasonable for psychologists to avoid social or other nonprofessional contacts with persons such as patients, clients, students, supervisees, or research participants. Psychologists must always be sensitive to the potential harmful effects of other contacts on their work and on those persons with whom they deal. A psychologist refrains from entering into or promising another personal, scientific, professional, financial, or other relationship with such persons if it appears likely that such a relationship reasonably might impair the psychologist's objectivity or otherwise interfere with the psychologist's effectively performing his or her function as a psychologist, or might harm or exploit the other party.

(b) Likewise, whenever feasible, a psychologist refrains from taking on professional or scientific obligations when preexisting relationships would create a risk of such harm.

(c) If a psychologist finds that, due to unforeseen factors, a potentially harmful multiple relationship has arisen, the psychologist attempts to resolve it with due regard for the best interests of the affected person and maximal compliance with the Ethics Code.

1.18 Barter (With Patients or Clients)

Psychologists ordinarily refrain from accepting goods, services, or other nonmonetary remuneration from patients or clients in return for psychological services because such arrangements create inherent potential for conflicts, exploitation, and distortion of the professional relationship. A psychologist may participate in bartering *only* if (1) it is not clinically contraindicated, *and* (2) the relationship is not exploitative. (See also Standards 1.17, Multiple Relationships, and 1.25, Fees and Financial Arrangements.)

1.19 Exploitative Relationships

(a) Psychologists do not exploit persons over whom they have supervisory, evaluative, or other authority such as students, supervisees, employees, research participants, and clients or patients. (See also Standards 4.05–4.07 regarding sexual involvement with clients or patients.)

(b) Psychologists do not engage in sexual relationships with students or supervisees in training over whom the psychologist has evaluative or direct authority, because such relationships are so likely to impair judgment or be exploitative.

1.20 Consultations and Referrals

(a) Psychologists arrange for appropriate consultations and referrals based principally on the best interests of their patients or clients, with appropriate consent, and subject to other relevant considerations, including applicable law and contractual obligations. (See also Standards 5.01, Discussing the Limits of Confidentiality, and 5.06, Consultations.)

(b) When indicated and professionally appropriate, psychologists cooperate with other professionals in order to serve their patients or clients effectively and appropriately.

(c) Psychologists' referral practices are consistent with law.

1.21 Third-Party Requests for Services

(a) When a psychologist agrees to provide services to a person or entity at the request of a third party, the psychologist clarifies to the extent feasible, at the outset of the service, the nature of the relationship with each party. This clarification includes the role of the psychologist (such as therapist, organizational consultant, diagnostician, or expert witness), the probable uses of the services provided or the information obtained, and the fact that there may be limits to confidentiality.

(b) If there is a foreseeable risk of the psychologist's being called upon to perform conflicting roles because of the involvement of a third party, the psychologist clarifies the nature and direction of his or her responsibilities, keeps all parties appropriately informed as matters develop, and resolves the situation in accordance with this Ethics Code.

1.22 Delegation to and Supervision of Subordinates

(a) Psychologists delegate to their employees, supervisees, and research assistants only those responsibilities that such persons can reasonably be expected to perform competently, on the basis of their education, training, or experience, either independently or with the level of supervision being provided.

(b) Psychologists provide proper training and supervision to their employees or supervisees and take reasonable steps to see that such persons perform services responsibly, competently, and ethically.

(c) If institutional policies, procedures, or practices prevent fulfillment of this obligation, psychologists attempt to modify their role or to correct the situation to the extent feasible.

1.23 Documentation of Professional and Scientific Work

(a) Psychologists appropriately document their professional and scientific work in order to facilitate provision of services later by them or by other professionals, to ensure accountability, and to meet other requirements of institutions or the law.

(b) When psychologists have reason to believe that records of their professional services will be used in legal proceedings involving recipients of or participants in their work, they have a responsibility to create and maintain documentation in the kind of detail and quality that would be consistent with reasonable scrutiny in an adjudicative forum. (See also Standard 7.01, Professionalism, under Forensic Activities.)

1.24 Records and Data

Psychologists create, maintain, disseminate, store, retain, and dispose of records and data relating to their research, practice, and other work in accordance with law and in a manner that permits compliance with the requirements of this Ethics Code. (See also Standard 5.04, Maintenance of Records.)

1.25 Fees and Financial Arrangements

(a) As early as is feasible in a professional or scientific relationship, the psychologist and the patient, client, or other appropriate recipient of psychological services reach an agreement specifying the compensation and the billing arrangements.

(b) Psychologists do not exploit recipients of services or payors with respect to fees.

(c) Psychologists' fee practices are consistent with law.

(d) Psychologists do not misrepresent their fees.

(e) If limitations to services can be anticipated because of limitations in financing, this is discussed with the patient, client, or other appropriate recipient of services as early as is feasible. (See also Standard 4.08, Interruption of Services.)

(f) If the patient, client, or other recipient of services does not pay for services as agreed, and if the psychologist wishes to use collection agencies or legal measures to collect the fees, the psychologist first informs the person that such measures will be taken and provides that person an opportunity to make prompt payment. (See also Standard 5.11, Withholding Records for Nonpayment.)

1.26 Accuracy in Reports to Payors and Funding Sources

In their reports to payors for services or sources of research funding, psychologists accurately state the nature of the research or service provided, the fees or charges, and where applicable, the identity of the provider, the findings, and the diagnosis. (See also Standard 5.05, Disclosures.)

1.27 Referrals and Fees

When a psychologist pays, receives payment from, or divides fees with another professional other than in an employer–employee relationship, the payment to each is based on the services (clinical, consultative, administrative, or other) provided and is not based on the referral itself.

2. Evaluation, Assessment, or Intervention

2.01 Evaluation, Diagnosis, and Interventions in Professional Context

(a) Psychologists perform evaluations, diagnostic services, or interventions only within the context of a defined professional relationship. (See also Standard 1.03, Professional and Scientific Relationship.)

(b) Psychologists' assessments, recommendations, reports, and psychological diagnostic or evaluative statements are based on information and techniques (including personal interviews of the individual when appropriate) sufficient to provide appropriate substantiation for their findings. (See also Standard 7.02, Forensic Assessments.)

2.02 Competence and Appropriate Use of Assessments and Interventions

(a) Psychologists who develop, administer, score, interpret, or use psychological assessment techniques, interviews, tests, or instruments do so in a manner and for purposes that are appropriate in light of the research on or evidence of the usefulness and proper application of the techniques.

(b) Psychologists refrain from misuse of assessment techniques, interventions, results, and interpretations and take reasonable steps to prevent others from misusing the information these techniques provide. This includes refraining from releasing raw test results or raw data to persons, other than to patients or clients as appropriate, who are not qualified to use such information. (See also Standards 1.02, Relationship of Ethics and Law, and 1.04, Boundaries of Competence.)

2.03 Test Construction

Psychologists who develop and conduct research with tests and other assessment techniques use specific procedures and current professional knowledge for test design, standardization, validation, reduction or elimination of bias, and recommendations for use.

2.04 Use of Assessment in General and With Special Populations

(a) Psychologists who perform interventions or administer, score, interpret, or use assessment techniques are familiar with the reliability, validation, and related standardization or outcome studies of, and proper applications and uses of, the techniques they use.

(b) Psychologists recognize limits to the certainty with which diagnoses, judgments, or predictions can be made about individuals.

(c) Psychologists attempt to identify situations in which particular interventions or assessment techniques or norms may not be applicable or may require adjustment in administration or interpretation because of factors such as individuals' gender, age, race, ethnicity, national origin, religion, sexual orientation, disability, language, or socioeconomic status.

2.05 Interpreting Assessment Results

When interpreting assessment results, including automated interpretations, psychologists take into account the various test factors and characteristics of the person being assessed that might affect psychologists' judgments or reduce the accuracy of their interpretations. They indicate any significant reservations they have about the accuracy or limitations of their interpretations.

2.06 Unqualified Persons

Psychologists do not promote the use of psychological assessment techniques by unqualified persons. (See also Standard 1.22, Delegation to and Supervision of Subordinates.)

2.07 Obsolete Tests and Outdated Test Results

(a) Psychologists do not base their assessment or intervention decisions or recommendations on data or test results that are outdated for the current purpose.

(b) Similarly, psychologists do not base such decisions or recommendations on tests and measures that are obsolete and not useful for the current purpose.

2.08 Test Scoring and Interpretation Services

(a) Psychologists who offer assessment or scoring procedures to other professionals accurately describe the purpose, norms, validity, reliability, and applications of the procedures and any special qualifications applicable to their use.

(b) Psychologists select scoring and interpretation services (including automated services) on the basis of evidence of the validity of the program and procedures as well as on other appropriate considerations.

(c) Psychologists retain appropriate responsibility for the appropriate application, interpretation, and use of assessment instruments, whether they score and interpret such tests themselves or use automated or other services.

2.09 Explaining Assessment Results

Unless the nature of the relationship is clearly explained to the person being assessed in advance and precludes provision of an explanation of results (such as in some organizational consulting, preemployment or security screenings, and forensic evaluations), psychologists ensure that an explanation of the results is provided using language that is reasonably understandable to the person assessed or to another legally authorized person on behalf of the client. Regardless of whether the scoring and interpretation are done by the psychologist, by assistants, or by automated or other outside services, psychologists take reasonable steps to ensure that appropriate explanations of results are given.

2.10 Maintaining Test Security

Psychologists make reasonable efforts to maintain the integrity and security of tests and other assessment techniques consistent with law, contractual obligations, and in a manner that permits compliance with the requirements of this Ethics Code. (See also Standard 1.02, Relationship of Ethics and Law.)

3. Advertising and Other Public Statements

3.01 Definition of Public Statements

Psychologists comply with this Ethics Code in public statements relating to their professional services, products, or publications or to the field of psychology. Public statements include but are not limited to paid or unpaid advertising, brochures, printed matter, directory listings, personal resumes or curricula vitae, interviews or comments for use in media, statements in legal proceedings, lectures and public oral presentations, and published materials.

3.02 Statements by Others

(a) Psychologists who engage others to create or place public statements that promote their professional practice, products, or activities retain professional responsibility for such statements.

(b) In addition, psychologists make reasonable efforts to prevent others whom they do not control (such as employers, publishers, sponsors, organizational clients, and representatives of the print or broadcast media) from making deceptive statements concerning psychologists' practice or professional or scientific activities.

(c) If psychologists learn of deceptive statements about their work made by others, psychologists make reasonable efforts to correct such statements.

(d) Psychologists do not compensate employees of press, radio, television, or other communication media in return for publicity in a news item.

(e) A paid advertisement relating to the psychologist's activities must be identified as such, unless it is already apparent from the context.

3.03 Avoidance of False or Deceptive Statements

(a) Psychologists do not make public statements that are false, deceptive, misleading, or fraudulent, either because of what they state, convey, or suggest or because of what they omit, concerning their research, practice, or other work activities or those of persons or organizations with which they are affiliated. As examples (and not in limitation) of this standard, psychologists do not make false or deceptive statements concerning (1) their training, experience, or competence; (2) their academic degrees; (3) their credentials; (4) their institutional or association affiliations; (5) their services; (6) the scientific or clinical basis for, or results or degree of success of, their services; (7) their fees; or (8) their publications or research findings. (See also Standards 6.15, Deception in Research, and 6.18, Providing Participants With Information About the Study.)

(b) Psychologists claim as credentials for their psychological work, only degrees that (1) were earned from a regionally accredited educational institution or (2) were the basis for psychology licensure by the state in which they practice.

3.04 Media Presentations

When psychologists provide advice or comment by means of public lectures, demonstrations, radio or television programs, prerecorded tapes, printed articles, mailed material, or other media, they take reasonable precautions to ensure that (1) the statements are based on appropriate psychological literature and practice, (2) the statements are otherwise consistent with this Ethics Code, and (3) the recipients of the information are not encouraged to infer that a relationship has been established with them personally.

3.05 *Testimonials*

Psychologists do not solicit testimonials from current psychotherapy clients or patients or other persons who because of their particular circumstances are vulnerable to undue influence.

3.06 *In-Person Solicitation*

Psychologists do not engage, directly or through agents, in uninvited in-person solicitation of business from actual or potential psychotherapy patients or clients or other persons who because of their particular circumstances are vulnerable to undue influence. However, this does not preclude attempting to implement appropriate collateral contacts with significant others for the purpose of benefiting an already engaged therapy patient.

4. *Therapy*

4.01 *Structuring the Relationship*

(a) Psychologists discuss with clients or patients as early as is feasible in the therapeutic relationship appropriate issues, such as the nature and anticipated course of therapy, fees, and confidentiality. (See also Standards 1.25, Fees and Financial Arrangements, and 5.01, Discussing the Limits of Confidentiality.)

(b) When the psychologist's work with clients or patients will be supervised, the above discussion includes that fact, and the name of the supervisor, when the supervisor has legal responsibility for the case.

(c) When the therapist is a student intern, the client or patient is informed of that fact.

(d) Psychologists make reasonable efforts to answer patients' questions and to avoid apparent misunderstandings about therapy. Whenever possible, psychologists provide oral and/or written information, using language that is reasonably understandable to the patient or client.

4.02 *Informed Consent to Therapy*

(a) Psychologists obtain appropriate informed consent to therapy or related procedures, using language that is reasonably understandable to participants. The content of informed consent will vary depending on many circumstances; however, informed consent generally implies that the person (1) has the capacity to consent, (2) has been informed of significant information concerning the procedure, (3) has freely and without undue influence expressed consent, and (4) consent has been appropriately documented.

(b) When persons are legally incapable of giving informed consent, psychologists obtain informed permission from a legally authorized person, if such substitute consent is permitted by law.

(c) In addition, psychologists (1) inform those persons who are legally incapable of giving informed consent about the proposed interventions in a manner commensurate with the persons' psychological capacities, (2) seek their assent to those interventions, and (3) consider such persons' preferences and best interests.

4.03 Couple and Family Relationships

(a) When a psychologist agrees to provide services to several persons who have a relationship (such as husband and wife or parents and children), the psychologist attempts to clarify at the outset (1) which of the individuals are patients or clients and (2) the relationship the psychologist will have with each person. This clarification includes the role of the psychologist and the probable uses of the services provided or the information obtained. (See also Standard 5.01, Discussing the Limits of Confidentiality.)

(b) As soon as it becomes apparent that the psychologist may be called on to perform potentially conflicting roles (such as marital counselor to husband and wife, and then witness for one party in a divorce proceeding), the psychologist attempts to clarify and adjust, or withdraw from, roles appropriately. (See also Standard 7.03, Clarification of Role, under Forensic Activities.)

4.04 Providing Mental Health Services to Those Served by Others

In deciding whether to offer or provide services to those already receiving mental health services elsewhere, psychologists carefully consider the treatment issues and the potential patient's or client's welfare. The psychologist discusses these issues with the patient or client, or another legally authorized person on behalf of the client, in order to minimize the risk of confusion and conflict, consults with the other service providers when appropriate, and proceeds with caution and sensitivity to the therapeutic issues.

4.05 Sexual Intimacies With Current Patients or Clients

Psychologists do not engage in sexual intimacies with current patients or clients.

4.06 Therapy With Former Sexual Partners

Psychologists do not accept as therapy patients or clients persons with whom they have engaged in sexual intimacies.

4.07 Sexual Intimacies With Former Therapy Patients

(a) Psychologists do not engage in sexual intimacies with a former therapy patient or client for at least two years after cessation or termination of professional services.

(b) Because sexual intimacies with a former therapy patient or client are so frequently harmful to the patient or client, and because such intimacies undermine public confidence in the psychology profession and thereby deter the public's use of needed services, psychologists do not engage in sexual intimacies with former therapy patients and clients even after a two-year interval except in the most unusual circumstances. The psychologist who engages in such activity after the two years following cessation or termination of treatment bears the burden of demonstrating that there has been no exploitation, in light of all relevant factors, including (1) the amount of time that has passed since therapy terminated, (2) the nature and duration of the therapy, (3) the circumstances of termination, (4) the patient's or client's personal history, (5) the patient's or client's current mental status, (6) the likelihood of adverse impact on the patient or client and others, and (7) any statements or actions made by the therapist during the course of therapy suggesting or inviting the possibility of a posttermination sexual or romantic relationship with the patient or client. (See also Standard 1.17, Multiple Relationships.)

4.08 Interruption of Services

(a) Psychologists make reasonable efforts to plan for facilitating care in the event that psychological services are interrupted by factors such as the psychologist's illness, death, unavailability, or relocation or by the client's relocation or financial limitations. (See also Standard 5.09, Preserving Records and Data.)

(b) When entering into employment or contractual relationships, psychologists provide for orderly and appropriate resolution of responsibility for patient or client care in the event that the employment or contractual relationship ends, with paramount consideration given to the welfare of the patient or client.

4.09 Terminating the Professional Relationship

(a) Psychologists do not abandon patients or clients. (See also Standard 1.25e, under Fees and Financial Arrangements.)

(b) Psychologists terminate a professional relationship when it becomes reasonably clear that the patient or client no longer needs the service, is not benefiting, or is being harmed by continued service.

(c) Prior to termination for whatever reason, except where precluded by the patient's or client's conduct, the psychologist discusses the patient's or client's views and needs, provides appropriate pretermination counseling, suggests alternative service providers as appropriate, and takes other reasonable steps to facilitate transfer of responsibility to another provider if the patient or client needs one immediately.

5. *Privacy and Confidentiality*

These Standards are potentially applicable to the professional and scientific activities of all psychologists.

5.01 *Discussing the Limits of Confidentiality*

(a) Psychologists discuss with persons and organizations with whom they establish a scientific, or professional relationship (including, to the extent feasible, minors and their legal representatives) (1) the relevant limitations on confidentiality, including limitations where applicable in group, marital, and family therapy or in organizational consulting, and (2) the foreseeable uses of the information generated through their services.

(b) Unless it is not feasible or is contraindicated, the discussion of confidentiality occurs at the outset of the relationship and thereafter as new circumstances may warrant.

(c) Permission for electronic recording of interviews is secured from clients and patients.

5.02 *Maintaining Confidentiality*

Psychologists have a primary obligation and take reasonable precautions to respect the confidentiality rights of those with whom they work or consult, recognizing that confidentiality may be established by law, institutional rules, or professional or scientific relationships. (See also Standard 6.26, Professional Reviewers.)

5.03 *Minimizing Intrusions on Privacy*

(a) In order to minimize intrusions on privacy, psychologists include in written and oral reports, consultations, and the like, only information germane to the purpose for which the communication is made.

(b) Psychologists discuss confidential information obtained in clinical or consulting relationships, or evaluative data concerning patients, individual or organizational clients, students, research participants, supervisees, and employees, only for appropriate scientific or professional purposes and only with persons clearly concerned with such matters.

5.04 *Maintenance of Records*

Psychologists maintain appropriate confidentiality in creating, storing, accessing, transferring, and disposing of records under their control, whether these are written, automated, or in any other medium. Psychologists maintain and dispose of records in accordance with law and in a manner that permits compliance with the requirements of this Ethics Code.

5.05 Disclosures

(a) Psychologists disclose confidential information without the consent of the individual only as mandated by law, or where permitted by law for a valid purpose, such as (1) to provide needed professional services to the patient or the individual or organizational client, (2) to obtain appropriate professional consultations, (3) to protect the patient or client or others from harm, or (4) to obtain payment for services, in which instance disclosure is limited to the minimum that is necessary to achieve the purpose.

(b) Psychologists also may disclose confidential information with the appropriate consent of the patient or the individual or organizational client (or of another legally authorized person on behalf of the patient or client), unless prohibited by law.

5.06 Consultations

When consulting with colleagues, (1) psychologists do not share confidential information that reasonably could lead to the identification of a patient, client, research participant, or other person or organization with whom they have a confidential relationship unless they have obtained the prior consent of the person or organization or the disclosure cannot be avoided, and (2) they share information only to the extent necessary to achieve the purposes of the consultation. (See also Standard 5.02, Maintaining Confidentiality.)

5.07 Confidential Information in Databases

(a) If confidential information concerning recipients of psychological services is to be entered into databases or systems of records available to persons whose access has not been consented to by the recipient, then psychologists use coding or other techniques to avoid the inclusion of personal identifiers.

(b) If a research protocol approved by an institutional review board or similar body requires the inclusion of personal identifiers, such identifiers are deleted before the information is made accessible to persons other than those of whom the subject was advised.

(c) If such deletion is not feasible, then before psychologists transfer such data to others or review such data collected by others, they take reasonable steps to determine that appropriate consent of personally identifiable individuals has been obtained.

5.08 Use of Confidential Information for Didactic or Other Purposes

(a) Psychologists do not disclose in their writings, lectures, or other public media, confidential, personally identifiable information concerning their patients, individual or organizational clients, students, research participants, or other recipients of their services that they obtained during the course of their work, unless the person or organization has consented in writing or unless there is other ethical or legal authorization for doing so.

(b) Ordinarily, in such scientific and professional presentations, psychologists disguise confidential information concerning such persons or organizations so that they are not individually identifiable to others and so that discussions do not cause harm to subjects who might identify themselves.

5.09 Preserving Records and Data

A psychologist makes plans in advance so that confidentiality of records and data is protected in the event of the psychologist's death, incapacity, or withdrawal from the position or practice.

5.10 Ownership of Records and Data

Recognizing that ownership of records and data is governed by legal principles, psychologists take reasonable and lawful steps so that records and data remain available to the extent needed to serve the best interests of patients, individual or organizational clients, research participants, or appropriate others.

5.11 Withholding Records for Nonpayment

Psychologists may not withhold records under their control that are requested and imminently needed for a patient's or client's treatment solely because payment has not been received, except as otherwise provided by law.

6. Teaching, Training Supervision, Research, and Publishing

6.01 Design of Education and Training Programs

Psychologists who are responsible for education and training programs seek to ensure that the programs are competently designed, provide the proper experiences, and meet the requirements for licensure, certification, or other goals for which claims are made by the program.

6.02 Descriptions of Education and Training Programs

(a) Psychologists responsible for education and training programs seek to ensure that there is a current and accurate description of the program content, training goals and objectives, and requirements that must be met for satisfactory completion of the program. This information must be made readily available to all interested parties.

(b) Psychologists seek to ensure that statements concerning their course outlines are accurate and not misleading, particularly regarding the subject matter to be covered, bases for evaluating progress, and the nature of course experiences. (See also Standard 3.03, Avoidance of False or Deceptive Statements.)

(c) To the degree to which they exercise control, psychologists responsible for announcements, catalogs, brochures, or advertisements describing workshops, seminars, or other non-degree-granting educational programs ensure that they accurately describe the audience for which the program is intended, the educational objectives, the presenters, and the fees involved.

6.03 Accuracy and Objectivity in Teaching

(a) When engaged in teaching or training, psychologists present psychological information accurately and with a reasonable degree of objectivity.

(b) When engaged in teaching or training, psychologists recognize the power they hold over students or supervisees and therefore make reasonable efforts to avoid engaging in conduct that is personally demeaning to students or supervisees. (See also Standards 1.09, Respecting Others, and 1.12, Other Harassment.)

6.04 Limitation on Teaching

Psychologists do not teach the use of techniques or procedures that require specialized training, licensure, or expertise, including but not limited to hypnosis, biofeedback, and projective techniques, to individuals who lack the prerequisite training, legal scope of practice, or expertise.

6.05 Assessing Student and Supervisee Performance

(a) In academic and supervisory relationships, psychologists establish an appropriate process for providing feedback to students and supervisees.

(b) Psychologists evaluate students and supervisees on the basis of their actual performance on relevant and established program requirements.

6.06 Planning Research

(a) Psychologists design, conduct, and report research in accordance with recognized standards of scientific competence and ethical research.

(b) Psychologists plan their research so as to minimize the possibility that results will be misleading.

(c) In planning research, psychologists consider its ethical acceptability under the Ethics Code. If an ethical issue is unclear, psychologists seek to resolve the issue through consultation with institutional review boards, animal care and use committees, peer consultations, or other proper mechanisms.

(d) Psychologists take responsible steps to implement appropriate protections for the rights and welfare of human participants, other persons affected by the research, and the welfare of animal subjects.

6.07 Responsibility

(a) Psychologists conduct research competently and with due concern for the dignity and welfare of the participants.

(b) Psychologists are responsible for the ethical conduct of research conducted by them or by others under their supervision or control.

(c) Researchers and assistants are permitted to perform only those tasks for which they are appropriately trained and prepared.

(d) As part of the process of development and implementation of research projects, psychologists consult those with expertise concerning any special population under investigation or most likely to be affected.

6.08 Compliance With Law and Standards

Psychologists plan and conduct research in a manner consistent with federal and state law and regulations, as well as professional standards governing the conduct of research, and particularly those standards governing research with human participants and animal subjects.

6.09 Institutional Approval

Psychologists obtain from host institutions or organizations appropriate approval prior to conducting research, and they provide accurate information about their research proposals. They conduct the research in accordance with the approved research protocol.

6.10 Research Responsibilities

Prior to conducting research (except research involving only anonymous surveys, naturalistic observations, or similar research), psychologists enter into an agreement with participants that clarifies the nature of the research and the responsibilities of each party.

6.11 Informed Consent to Research

(a) Psychologists use language that is reasonably understandable to research participants in obtaining their appropriate informed consent (except as provided in Standard 6.12, Dispensing With Informed Consent). Such informed consent is appropriately documented.

(b) Using language that is reasonably understandable to participants, psychologists inform participants of the nature of the research; they inform participants that they are free to participate or to decline to participate or to withdraw from the research; they explain the foreseeable consequences of declining or withdrawing; they inform participants of significant factors that may be expected to influence their willingness to participate (such as risks, discomfort, adverse effects, or limitations on confidentiality, except as provided in Standard 6.15, Deception in Research); and they explain other aspects about which the prospective participants inquire.

(c) When psychologists conduct research with individuals such as students or subordinates, psychologists take special care to protect the prospective participants from adverse consequences of declining or withdrawing from participation.

(d) When research participation is a course requirement or opportunity for extra credit, the prospective participant is given the choice of equitable alternative activities.

(e) For persons who are legally incapable of giving informed consent, psychologists nevertheless (1) provide an appropriate explanation, (2) obtain the participant's assent, and (3) obtain appropriate permission from a legally authorized person, if such substitute consent is permitted by law.

6.12 Dispensing With Informed Consent

Before determining that planned research (such as research involving only anonymous questionnaires, naturalistic observations, or certain kinds of archival research) does not require the informed consent of research participants, psychologists consider applicable regulations and institutional review board requirements, and they consult with colleagues as appropriate.

6.13 Informed Consent in Research Filming or Recording

Psychologists obtain informed consent from research participants prior to filming or recording them in any form, unless the research involves simply naturalistic observations in public places and it is not anticipated that the recording will be used in a manner that could cause personal identification or harm.

6.14 Offering Inducement for Research Participants

(a) In offering professional services as an inducement to obtain research participants, psychologists make clear the nature of the services, as well as the risks, obligations, and limitations. (See also Standard 1.18, Barter [With Patients or Clients].)

(b) Psychologists do not offer excessive or inappropriate financial or other inducements to obtain research participants, particularly when it might tend to coerce participation.

6.15 Deception in Research

(a) Psychologists do not conduct a study involving deception unless they have determined that the use of deceptive techniques is justified by the study's prospective scientific, educational, or applied value and that equally effective alternative procedures that do not use deception are not feasible.

(b) Psychologists never deceive research participants about significant aspects that would affect their willingness to participate, such as physical risks, discomfort, or unpleasant emotional experiences.

(c) Any other deception that is an integral feature of the design and conduct of an experiment must be explained to participants as early as is feasible, preferably at the conclusion of their participation, but no later than at the conclusion of the research. (See also Standard 6.18, Providing Participants With Information About the Study.)

6.16 Sharing and Utilizing Data

Psychologists inform research participants of their anticipated sharing or further use of personally identifiable research data and of the possibility of unanticipated future uses.

6.17 Minimizing Invasiveness

In conducting research, psychologists interfere with the participants or milieu from which data are collected only in a manner that is warranted by an appropriate research design and that is consistent with psychologists' roles as scientific investigators.

6.18 Providing Participants With Information About the Study

(a) Psychologists provide a prompt opportunity for participants to obtain appropriate information about the nature, results, and conclusions of the research, and psychologists attempt to correct any misconceptions that participants may have.

(b) If scientific or humane values justify delaying or withholding this information, psychologists take reasonable measures to reduce the risk of harm.

6.19 Honoring Commitments

Psychologists take reasonable measures to honor all commitments they have made to research participants.

6.20 Care and Use of Animals in Research

(a) Psychologists who conduct research involving animals treat them humanely.

(b) Psychologists acquire, care for, use, and dispose of animals in compliance with current federal, state, and local laws and regulations, and with professional standards.

(c) Psychologists trained in research methods and experienced in the care of laboratory animals supervise all procedures involving animals and are responsible for ensuring appropriate consideration of their comfort, health, and humane treatment.

(d) Psychologists ensure that all individuals using animals under their supervision have received instruction in research methods and in the care, maintenance, and handling of the species being used, to the extent appropriate to their role.

(e) Responsibilities and activities of individuals assisting in a research project are consistent with their respective competencies.

(f) Psychologists make reasonable efforts to minimize the discomfort, infection, illness, and pain of animal subjects.

(g) A procedure subjecting animals to pain, stress, or privation is used only when an alternative procedure is unavailable and the goal is justified by its prospective scientific, educational, or applied value.

(h) Surgical procedures are performed under appropriate anesthesia; techniques to avoid infection and minimize pain are followed during and after surgery.

(i) When it is appropriate that the animal's life be terminated, it is done rapidly, with an effort to minimize pain, and in accordance with accepted procedures.

6.21 Reporting of Results

(a) Psychologists do not fabricate data or falsify results in their publications.

(b) If psychologists discover significant errors in their published data, they take reasonable steps to correct such errors in a correction, retraction, erratum, or other appropriate publication means.

6.22 Plagiarism

Psychologists do not present substantial portions or elements of another's work or data as their own, even if the other work or data source is cited occasionally.

6.23 Publication Credit

(a) Psychologists take responsibility and credit, including authorship credit, only for work they have actually performed or to which they have contributed.

(b) Principal authorship and other publication credits accurately reflect the relative scientific or professional contributions of the individuals involved, regardless of their relative status. Mere possession of an institutional position, such as Department Chair, does not justify authorship credit. Minor contributions to the research or to the writing for publications are appropriately acknowledged, such as in footnotes or in an introductory statement.

(c) A student is usually listed as principal author on any multiple-authored article that is substantially based on the student's dissertation or thesis.

6.24 Duplicate Publication of Data

Psychologists do not publish, as original data, data that have been previously published. This does not preclude republishing data when they are accompanied by proper acknowledgment.

6.25 Sharing Data

After research results are published, psychologists do not withhold the data on which their conclusions are based from other competent professionals who seek to verify the substantive claims through reanalysis and who intend to use such data only for that purpose, provided that the confidentiality of the participants can be protected and unless legal rights concerning proprietary data preclude their release.

6.26 Professional Reviewers

Psychologists who review material submitted for publication, grant, or other research proposal review respect the confidentiality of and the proprietary rights in such information of those who submitted it.

7. *Forensic Activities*

7.01 *Professionalism*

Psychologists who perform forensic functions, such as assessments, interviews, consultations, reports, or expert testimony, must comply with all other provisions of this Ethics Code to the extent that they apply to such activities. In addition, psychologists base their forensic work on appropriate knowledge of and competence in the areas underlying such work, including specialized knowledge concerning special populations. (See also Standards 1.06, Basis for Scientific and Professional Judgments; 1.08, Human Differences; 1.15, Misuse of Psychologists' Influence; and 1.23, Documentation of Professional and Scientific Work.)

7.02 *Forensic Assessments*

(a) Psychologists' forensic assessments, recommendations, and reports are based on information and techniques (including personal interviews of the individual, when appropriate) sufficient to provide appropriate substantiation for their findings. (See also Standards 1.03, Professional and Scientific Relationship; 1.23, Documentation of Professional and Scientific Work; 2.01, Evaluation, Diagnosis, and Interventions in Professional Context; and 2.05, Interpreting Assessment Results.)

(b) Except as noted in (c), below, psychologists provide written or oral forensic reports or testimony of the psychological characteristics of an individual only after they have conducted an examination of the individual adequate to support their statements or conclusions.

(c) When, despite reasonable efforts, such an examination is not feasible, psychologists clarify the impact of their limited information on the reliability and validity of their reports and testimony, and they appropriately limit the nature and extent of their conclusions or recommendations.

7.03 *Clarification of Role*

In most circumstances, psychologists avoid performing multiple and potentially conflicting roles in forensic matters. When psychologists may be called on to serve in more than one role in a legal proceeding—for example, as consultant or expert for one party or for the court and as a fact witness—they clarify role expectations and the extent of confidentiality in advance to the extent feasible, and thereafter as changes occur, in order to avoid compromising their professional judgment and objectivity and in order to avoid misleading others regarding their role.

7.04 Truthfulness and Candor

(a) In forensic testimony and reports, psychologists testify truthfully, honestly, and candidly and, consistent with applicable legal procedures, describe fairly the bases for their testimony and conclusions.

(b) Whenever necessary to avoid misleading, psychologists acknowledge the limits of their data or conclusions.

7.05 Prior Relationships

A prior professional relationship with a party does not preclude psychologists from testifying as fact witnesses or from testifying to their services to the extent permitted by applicable law. Psychologists appropriately take into account ways in which the prior relationship might affect their professional objectivity or opinions and disclose the potential conflict to the relevant parties.

7.06 Compliance With Law and Rules

In performing forensic roles, psychologists are reasonably familiar with the rules governing their roles. Psychologists are aware of the occasionally competing demands placed upon them by these principles and the requirements of the court system, and attempt to resolve these conflicts by making known their commitment to this Ethics Code and taking steps to resolve the conflict in a responsible manner. (See also Standard 1.02, Relationship of Ethics and Law.)

8. *Resolving Ethical Issues*

8.01 Familiarity With Ethics Code

Psychologists have an obligation to be familiar with this Ethics Code, other applicable ethics codes, and their application to psychologists' work. Lack of awareness or misunderstanding of an ethical standard is not itself a defense to a charge of unethical conduct.

8.02 Confronting Ethical Issues

When a psychologist is uncertain whether a particular situation or course of action would violate this Ethics Code, the psychologist ordinarily consults with other psychologists knowledgeable about ethical issues, with state or national psychology ethics committees, or with other appropriate authorities in order to choose a proper response.

8.03 Conflicts Between Ethics and Organizational Demands

If the demands of an organization with which psychologists are affiliated conflict with this Ethics Code, psychologists clarify the nature of the conflict, make known their commitment to the Ethics Code, and to the extent feasible, seek to resolve the conflict in a way that permits the fullest adherence to the Ethics Code.

8.04 Informal Resolution of Ethical Violations

When psychologists believe that there may have been an ethical violation by another psychologist, they attempt to resolve the issue by bringing it to the attention of that individual if an informal resolution appears appropriate and the intervention does not violate any confidentiality rights that may be involved.

8.05 Reporting Ethical Violations

If an apparent ethical violation is not appropriate for informal resolution under Standard 8.04 or is not resolved properly in that fashion, psychologists take further action appropriate to the situation, unless such action conflicts with confidentiality rights in ways that cannot be resolved. Such action might include referral to state or national committees on professional ethics or to state licensing boards.

8.06 Cooperating With Ethics Committees

Psychologists cooperate in ethics investigations, proceedings, and resulting requirements of the APA or any affiliated state psychological association to which they belong. In doing so, they make reasonable efforts to resolve any issues as to confidentiality. Failure to cooperate is itself an ethics violation.

8.07 Improper Complaints

Psychologists do not file or encourage the filing of ethics complaints that are frivolous and are intended to harm the respondent rather than to protect the public.

Appendix B:
Protection of Human Subjects

TITLE 45
CODE OF FEDERAL REGULATIONS
PART 46

REVISED JUNE 18, 1991
REPRINTED APRIL 2, 1996

THE PUBLIC HEALTH SERVICE ACT
AS AMENDED BY
THE HEALTH RESEARCH EXTENSION ACT OF 1985
PUBLIC LAW 99-158
NOVEMBER 20, 1985

"INSTITUTIONAL REVIEW BOARDS; ETHICS GUIDANCE PROGRAM

"SEC. 491. (a) The Secretary shall by regulation require that each entity which applies for a grant, contract, or cooperative agreement under this Act for any project or program which involves the conduct of biomedical or behavioral research involving human subjects submit in or with its application for such grant, contract, or cooperative agreement assurances satisfactory to the Secretary that it has established (in accordance with regulations which the Secretary shall prescribe) a board (to be known as an 'Institutional Review Board') to review biomedical and behavioral research involving human subjects conducted at or supported by such entity in order to protect the rights of the human subjects of such research.

"(b)(1) The Secretary shall establish a program within the Department of Health and Human Services under which requests for clarification and guidance with respect to ethical issues raised in connection with biomedical or behavioral research involving human subjects are responded to promptly and appropriately.

"(2) The Secretary shall establish a process for the prompt and appropriate response to information provided to the Director of NIH respecting incidences of violations of the rights of human subjects of research for which funds have been made available under this Act. The process shall

include procedures for the receiving of reports of such information from recipients of funds under this Act and taking appropriate action with respect to such violations.

"FETAL RESEARCH

"Sec. 498. (a) The Secretary may not conduct or support any research or experimentation, in the United States or in any other country, on a nonviable living human fetus ex utero or a living human fetus ex utero for whom viability has not been ascertained unless the research or experimentation—*

> "*(1) may enhance the well-being or meet the health needs of the fetus or enhance the probability of its survival to viability; or*
>
> "*(2) will pose no added risk of suffering, injury, or death to the fetus and the purpose of the research or experimentation is the development of important biomedical knowledge which cannot be obtained by other means.*

"*(b) In administering the regulations for the protection of human research subjects which—*

> "*(1) apply to research conducted or supported by the Secretary;*
>
> "*(2) involve living human fetuses in utero; and*
>
> "*(3) are published in Section 46.208 of Part 46 of Title 45 of the Code of Federal Regulations;*

or any successor to such regulations, the Secretary shall require that the risk standard (published in Section 46.102(g) of such Part 46 or any successor to such regulations) be the same for fetuses which are intended to be aborted and fetuses which are intended to be carried to term.

NOTE: Section 46.102(g) becomes Section 46.102(i) in Title 45 CFR Part 46 as revised on June 18, 1991.

THE PUBLIC HEALTH SERVICE ACT
AS AMENDED BY
THE NATIONAL INSTITUTES OF HEALTH
REVITALIZATION ACT OF 1993
PUBLIC LAW 103-43
JUNE 10, 1993

"CERTAIN PROVISIONS REGARDING REVIEW AND APPROVAL OF PROPOSALS FOR RESEARCH

"SEC. 492A. (a) REVIEW AS PRECONDITION TO RESEARCH.—
"(1) PROTECTION OF HUMAN RESEARCH SUBJECTS.—

"(A) In the case of any application submitted to the Secretary for financial assistance to conduct research, the Secretary may not approve or fund any application that is subject to review under section 491(a) by an Institutional Review Board unless the application has undergone review in accordance with such section and has been recommended for approval by a majority of the members of the Board conducting such review.

"(B) In the case of research that is subject to review under procedures established by the Secretary for the protection of human subjects in clinical research conducted by the National Institutes of Health, the Secretary may not authorize the conduct of the research unless the research has, pursuant to such procedures, been recommended for approval.

THE CODE OF FEDERAL REGULATIONS
TITLE 45 CFR PART 46
IMPLEMENTS THESE AMENDMENTS
TO THE PUBLIC HEALTH SERVICE ACT

PART 46—PROTECTION OF HUMAN SUBJECTS

Subpart A—Federal Policy for the Protection of Human Subjects (Basic DHHS Policy for Protection of Human Research Subjects)

Sec.
46.101 To what does this policy apply?
46.102 Definitions.
46.103 Assuring compliance with this policy—research conducted or supported by any Federal Department or Agency.
46.104–46.106 [Reserved]
46.107 IRB membership.
46.108 IRB functions and operations.
46.109 IRB review of research.
46.110 Expedited review procedures for certain kinds of research involving no more than minimal risk, and for minor changes in approved research.
46.111 Criteria for IRB approval of research.
46.112 Review by institution.
46.113 Suspension or termination of IRB approval of research.
46.114 Cooperative research.
46.115 IRB records.
46.116 General requirements for informed consent.
46.117 Documentation of informed consent.
46.118 Applications and proposals lacking definite plans for involvement of human subjects.
46.119 Research undertaken without the intention of involving human subjects.
46.120 Evaluation and disposition of applications and proposals for research to be conducted or supported by a Federal Department or Agency.
46.121 [Reserved]
46.122 Use of Federal funds.
46.123 Early termination of research support: Evaluation of applications and proposals.
46.124 Conditions.

Subpart B—Additional DHHS Protections Pertaining to Research, Development, and Related Activities Involving Fetuses, Pregnant Women, and Human In Vitro Fertilization

Sec.
46.201 Applicability.
46.202 Purpose.
46.203 Definitions.
46.204 Ethical Advisory Boards.
46.205 Additional duties of the Institutional Review Boards in connection with activities involving fetuses, pregnant women, or human in vitro fertilization.
46.206 General limitations.
46.207 Activities directed toward pregnant women as subjects.
46.208 Activities directed toward fetuses *in utero* as subjects.
46.209 Activities directed toward fetuses *ex utero*, including nonviable fetuses, as subjects.
46.210 Activities involving the dead fetus, fetal material, or the placenta.
46.211 Modification or waiver of specific requirements.

Subpart C—Additional DHHS Protections Pertaining to Biomedical and Behavioral Research Involving Prisoners as Subjects

Sec.
46.301   Applicability.
46.302   Purpose.
46.303   Definitions.
46.304   Composition of Institutional Review Boards where prisoners are involved.
46.305   Additional duties of the Institutional Review Boards where prisoners are involved.
46.306   Permitted research involving prisoners.

Subpart D—Additional DHHS Protections for Children Involved as Subjects in Research

Sec.
46.401   To what do these regulations apply?
46.402   Definitions.
46.403   IRB duties.
46.404   Research not involving greater than minimal risk.
46.405   Research involving greater than minimal risk but presenting the prospect of direct benefit to the individual subjects.
46.406   Research involving greater than minimal risk and no prospect of direct benefit to individual subjects, but likely to yield generalizable knowledge about the subject's disorder or condition.
46.407   Research not otherwise approvable which presents an opportunity to understand, prevent, or alleviate a serious problem affecting the health or welfare of children.
46.408   Requirements for permission by parents or guardians and for assent by children.
46.409   Wards.

Authority: 5 U.S.C. 301; Sec. 474(a), 88 Stat. 352 (42 U.S.C. 2891–3(a)).

Note: As revised, Subpart A of the DHHS regulations incorporates the Common Rule (Federal Policy) for the Protection of Human Subjects (56 FR 28003). Subpart D of the HHS regulations has been amended at Section 46.401(b) to reference the revised Subpart A.

The Common Rule (Federal Policy) is also codified at
7 CFR Part 1c Department of Agriculture
10 CFR Part 745 Department of Energy
14 CFR Part 1230 National Aeronautics and Space Administration
15 CFR Part 27 Department of Commerce
16 CFR Part 1028 Consumer Product Safety Commission
22 CFR Part 225 International Development Cooperation Agency, Agency for International Development
24 CFR Part 60 Department of Housing and Urban Development
28 CFR Part 46 Department of Justice
32 CFR Part 219 Department of Defense
34 CFR Part 97 Department of Education
38 CFR Part 16 Department of Veterans Affairs
40 CFR Part 26 Environmental Protection Agency

45 CFR Part 690 National Science Foundation
49 CFR Part 11 Department of Transportation

PART 46—PROTECTION OF HUMAN SUBJECTS

Subpart A—Federal Policy for the Protection of Human Subjects (Basic DHHS Policy for Protection of Human Research Subjects)

Source: 56 FR 28003, June 18, 1991.

§ 46.101   To what does this policy apply?

(a) Except as provided in paragraph (b) of this section, this policy applies to all research involving human subjects conducted, supported or otherwise subject to regulation by any Federal Department or Agency which takes appropriate administrative action to make the policy applicable to such research. This includes research conducted by Federal civilian employees or military personnel, except that each Department or Agency head may adopt such procedural modifications as may be appropriate from an administrative standpoint. It also includes research conducted, supported, or otherwise subject to regulation by the Federal Government outside the United States.

(1) Research that is conducted or supported by a Federal Department or Agency, whether or not it is regulated as defined in § 46.102(e), must comply with all sections of this policy.

(2) Research that is neither conducted nor supported by a Federal Department or Agency but is subject to regulation as defined in § 46.102(e) must be reviewed and approved, in compliance with § 46.101, § 46.102, and § 46.107 through § 46.117 of this policy, by an Institutional Review Board (IRB) that operates in accordance with the pertinent requirements of this policy.

(b) Unless otherwise required by Department or Agency heads, research activities in which the only involvement of human subjects will be in one or more of the following categories are exempt from this policy:

(1) Research conducted in established or commonly accepted educational settings, involving normal educational practices, such as (i) research on regular and special education instructional strategies, or (ii) research on the effectiveness of or the comparison among instructional techniques, curricula, or classroom management methods.

(2) Research involving the use of educational tests (cognitive, diagnostic, aptitude, achievement), survey procedures, interview procedures or observation of public behavior, unless:

(i) information obtained is recorded in such a manner that human subjects can be identified, directly or through identifiers linked to the subjects; and (ii) any disclosure of the human subjects' responses outside the research could reasonably place the subjects at risk of criminal or civil liability or be damaging to the subjects' financial standing, employability, or reputation.

(3) Research involving the use of educational tests (cognitive, diagnostic, aptitude, achievement), survey procedures, interview procedures, or observation of public behavior that is not exempt under paragraph (b)(2) of this section, if:

(i) the human subjects are elected or appointed public officials or candidates for public office; or (ii) Federal statute(s) require(s) without exception that the confidentiality of the personally identifiable information will be maintained throughout the research and thereafter.

(4) Research involving the collection or study of existing data, documents, records, pathological specimens, or diagnostic specimens, if these sources are publicly available or if the information is recorded by the investigator in such a manner that subjects cannot be identified, directly or through identifiers linked to the subjects.

(5) Research and demonstration projects which are conducted by or subject to the approval of Department or Agency heads, and which are designed to study, evaluate, or otherwise examine:

(i) Public benefit or service programs; (ii) procedures for obtaining benefits or services under those programs; (iii) possible changes in or alternatives to those programs or procedures; or (iv) possible changes in methods or levels of payment for benefits or services under those programs.

(6) Taste and food quality evaluation and consumer acceptance studies, (i) if wholesome foods without additives are consumed or (ii) if a food is consumed that contains a food ingredient at or below the level and for a use found to be safe, or agricultural chemical or environmental contaminant at or below the level found to be safe, by the Food and Drug Administration or approved by the Environmental Protection Agency or the Food Safety and Inspection Service of the U.S. Department of Agriculture.

(c) Department or Agency heads retain final judgment as to whether a particular activity is covered by this policy.

(d) Department or Agency heads may require that specific research activities or classes of research activities conducted, supported, or otherwise subject to regulation by the Department or Agency but not otherwise covered by this policy, comply with some or all of the requirements of this policy.

(e) Compliance with this policy requires compliance with pertinent Federal laws or regulations which provide additional protections for human subjects.

(f) This policy does not affect any State or local laws or regulations which may otherwise be applicable and which provide additional protections for human subjects.

(g) This policy does not affect any foreign laws or regulations which may otherwise be applicable and which provide additional protections to human subjects of research.

(h) When research covered by this policy takes place in foreign countries, procedures normally followed in the foreign countries to protect human subjects may differ from those set forth in this policy. [An example is a foreign institution which complies with guidelines consistent with the World Medical Assembly Declaration (Declaration of Helsinki amended 1989) issued either by sovereign states or by an organization whose function for the protection of human research subjects is internationally recognized.] In these circumstances, if a Department or Agency head determines that the procedures prescribed by the institution afford protections that are at least equivalent to those provided in this policy, the Department or Agency head may approve the substitution of the foreign procedures in lieu of the procedural requirements provided in this policy. Except when otherwise required by statute, Executive Order, or the Department or Agency head, notices of these actions as they occur will be published in the **Federal Register** or will be otherwise published as provided in Department or Agency procedures.

(i) Unless otherwise required by law, Department or Agency heads may waive the applicability of some or all of the provisions of this policy to specific research activities or classes of research activities otherwise covered by this policy. Except when otherwise required by statute or Executive Order, the Department or Agency head shall forward advance notices of these actions to the Office for Protection from Research Risks, National Institutes of Health, Department of Health and Human Services (DHHS), and shall also publish them in the **Federal Register** or in such other manner as provided in Department or Agency procedures.[1]

§ 46.102 Definitions.

(a) *Department or Agency head* means the head of any Federal Department or Agency and any other officer or employee of any Department or Agency to whom authority has been delegated.

(b) *Institution* means any public or private entity or Agency (including Federal, State, and other agencies).

(c) *Legally authorized representative* means an individual or judicial or other body authorized under applicable law to consent on behalf of a prospective subject to the subject's participation in the procedure(s) involved in the research.

(d) *Research* means a systematic investigation, including research development, testing and evaluation, designed to develop or contribute to generalizable knowledge. Activities which meet this definition constitute research for purposes of this policy, whether or not they are conducted or supported under a program which is considered research for other purposes. For example, some demonstration and service programs may include research activities.

(e) *Research subject to regulation*, and similar terms are intended to encompass those research activities for which a Federal Department or Agency has specific responsibility for regulating as a research activity, (for example, Investigational New Drug requirements administered by the Food and Drug Administration). It does not include research activities which are incidentally regulated by a Federal Department or Agency solely as part of the Department's or Agency's broader responsibility to regulate certain types of activities whether research or non-research in nature (for example, Wage and Hour requirements administered by the Department of Labor).

(f) *Human subject* means a living individual about whom an investigator (whether professional or student) conducting research obtains

(1) data through intervention or interaction with the individual, or

(2) identifiable private information. *Intervention* includes both physical procedures by which data are gathered (for example, venipuncture) and manipulations of the subject or the subject's environment that are performed for research purposes. Interaction includes communication or interpersonal contact between investigator and subject. *Private information* includes information about behavior that occurs in a context in which an individual can reasonably expect that no observation or recording is taking place, and information which has been provided for specific purposes by an individual and which the individual can reasonably expect will not be made public (for example, a medical record). Private information must be individually identifiable (i.e., the identity of the subject is or may readily be ascertained by the investigator or associated with the information) in order for obtaining the information to constitute research involving human subjects.

---

[1]Institutions with DHHS-approved assurances on file will abide by provisions of Title 45 CFR Part 46 Subparts A–D. Some of the other departments and agencies have incorporated all provisions of Title 45 CFR Part 46 into their policies and procedures as well. However, the exemptions at 45 CFR 46.101(b) do not apply to research involving prisoners, fetuses, pregnant women, or human in vitro fertilization, Subparts B and C. The exemption at 45 CFR 46.101(b)(2), for research involving survey or interview procedures or observation of public behavior, does not apply to research with children, Subpart D, except for research involving observations of public behavior when the investigator(s) do not participate in the activities being observed.

(g) *IRB* means an Institutional Review Board established in accord with and for the purposes expressed in this policy.

(h) *IRB approval* means the determination of the IRB that the research has been reviewed and may be conducted at an institution within the constraints set forth by the IRB and by other institutional and Federal requirements.

(i) *Minimal risk* means that the probability and magnitude of harm or discomfort anticipated in the research are not greater in and of themselves than those ordinarily encountered in daily life or during the performance of routine physical or psychological examinations or tests.

(j) *Certification* means the official notification by the institution to the supporting Department or Agency, in accordance with the requirements of this policy, that a research project or activity involving human subjects has been reviewed and approved by an IRB in accordance with an approved assurance.

§ 46.103 Assuring compliance with this policy—research conducted or supported by any Federal Department or Agency.

(a) Each institution engaged in research which is covered by this policy and which is conducted or supported by a Federal Department or Agency shall provide written assurance satisfactory to the Department or Agency head that it will comply with the requirements set forth in this policy. In lieu of requiring submission of an assurance, individual Department or Agency heads shall accept the existence of a current assurance, appropriate for the research in question, on file with the Office for Protection from Research Risks, National Institutes of Health, DHHS, and approved for Federalwide use by that office. When the existence of an DHHS-approved assurance is accepted in lieu of requiring submission of an assurance, reports (except certification) required by this policy to be made to Department and Agency heads shall also be made to the Office for Protection from Research Risks, National Institutes of Health, DHHS.

(b) Departments and agencies will conduct or support research covered by this policy only if the institution has an assurance approved as provided in this section, and only if the institution has certified to the Department or Agency head that the research has been reviewed and approved by an IRB provided for in the assurance, and will be subject to continuing review by the IRB. Assurances applicable to federally supported or conducted research shall at a minimum include:

(1) A statement of principles governing the institution in the discharge of its responsibilities for protecting the rights and welfare of human subjects of research conducted at or sponsored by the institution, regardless of whether the research is subject to Federal regulation. This may include an appropriate existing code, declaration, or statement of ethical principles, or a statement formulated by the institution itself. This requirement does not preempt provisions of this policy applicable to Department- or Agency-supported or regulated research and need not be applicable to any research exempted or waived under § 46.101 (b) or (i).

(2) Designation of one or more IRBs established in accordance with the requirements of this policy, and for which provisions are made for meeting space and sufficient staff to support the IRB's review and recordkeeping duties.

(3) A list of IRB members identified by name; earned degrees; representative capacity; indications of experience such as board certifications, licenses, etc., sufficient to describe each member's chief anticipated contributions to IRB deliberations; and any employment or other relationship between each member and the institution; for example: full-time employee, part-time employee, member of governing panel or board, stockholder, paid or unpaid consultant. Changes in IRB membership shall be reported to the Department or Agency head, unless in accord

with § 46.103(a) of this policy, the existence of a DHHS-approved assurance is accepted. In this case, change in IRB membership shall be reported to the Office for Protection from Research Risks, National Institutes of Health, DHHS.

(4) Written procedures which the IRB will follow (i) for conducting its initial and continuing review of research and for reporting its findings and actions to the investigator and the institution; (ii) for determining which projects require review more often than annually and which projects need verification from sources other than the investigators that no material changes have occurred since previous IRB review; and (iii) for ensuring prompt reporting to the IRB of proposed changes in a research activity, and for ensuring that such changes in approved research, during the period for which IRB approval has already been given, may not be initiated without IRB review and approval except when necessary to eliminate apparent immediate hazards to the subject.

(5) Written procedures for ensuring prompt reporting to the IRB, appropriate institutional officials, and the Department or Agency head of (i) any unanticipated problems involving risks to subjects or others or any serious or continuing non-compliance with this policy or the requirements or determinations of the IRB; and (ii) any suspension or termination of IRB approval.

(c) The assurance shall be executed by an individual authorized to act for the institution and to assume on behalf of the institution the obligations imposed by this policy and shall be filed in such form and manner as the Department or Agency head prescribes.

(d) The Department or Agency head will evaluate all assurances submitted in accordance with this policy through such officers and employees of the Department or Agency and such experts or consultants engaged for this purpose as the Department or Agency head determines to be appropriate. The Department or Agency head's evaluation will take into consideration the adequacy of the proposed IRB in light of the anticipated scope of the institution's research activities and the types of subject populations likely to be involved, the appropriateness of the proposed initial and continuing review procedures in light of the probable risks, and the size and complexity of the institution.

(e) On the basis of this evaluation, the Department or Agency head may approve or disapprove the assurance, or enter into negotiations to develop an approvable one. The Department or Agency head may limit the period during which any particular approved assurance or class of approved assurances shall remain effective or otherwise condition or restrict approval.

(f) Certification is required when the research is supported by a Federal Department or Agency and not otherwise exempted or waived under § 46.101 (b) or (i). An institution with an approved assurance shall certify that each application or proposal for research covered by the assurance and by § 46.103 of this policy has been reviewed and approved by the IRB. Such certification must be submitted with the application or proposal or by such later date as may be prescribed by the Department or Agency to which the application or proposal is submitted. Under no condition shall research covered by § 46.103 of the policy be supported prior to receipt of the certification that the research has been reviewed and approved by the IRB. Institutions without an approved assurance covering the research shall certify within 30 days after receipt of a request for such a certification from the Department or Agency, that the application or proposal has been approved by the IRB. If the certification is not submitted within these time limits, the application or proposal may be returned to the institution.

(Approved by the Office of Management and Budget under Control Number 9999-0020.)

§§ 46.104—46.106   [Reserved]

§ 46.107   IRB membership.

(a) Each IRB shall have at least five members, with varying backgrounds to promote complete and adequate review of research activities commonly conducted by the institution. The IRB shall be sufficiently qualified through the experience and expertise of its members, and the diversity of the members, including consideration of race, gender, and cultural backgrounds and sensitivity to such issues as community attitudes, to promote respect for its advice and counsel in safeguarding the rights and welfare of human subjects. In addition to possessing the professional competence necessary to review specific research activities, the IRB shall be able to ascertain the acceptability of proposed research in terms of institutional commitments and regulations, applicable law, and standards of professional conduct and practice. The IRB shall therefore include persons knowledgeable in these areas. If an IRB regularly reviews research that involves a vulnerable category of subjects, such as children, prisoners, pregnant women, or handicapped or mentally disabled persons, consideration shall be given to the inclusion of one or more individuals who are knowledgeable about and experienced in working with these subjects.

(b) Every nondiscriminatory effort will be made to ensure that no IRB consists entirely of men or entirely of women, including the institution's consideration of qualified persons of both sexes, so long as no selection is made to the IRB on the basis of gender. No IRB may consist entirely of members of one profession.

(c) Each IRB shall include at least one member whose primary concerns are in scientific areas and at least one member whose primary concerns are in nonscientific areas.

(d) Each IRB shall include at least one member who is not otherwise affiliated with the institution and who is not part of the immediate family of a person who is affiliated with the institution.

(e) No IRB may have a member participate in the IRB's initial or continuing review of any project in which the member has a conflicting interest, except to provide information requested by the IRB.

(f) An IRB may, in its discretion, invite individuals with competence in special areas to assist in the review of issues which require expertise beyond or in addition to that available on the IRB. These individuals may not vote with the IRB.

§ 46.108   IRB functions and operations.

In order to fulfill the requirements of this policy each IRB shall:

(a) Follow written procedures in the same detail as described in § 46.103(b)(4) and to the extent required by § 46.103(b)(5).

(b) Except when an expedited review procedure is used (see § 46.110), review proposed research at convened meetings at which a majority of the members of the IRB are present, including at least one member whose primary concerns are in nonscientific areas. In order for the research to be approved, it shall receive the approval of a majority of those members present at the meeting.

§ 46.109   IRB review of research.

(a) An IRB shall review and have authority to approve, require modifications in (to secure approval), or disapprove all research activities covered by this policy.

(b) An IRB shall require that information given to subjects as part of informed consent is in accordance with § 46.116. The IRB may require that information, in addition to that specifically mentioned in § 46.116, be given to the subjects when in the IRB's judgment the information would meaningfully add to the protection of the rights and welfare of subjects.

(c) An IRB shall require documentation of informed consent or may waive documentation in accordance with § 46.117.

(d) An IRB shall notify investigators and the institution in writing of its decision to approve or disapprove the proposed research activity, or of modifications required to secure IRB approval of the research activity. If the IRB decides to disapprove a research activity, it shall include in its written notification a statement of the reasons for its decision and give the investigator an opportunity to respond in person or in writing.

(e) An IRB shall conduct continuing review of research covered by this policy at intervals appropriate to the degree of risk, but not less than once per year, and shall have authority to observe or have a third party observe the consent process and the research.

(Approved by the Office of Management and Budget under Control Number 9999-0020.)

§ 46.110   Expedited review procedures for certain kinds of research involving no more than minimal risk, and for minor changes in approved research.

(a) The Secretary, HHS, has established, and published as a Notice in the **Federal Register**, a list of categories of research that may be reviewed by the IRB through an expedited review procedure. The list will be amended, as appropriate, after consultation with other departments and agencies, through periodic republication by the Secretary, HHS, in the **Federal Register**. A copy of the list is available from the Office for Protection from Research Risks, National Institutes of Health, DHHS, Bethesda, Maryland 20892.

(b) An IRB may use the expedited review procedure to review either or both of the following:

(1) some or all of the research appearing on the list and found by the reviewer(s) to involve no more than minimal risk,

(2) minor changes in previously approved research during the period (of one year or less) for which approval is authorized.

Under an expedited review procedure, the review may be carried out by the IRB chairperson or by one or more experienced reviewers designated by the chairperson from among members of the IRB. In reviewing the research, the reviewers may exercise all of the authorities of the IRB except that the reviewers may not disapprove the research. A research activity may be disapproved only after review in accordance with the non-expedited procedure set forth in § 46.108(b).

(c) Each IRB which uses an expedited review procedure shall adopt a method for keeping all members advised of research proposals which have been approved under the procedure.

(d) The Department or Agency head may restrict, suspend, terminate, or choose not to authorize an institution's or IRB's use of the expedited review procedure.

§ 46.111   Criteria for IRB approval of research.

(a) In order to approve research covered by this policy the IRB shall determine that all of the following requirements are satisfied:

(1) Risks to subjects are minimized: (i) by using procedures which are consistent with sound research design and which do not unnecessarily expose subjects to risk, and (ii) whenever appropriate, by using procedures already being performed on the subjects for diagnostic or treatment purposes.

(2) Risks to subjects are reasonable in relation to anticipated benefits, if any, to subjects, and the importance of the knowledge that may reasonably be expected

to result. In evaluating risks and benefits, the IRB should consider only those risks and benefits that may result from the research (as distinguished from risks and benefits of therapies subjects would receive even if not participating in the research). The IRB should not consider possible long-range effects of applying knowledge gained in the research (for example, the possible effects of the research on public policy) as among those research risks that fall within the purview of its responsibility.

(3) Selection of subjects is equitable. In making this assessment the IRB should take into account the purposes of the research and the setting in which the research will be conducted and should be particularly cognizant of the special problems of research involving vulnerable populations, such as children, prisoners, pregnant women, mentally disabled persons, or economically or educationally disadvantaged persons.

(4) Informed consent will be sought from each prospective subject or the subject's legally authorized representative, in accordance with, and to the extent required by § 46.116.

(5) Informed consent will be appropriately documented, in accordance with, and to the extent required by § 46.117.

(6) When appropriate, the research plan makes adequate provision for monitoring the data collected to ensure the safety of subjects.

(7) When appropriate, there are adequate provisions to protect the privacy of subjects and to maintain the confidentiality of data.

(b) When some or all of the subjects are likely to be vulnerable to coercion or undue influence, such as children, prisoners, pregnant women, mentally disabled persons, or economically or educationally disadvantaged persons, additional safeguards have been included in the study to protect the rights and welfare of these subjects.

§ 46.112   Review by institution.

Research covered by this policy that has been approved by an IRB may be subject to further appropriate review and approval or disapproval by officials of the institution. However, those officials may not approve the research if it has not been approved by an IRB.

§ 46.113   Suspension or termination of IRB approval of research.

An IRB shall have authority to suspend or terminate approval of research that is not being conducted in accordance with the IRB's requirements or that has been associated with unexpected serious harm to subjects. Any suspension or termination of approval shall include a statement of the reasons for the IRB's action and shall be reported promptly to the investigator, appropriate institutional officials, and the Department or Agency head.

(Approved by the Office of Management and Budget under Control Number 9999-0020.)

§ 46.114   Cooperative research.

Cooperative research projects are those projects covered by this policy which involve more than one institution. In the conduct of cooperative research projects, each institution is responsible for safeguarding the rights and welfare of human subjects and for complying with this policy. With the approval of the Department or Agency head, an institution participating in a cooperative project may enter into a joint review arrangement, rely upon the review of another qualified IRB, or make similar arrangements for avoiding duplication of effort.

§ 46.115   IRB records.

(a) An institution, or when appropriate an IRB, shall prepare and maintain adequate documentation of IRB activities, including the following:

(1) Copies of all research proposals reviewed, scientific evaluations, if any, that accompany the proposals, approved sample consent documents, progress reports submitted by investigators, and reports of injuries to subjects.

(2) Minutes of IRB meetings which shall be in sufficient detail to show attendance at the meetings; actions taken by the IRB; the vote on these actions including the number of members voting for, against, and abstaining; the basis for requiring changes in or disapproving research; and a written summary of the discussion of controverted issues and their resolution.

(3) Records of continuing review activities.

(4) Copies of all correspondence between the IRB and the investigators.

(5) A list of IRB members in the same detail as described in § 46.103(b)(3).

(6) Written procedures for the IRB in the same detail as described in § 46.103(b)(4) and § 46.103(b)(5).

(7) Statements of significant new findings provided to subjects, as required by § 46.116(b)(5).

(b) The records required by this policy shall be retained for at least 3 years, and records relating to research which is conducted shall be retained for at least 3 years after completion of the research. All records shall be accessible for inspection and copying by authorized representatives of the Department or Agency at reasonable times and in a reasonable manner.

(Approved by the Office of Management and Budget under Control Number 9999-0020.)

§ 46.116   General requirements for informed consent.

Except as provided elsewhere in this policy, no investigator may involve a human being as a subject in research covered by this policy unless the investigator has obtained the legally effective informed consent of the subject or the subject's legally authorized representative. An investigator shall seek such consent only under circumstances that provide the prospective subject or the representative sufficient opportunity to consider whether or not to participate and that minimize the possibility of coercion or undue influence. The information that is given to the subject or the representative shall be in language understandable to the subject or the representative. No informed consent, whether oral or written, may include any exculpatory language through which the subject or the representative is made to waive or appear to waive any of the subject's legal rights, or releases or appears to release the investigator, the sponsor, the institution or its agents from liability for negligence.

(a) Basic elements of informed consent. Except as provided in paragraph (c) or (d) of this section, in seeking informed consent the following information shall be provided to each subject:

(1) a statement that the study involves research, an explanation of the purposes of the research and the expected duration of the subject's participation, a description of the procedures to be followed, and identification of any procedures which are experimental;

(2) a description of any reasonably foreseeable risks or discomforts to the subject;

(3) a description of any benefits to the subject or to others which may reasonably be expected from the research;

(4) a disclosure of appropriate alternative procedures or courses of treatment, if any, that might be advantageous to the subject;

(5) a statement describing the extent, if any, to which confidentiality of records identifying the subject will be maintained;

(6) for research involving more than minimal risk, an explanation as to whether any compensation and an explanation as to whether any medical treatments are available if injury occurs and, if so, what they consist of, or where further information may be obtained;

(7) an explanation of whom to contact for answers to pertinent questions about the research and research subjects' rights, and whom to contact in the event of a research-related injury to the subject; and

(8) a statement that participation is voluntary, refusal to participate will involve no penalty or loss of benefits to which the subject is otherwise entitled, and the subject may discontinue participation at any time without penalty or loss of benefits to which the subject is otherwise entitled.

(b) additional elements of informed consent. When appropriate, one or more of the following elements of information shall also be provided to each subject:

(1) a statement that the particular treatment or procedure may involve risks to the subject (or to the embryo or fetus, if the subject is or may become pregnant) which are currently unforeseeable;

(2) anticipated circumstances under which the subject's participation may be terminated by the investigator without regard to the subject's consent;

(3) any additional costs to the subject that may result from participation in the research;

(4) the consequences of a subject's decision to withdraw from the research and procedures for orderly termination of participation by the subject;

(5) A statement that significant new findings developed during the course of the research which may relate to the subject's willingness to continue participation will be provided to the subject, and

(6) the approximate number of subjects involved in the study.

(c) An IRB may approve a consent procedure which does not include, or which alters, some or all of the elements of informed consent set forth above, or waive the requirement to obtain informed consent provided the IRB finds and documents that:

(1) the research or demonstration project is to be conducted by or subject to the approval of state or local government officials and is designed to study, evaluate, or otherwise examine: (i) public benefit or service programs; (ii) procedures for obtaining benefits or services under those programs; (iii) possible changes in or alternatives to those programs or procedures; or (iv) possible changes in methods or levels of payment for benefits or services under those programs; and

(2) the research could not practicably be carried out without the waiver or alteration.

(d) An IRB may approve a consent procedure which does not include, or which alters, some or all of the elements of informed consent set forth in this section, or waive the requirements to obtain informed consent provided the IRB finds and documents that:

(1) the research involves no more than minimal risk to the subjects;

(2) the waiver or alteration will not adversely affect the rights and welfare of the subjects;

(3) the research could not practicably be carried out without the waiver or alteration; and

(4) whenever appropriate, the subjects will be provided with additional pertinent information after participation.

(e) The informed consent requirements in this policy are not intended to preempt any applicable Federal, State, or local laws which require additional information to be disclosed in order for informed consent to be legally effective.

(f) Nothing in this policy is intended to limit the authority of a physician to provide emergency medical care, to the extent the physician is permitted to do so under applicable Federal, State, or local law.

(Approved by the Office of Management and Budget under Control Number 9999-0020.)

§ 46.117 Documentation of informed consent.

(a) Except as provided in paragraph (c) of this section, informed consent shall be documented by the use of a written consent form approved by the IRB and signed by the subject or the subject's legally authorized representative. A copy shall be given to the person signing the form.

(b) Except as provided in paragraph (c) of this section, the consent form may be either of the following:

(1) A written consent document that embodies the elements of informed consent required by § 46.116. This form may be read to the subject or the subject's legally authorized representative, but in any event, the investigator shall give either the subject or the representative adequate opportunity to read it before it is signed; or

(2) A short form written consent document stating that the elements of informed consent required by § 46.116 have been presented orally to the subject or the subject's legally authorized representative. When this method is used, there shall be a witness to the oral presentation. Also, the IRB shall approve a written summary of what is to be said to the subject or the representative. Only the short form itself is to be signed by the subject or the representative. However, the witness shall sign both the short form and a copy of the summary, and the person actually obtaining consent shall sign a copy of the summary. A copy of the summary shall be given to the subject or the representative, in addition to a copy of the short form.

(c) An IRB may waive the requirement for the investigator to obtain a signed consent form for some or all subjects if it finds either:

(1) That the only record linking the subject and the research would be the consent document and the principal risk would be potential harm resulting from a breach of confidentiality. Each subject will be asked whether the subject wants documentation linking the subject with the research, and the subject's wishes will govern; or

(2) That the research presents no more than minimal risk of harm to subjects and involves no procedures for which written consent is normally required outside of the research context.

In cases in which the documentation requirement is waived, the IRB may require the investigator to provide subjects with a written statement regarding the research.

(Approved by the Office of Management and Budget under Control Number 9999-0020.)

§ 46.118 Applications and proposals lacking definite plans for involvement of human subjects.

Certain types of applications for grants, cooperative agreements, or contracts are submitted to departments or agencies with the knowledge that subjects may be involved within the period of support, but definite plans would not normally be set forth in the application or proposal. These include activities such as institutional type grants when selection of specific projects is the institution's responsibility; research training grants in which the activities involving subjects remain to be selected; and projects in which human subjects' involvement will depend upon completion of instruments, prior animal studies, or purification of compounds. These applications need not be reviewed by an IRB before an award may be made. However, except for research exempted or waived under § 46.101 (b) or (i), no human subjects may be involved in any project supported by these awards until the project has been reviewed and approved by the IRB, as provided in this policy, and certification submitted, by the institution, to the Department or Agency.

§ 46.119   Research undertaken without the intention of involving human subjects.

In the event research is undertaken without the intention of involving human subjects, but it is later proposed to involve human subjects in the research, the research shall first be reviewed and approved by an IRB, as provided in this policy, a certification submitted, by the institution, to the Department or Agency, and final approval given to the proposed change by the Department or Agency.

§ 46.120   Evaluation and disposition of applications and proposals for research to be conducted or supported by a Federal Department or Agency.

(a) The Department or Agency head will evaluate all applications and proposals involving human subjects submitted to the Department or Agency through such officers and employees of the Department or Agency and such experts and consultants as the Department or Agency head determines to be appropriate. This evaluation will take into consideration the risks to the subjects, the adequacy of protection against these risks, the potential benefits of the research to the subjects and others, and the importance of the knowledge gained or to be gained.

(b) On the basis of this evaluation, the Department or Agency head may approve or disapprove the application or proposal, or enter into negotiations to develop an approvable one.

§ 46.121   [Reserved]

§ 46.122   Use of Federal funds.

Federal funds administered by a Department or Agency may not be expended for research involving human subjects unless the requirements of this policy have been satisfied.

§ 46.123   Early termination of research support: Evaluation of applications and proposals.

(a) The Department or Agency head may require that Department or Agency support for any project be terminated or suspended in the manner prescribed in applicable program requirements, when the Department or Agency head finds an institution has materially failed to comply with the terms of this policy.

(b) In making decisions about supporting or approving applications or proposals covered by this policy the Department or Agency head may take into account, in addition to all other eligibility requirements and program criteria, factors such as whether the applicant has been subject to a termination or suspension under paragraph (a) of this section and whether the applicant or the person or persons who would direct or has/have directed the scientific and technical aspects of an activity has/have, in the judgment of the Department or Agency head, materially failed to discharge responsibility for the protection of the rights and welfare of human subjects (whether or not the research was subject to Federal regulation).

§ 46.124   Conditions.

With respect to any research project or any class of research projects the Department or Agency head may impose additional conditions prior to or at the time of approval when in the judgment of the Department or Agency head additional conditions are necessary for the protection of human subjects.

Subpart B—Additional DHHS Protections Pertaining to Research, Development, and Related Activities Involving Fetuses, Pregnant Women, and Human In Vitro Fertilization

Source: 40 FR 33528, Aug. 8, 1975, 43 FR 1758, January 11, 1978; 43 FR 51559, November 3, 1978.

§ 46.201   Applicability.

(a) The regulations in this subpart are applicable to all Department of Health and Human Services grants and contracts supporting research, development, and related activities involving: (1) the fetus, (2) pregnant women, and (3) human *in vitro* fertilization.

(b) Nothing in this subpart shall be construed as indicating that compliance with the procedures set forth herein will in any way render inapplicable pertinent State or local laws bearing upon activities covered by this subpart.

(c) The requirements of this subpart are in addition to those imposed under the other subparts of this part.

§ 46.202   Purpose.

It is the purpose of this subpart to provide additional safeguards in reviewing activities to which this subpart is applicable to assure that they conform to appropriate ethical standards and relate to important societal needs.

§ 46.203   Definitions.

As used in this subpart:

(a) "Secretary" means the Secretary of Health and Human Services and any other officer or employee of the Department of Health and Human Services (DHHS) to whom authority has been delegated.

(b) "Pregnancy" encompasses the period of time from confirmation of implantation (through any of the presumptive signs of pregnancy, such as missed menses, or by a medically acceptable pregnancy test), until expulsion or extraction of the fetus.

(c) "Fetus" means the product of conception from the time of implantation (as evidenced by any of the presumptive signs of pregnancy, such as missed menses, or a medically acceptable pregnancy test), until a determination is made, following expulsion or extraction of the fetus, that it is viable.

(d) "Viable" as it pertains to the fetus means being able, after either spontaneous or induced delivery, to survive (given the benefit of available medical therapy) to the point of independently maintaining heart beat and respiration. The Secretary may from time to time, taking into account medical advances, publish in the **Federal Register** guidelines to assist in determining whether a fetus is viable for purposes of this subpart. If a fetus is viable after delivery, it is a premature infant.

(e) "Nonviable fetus" means a fetus *ex utero* which, although living, is not viable.

(f) "Dead fetus" means a fetus *ex utero* which exhibits neither heartbeat, spontaneous respiratory activity, spontaneous movement of voluntary muscles, nor pulsation of the umbilical cord (if still attached).

(g) *"In vitro* fertilization" means any fertilization of human ova which occurs outside the body of a female, either through admixture of donor human sperm and ova or by any other means.

§ 46.204   Ethical Advisory Boards.

(a) One or more Ethical Advisory Boards shall be established by the Secretary. Members of these Board(s) shall be so selected that the Board(s) will be competent to deal with medical, legal, social, ethical, and related issues and may include, for example, research scientists, physicians, psychologists, sociologists, educators, lawyers, and ethicists, as well as representatives of the general public. No Board member may be a regular, full-time employee of the Department of Health and Human Services.

(b) At the request of the Secretary, the Ethical Advisory Board shall render advice consistent with the policies and requirements of this part as to ethical issues, involving activities covered by this subpart, raised by individual applications or proposals. In addition, upon request by the Secretary, the Board shall render advice as to classes of applications or proposals and general policies, guidelines, and procedures.

(c) A Board may establish, with the approval of the Secretary, classes of applications or proposals which: (1) must be submitted to the Board, or (2) need not be submitted to the Board. Where the Board so establishes a class of applications or proposals which must be submitted, no application or proposal within the class may be funded by the Department or any component thereof until the application or proposal has been reviewed by the Board and the Board has rendered advice as to its acceptability from an ethical standpoint.

§ 46.205   Additional duties of the Institutional Review Boards in connection with activities involving fetuses, pregnant women, or human in vitro fertilization.

(a) In addition to the responsibilities prescribed for Institutional Review Boards under Subpart A of this part, the applicant's or offeror's Board shall, with respect to activities covered by this subpart, carry out the following additional duties:

(1) determine that all aspects of the activity meet the requirement of this subpart;

(2) determine that adequate consideration has been given to the manner in which potential subjects will be selected, and adequate provision has been made by the applicant or offeror for monitoring the actual informed consent process (e.g., through such mechanisms, when appropriate, as participation by the Institutional Review Board or subject advocates in: (i) overseeing the actual process by which individual consents required by this subpart are secured either by approving induction of each individual into the activity or verifying, perhaps through sampling, that approved procedures for induction of individuals into the activity are being followed, and (ii) monitoring the progress of the activity and intervening as necessary through such steps as visits to the activity site and continuing evaluation to determine if any unanticipated risks have arisen);

(3) carry out such other responsibilities as may be assigned by the Secretary.

(b) No award may be issued until the applicant or offeror has certified to the Secretary that the Institutional Review Board has made the determinations required under paragraph (a) of this section and the Secretary has approved these determinations, as provided in § 46.120 of Subpart A of this part.

(c) Applicants or offerors seeking support for activities covered by this subpart must provide for the designation of an Institutional Review Board, subject to approval by the Secretary, where no such Board has been established under Subpart A of this part.

§ 46.206   General limitations.

(a) No activity to which this subpart is applicable may be undertaken unless:

(1) appropriate studies on animals and nonpregnant individuals have been completed;

(2) except where the purpose of the activity is to meet the health needs of the mother or the particular fetus, the risk to the fetus is minimal and, in all cases, is the least possible risk for achieving the objectives of the activity;

(3) individuals engaged in the activity will have no part in: (i) any decisions as to the timing, method, and procedures used to terminate the pregnancy, and (ii) determining the viability of the fetus at the termination of the pregnancy; and

(4) no procedural changes which may cause greater than minimal risk to the fetus or the pregnant woman will be introduced into the procedure for terminating the pregnancy solely in the interest of the activity.

(b) No inducements, monetary or otherwise, may be offered to terminate pregnancy for purposes of the activity.

Source: 40 FR 33528, Aug. 8, 1975, as amended at 40 FR 51638, Nov. 6, 1975.

§ 46.207   Activities directed toward pregnant women as subjects.

(a) No pregnant woman may be involved as a subject in an activity covered by this subpart unless: (1) the purpose of the activity is to meet the health needs of the mother and the fetus will be placed at risk only to the minimum extent necessary to meet such needs, or (2) the risk to the fetus is minimal.

(b) An activity permitted under paragraph (a) of this section may be conducted only if the mother and father are legally competent and have given their informed consent after having been fully informed regarding possible impact on the fetus, except that the father's informed consent need not be secured if: (1) the purpose of the activity is to meet the health needs of the mother; (2) his identity or whereabouts cannot reasonably be ascertained; (3) he is not reasonably available; or (4) the pregnancy resulted from rape.

§ 46.208   Activities directed toward fetuses *in utero* as subjects.

(a) No fetus *in utero* may be involved as a subject in any activity covered by this subpart unless: (1) the purpose of the activity is to meet the health needs of the particular fetus and the fetus will be placed at risk only to the minimum extent necessary to meet such needs, or (2) the risk to the fetus imposed by the research is minimal and the purpose of the activity is the development of important biomedical knowledge which cannot be obtained by other means.

(b) An activity permitted under paragraph (a) of this section may be conducted only if the mother and father are legally competent and have given their informed consent, except that the father's consent need not be secured if: (1) his identity or whereabouts cannot reasonably be ascertained, (2) he is not reasonably available, or (3) the pregnancy resulted from rape.

§ 46.209   Activities directed toward fetuses *ex utero*, including nonviable fetuses, as subjects.

(a) Until it has been ascertained whether or not a fetus *ex utero* is viable, a fetus *ex utero* may not be involved as a subject in an activity covered by this subpart unless:

(1) there will be no added risk to the fetus resulting from the activity, and the purpose of the activity is the development of important biomedical knowledge which cannot be obtained by other means, or

(2) the purpose of the activity is to enhance the possibility of survival of the particular fetus to the point of viability.

(b) No nonviable fetus may be involved as a subject in an activity covered by this subpart unless:

(1) vital functions of the fetus will not be artificially maintained,

(2) experimental activities which of themselves would terminate the heartbeat or respiration of the fetus will not be employed, and

(3) the purpose of the activity is the development of important biomedical knowledge which cannot be obtained by other means.

(c) In the event the fetus *ex utero* is found to be viable, it may be included as a subject in the activity only to the extent permitted by and in accordance with the requirements of other subparts of this part.

(d) An activity permitted under paragraph (a) or (b) of this section may be conducted only if the mother and father are legally competent and have given their informed consent, except that the father's informed consent need not be secured if: (1) his identity or whereabouts cannot reasonably be ascertained, (2) he is not reasonably available, or (3) the pregnancy resulted from rape.

§ 46.210   Activities involving the dead fetus, fetal material, or the placenta.

Activities involving the dead fetus, mascerated fetal material, or cells, tissue, or organs excised from a dead fetus shall be conducted only in accordance with any applicable State or local laws regarding such activities.

§ 46.211   Modification or waiver of specific requirements.

Upon the request of an applicant or offeror (with the approval of its Institutional Review Board), the Secretary may modify or waive specific requirements of this subpart, with the approval of the Ethical Advisory Board after such opportunity for public comment as the Ethical Advisory Board considers appropriate in the particular instance. In making such decisions, the Secretary will consider whether the risks to the subject are so outweighed by the sum of the benefit to the subject and the importance of the knowledge to be gained as to warrant such modification or waiver and that such benefits cannot be gained except through a modification or waiver. Any such modifications or waivers will be published as notices in the **Federal Register.**

Subpart C—Additional DHHS Protections Pertaining to Biomedical and Behavioral Research Involving Prisoners as Subjects

Source: 43 FR 53655, Nov. 16, 1978.

§ 46.301   Applicability.

(a) The regulations in this subpart are applicable to all biomedical and behavioral research conducted or supported by the Department of Health and Human Services involving prisoners as subjects.

(b) Nothing in this subpart shall be construed as indicating that compliance with the procedures set forth herein will authorize research involving prisoners as subjects, to the extent such research is limited or barred by applicable State or local law.

(c) The requirements of this subpart are in addition to those imposed under the other subparts of this part.

§ 46.302   Purpose.

Inasmuch as prisoners may be under constraints because of their incarceration which could affect their ability to make a truly voluntary and uncoerced decision whether or not to participate as subjects in research, it is the purpose of this subpart to provide additional safeguards for the protection of prisoners involved in activities to which this subpart is applicable.

§ 46.303   Definitions.

As used in this subpart:

(a) "Secretary" means the Secretary of Health and Human Services and any other officer or employee of the Department of Health and Human Services to whom authority has been delegated.

(b) "DHHS" means the Department of Health and Human Services.

(c) "Prisoner" means any individual involuntarily confined or detained in a penal institution. The term is intended to encompass individuals sentenced to such an institution under a criminal or civil statute, individuals detained in other facilities by virtue of statutes or commitment procedures which provide alternatives to criminal prosecution or incarceration in a penal institution, and individuals detained pending arraignment, trial, or sentencing.

(d) "Minimal risk" is the probability and magnitude of physical or psychological harm that is normally encountered in the daily lives, or in the routine medical, dental, or psychological examination of healthy persons.

§ 46.304   Composition of Institutional Review Boards where prisoners are involved.

In addition to satisfying the requirements in § 46.107 of this part, an Institutional Review Board, carrying out responsibilities under this part with respect to research covered by this subpart, shall also meet the following specific requirements:

(a) A majority of the Board (exclusive of prisoner members) shall have no association with the prison(s) involved, apart from their membership on the Board.

(b) At least one member of the Board shall be a prisoner, or a prisoner representative with appropriate background and experience to serve in that capacity, except that where a particular research project is reviewed by more than one Board only one Board need satisfy this requirement.

§ 46.305   Additional duties of the Institutional Review Boards where prisoners are involved.

(a) In addition to all other responsibilities prescribed for Institutional Review Boards under this part, the Board shall review research covered by this subpart and approve such research only if it finds that:

(1) the research under review represents one of the categories of research permissible under § 46.306(a)(2);

(2) any possible advantages accruing to the prisoner through his or her participation in the research, when compared to the general living conditions, medical care, quality of food, amenities and opportunity for earnings in the prison, are not of such a magnitude that his or her ability to weigh the risks of the research against the value of such advantages in the limited choice environment of the prison is impaired;

(3) the risks involved in the research are commensurate with risks that would be accepted by nonprisoner volunteers;

(4) procedures for the selection of subjects within the prison are fair to all prisoners and immune from arbitrary intervention by prison authorities or prisoners. Unless the principal investigator provides to the Board justification in writing for following some other procedures, control subjects must be selected randomly from the group of available prisoners who meet the characteristics needed for that particular research project;

(5) the information is presented in language which is understandable to the subject population;

(6) adequate assurance exists that parole boards will not take into account a prisoner's participation in the research in making decisions regarding parole, and each prisoner is clearly informed in advance that participation in the research will have no effect on his or her parole; and

(7) where the Board finds there may be a need for follow-up examination or care of participants after the end of their participation, adequate provision has been made for such examination or care, taking into account the varying lengths of individual prisoners' sentences, and for informing participants of this fact.

(b) The Board shall carry out such other duties as may be assigned by the Secretary.

(c) The institution shall certify to the Secretary, in such form and manner as the Secretary may require, that the duties of the Board under this section have been fulfilled.

§ 46.306 Permitted research involving prisoners.

(a) Biomedical or behavioral research conducted or supported by DHHS may involve prisoners as subjects only if:

(1) the institution responsible for the conduct of the research has certified to the Secretary that the Institutional Review Board has approved the research under § 46.305 of this subpart; and

(2) in the judgment of the Secretary the proposed research involves solely the following:

(A) study of the possible causes, effects, and processes of incarceration, and of criminal behavior, provided that the study presents no more than minimal risk and no more than inconvenience to the subjects;

(B) study of prisons as institutional structures or of prisoners as incarcerated persons, provided that the study presents no more than minimal risk and no more than inconvenience to the subjects;

(C) research on conditions particularly affecting prisoners as a class (for example, vaccine trials and other research on hepatitis which is much more prevalent in prisons than elsewhere; and research on social and psychological problems such as alcoholism, drug addiction, and sexual assaults) provided that the study may proceed only after the Secretary has consulted with appropriate experts including experts in penology, medicine, and ethics, and published notice, in the **Federal Register**, of his intent to approve such research; or

(D) research on practices, both innovative and accepted, which have the intent and reasonable probability of improving the health or well-being of the subject. In cases in which those studies require the assignment of prisoners in a manner consistent with protocols approved by the IRB to control groups which may not benefit from the research, the study may proceed only after the Secretary has consulted with appropriate experts, including experts in penology, medicine, and ethics, and published notice, in the **Federal Register**, of the intent to approve such research.

(b) Except as provided in paragraph (a) of this section, biomedical or behavioral research conducted or supported by DHHS shall not involve prisoners as subjects.

Subpart D—Additional DHHS Protections for Children Involved as Subjects in Research.

Source: 48 FR 9818, March 8, 1983; 56 FR 28032, June 18, 1991.

§ 46.401   To what do these regulations apply?

(a) This subpart applies to all research involving children as subjects, conducted or supported by the Department of Health and Human Services.

(1) This includes research conducted by Department employees, except that each head of an Operating Division of the Department may adopt such nonsubstantive, procedural modifications as may be appropriate from an administrative standpoint.

(2) It also includes research conducted or supported by the Department of Health and Human Services outside the United States, but in appropriate circumstances, the Secretary may, under paragraph (i) of § 46.101 of Subpart A, waive the applicability of some or all of the requirements of these regulations for research of this type.

(b) Exemptions at § 46.101(b)(1) and (b)(3) through (b)(6) are applicable to this subpart. The exemption at § 46.101(b)(2) regarding educational tests is also applicable to this subpart. However, the exemption at § 46.101(b)(2) for research involving survey or interview procedures or observations of public behavior does not apply to research covered by this subpart, except for research involving observation of public behavior when the investigator(s) do not participate in the activities being observed.

(c) The exceptions, additions, and provisions for waiver as they appear in paragraphs (c) through (i) of § 46.101 of Subpart A are applicable to this subpart.

§ 46.402   Definitions.

The definitions in § 46.102 of Subpart A shall be applicable to this subpart as well. In addition, as used in this subpart:

(a) "Children" are persons who have not attained the legal age for consent to treatments or procedures involved in the research, under the applicable law of the jurisdiction in which the research will be conducted.

(b) "Assent" means a child's affirmative agreement to participate in research. Mere failure to object should not, absent affirmative agreement, be construed as assent.

(c) "Permission" means the agreement of parent(s) or guardian to the participation of their child or ward in research.

(d) "Parent" means a child's biological or adoptive parent.

(e) "Guardian" means an individual who is authorized under applicable State or local law to consent on behalf of a child to general medical care.

§ 46.403   IRB duties.

In addition to other responsibilities assigned to IRBs under this part, each IRB shall review research covered by this subpart and approve only research which satisfies the conditions of all applicable sections of this subpart.

§ 46.404 Research not involving greater than minimal risk.

DHHS will conduct or fund research in which the IRB finds that no greater than minimal risk to children is presented, only if the IRB finds that adequate provisions are made for soliciting the assent of the children and the permission of their parents or guardians, as set forth in § 46.408.

§ 46.405 Research involving greater than minimal risk but presenting the prospect of direct benefit to the individual subjects.

DHHS will conduct or fund research in which the IRB finds that more than minimal risk to children is presented by an intervention or procedure that holds out the prospect of direct benefit for the individual subject, or by a monitoring procedure that is likely to contribute to the subject's well-being, only if the IRB finds that:

(a) the risk is justified by the anticipated benefit to the subjects;

(b) the relation of the anticipated benefit to the risk is at least as favorable to the subjects as that presented by available alternative approaches; and

(c) adequate provisions are made for soliciting the assent of the children and permission of their parents or guardians, as set forth in § 46.08.

§ 46.406 Research involving greater than minimal risk and no prospect of direct benefit to individual subjects, but likely to yield generalizable knowledge about the subject's disorder or condition.

DHHS will conduct or fund research in which the IRB finds that more than minimal risk to children is presented by an intervention or procedure that does not hold out the prospect of direct benefit for the individual subject, or by a monitoring procedure which is not likely to contribute to the well-being of the subject, only if the IRB finds that:

(a) the risk represents a minor increase over minimal risk;

(b) the intervention or procedure presents experiences to subjects that are reasonably commensurate with those inherent in their actual or expected medical, dental, psychological, social, or educational situations;

(c) the intervention or procedure is likely to yield generalizable knowledge about the subjects' disorder or condition which is of vital importance for the understanding or amelioration of the subjects' disorder or condition; and

(d) adequate provisions are made for soliciting assent of the children and permission of their parents or guardians, as set forth in § 46.408.

§ 46.407 Research not otherwise approvable which presents an opportunity to understand, prevent, or alleviate a serious problem affecting the health or welfare of children.

DHHS will conduct or fund research that the IRB does not believe meets the requirements of § 46.404, § 46.405, or § 46.406 only if:

(a) the IRB finds that the research presents a reasonable opportunity to further the understanding, prevention, or alleviation of a serious problem affecting the health or welfare of children; and

(b) the Secretary, after consultation with a panel of experts in pertinent disciplines (for example: science, medicine, education, ethics, law) and following opportunity for public review and comment, has determined either:

(1) that the research in fact satisfies the conditions of § 46.404, § 46.405, or § 46.406, as applicable, or (2) the following:

(i) the research presents a reasonable opportunity to further the understanding, prevention, or alleviation of a serious problem affecting the health or welfare of children;

(ii) the research will be conducted in accordance with sound ethical principles;

(iii) adequate provisions are made for soliciting the assent of children and the permission of their parents or guardians, as set forth in § 46.408.

§ 46.408   Requirements for permission by parents or guardians and for assent by children.

(a) In addition to the determinations required under other applicable sections of this subpart, the IRB shall determine that adequate provisions are made for soliciting the assent of the children, when in the judgment of the IRB the children are capable of providing assent. In determining whether children are capable of assenting, the IRB shall take into account the ages, maturity, and psychological state of the children involved. This judgment may be made for all children to be involved in research under a particular protocol, or for each child, as the IRB deems appropriate. If the IRB determines that the capability of some or all of the children is so limited that they cannot reasonably be consulted or that the intervention or procedure involved in the research holds out a prospect of direct benefit that is important to the health or well-being of the children and is available only in the context of the research, the assent of the children is not a necessary condition for proceeding with the research. Even where the IRB determines that the subjects are capable of assenting, the IRB may still waive the assent requirement under circumstances in which consent may be waived in accord with § 46.116 of Subpart A.

(b) In addition to the determinations required under other applicable sections of this subpart, the IRB shall determine, in accordance with and to the extent that consent is required by § 46.116 of Subpart A, that adequate provisions are made for soliciting the permission of each child's parents or guardian. Where parental permission is to be obtained, the IRB may find that the permission of one parent is sufficient for research to be conducted under § 46.404 or § 46.405. Where research is covered by § 46.406 and § 46.407 and permission is to be obtained from parents, both parents must give their permission unless one parent is deceased, unknown, incompetent, or not reasonably available, or when only one parent has legal responsibility for the care and custody of the child.

(c) In addition to the provisions for waiver contained in § 46.116 of Subpart A if the IRB determines that a research protocol is designed for conditions or for a subject population for which parental or guardian permission is not a reasonable requirement to protect the subjects (for example, neglected or abused children), it may waive the consent requirements in Subpart A of this part and paragraph (b) of this section, provided an appropriate mechanism for protecting the children who will participate as subjects in the research is substituted, and provided further that the waiver is not inconsistent with Federal, State, or local law. The choice of an appropriate mechanism would depend upon the nature and purpose of the activities described in the protocol, the risk and anticipated benefit to the research subjects, and their age, maturity, status, and condition.

(d) Permission by parents or guardians shall be documented in accordance with and to the extent required by § 46.117 of Subpart A.

(e) When the IRB determines that assent is required, it shall also determine whether and how assent must be documented.

§ 46.409 Wards.

(a) Children who are wards of the State or any other agency, institution, or entity can be included in research aproved under § 46.406 or § 46.407 only if such research is:

(1) related to their status as wards; or

(2) conducted in schools, camps, hospitals, institutions, or similar settings in which the majority of children involved as subjects are not wards.

(b) If the research is approved under paragraph (a) of this section, the IRB shall require appointment of an advocate for each child who is a ward, in addition to any other individual acting on behalf of the child as guardian or in loco parentis. One individual may serve as advocate for more than one child. The advocate shall be an individual who has the background and experience to act in, and agrees to act in, the best interests of the child for the duration of the child's participation in the research and who is not associated in any way (except in the role as advocate or member of the IRB) with the research, the investigator(s), or the guardian organization.

RESEARCH ACTIVITIES WHICH MAY BE REVIEWED THROUGH EXPEDITED REVIEW PROCEDURES

Research activities involving no more than minimal risk *and* in which the only involvement of human subjects will be in one or more of the following categories (carried out through standard methods) may be reviewed by the Institutional Review Board through the expedited review procedure authorized in § 46.110 of 45 CFR Part 46.

(1) Collection of: hair and nail clippings, in a nondisfiguring manner; deciduous teeth; and permanent teeth if patient care indicates a need for extraction.

(2) Collection of excreta and external secretions including sweat, uncannulated saliva, placenta removed at delivery, and amniotic fluid at the time of rupture of the membrane prior to or during labor.

(3) Recording of data from subjects 18 years of age or older using noninvasive procedures routinely employed in clinical practice. This includes the use of physical sensors that are applied either to the surface of the body or at a distance and do not involve input of matter or significant amounts of energy into the subject or an invasion of the subject's privacy. It also includes such procedures as weighing, testing sensory acuity, electrocardiography, electroencephalography, thermography, detection of naturally occurring radioactivity, diagnostic echography, and electroretinography. It does not include exposure to electromagnetic radiation outside the visible range (for example, x-rays, microwaves).

(4) Collection of blood samples by venipuncture, in amounts not exceeding 450 milliliters in an eight-week period and no more often than two times per week, from subjects 18 years of age or older and who are in good health and not pregnant.

(5) Collection of both supra- and subgingival dental plaque and calculus, provided the procedure is not more invasive than routine prophylactic scaling of the teeth and the process is accomplished in accordance with accepted prophylactic techniques.

(6) Voice recordings made for research purposes such as investigations of speech defects.

(7) Moderate exercise by healthy volunteers.

(8) The study of existing data, documents, records, pathological specimens, or diagnostic specimens.

(9) Research on individual or group behavior or characteristics of individuals, such as studies of perception, cognition, game theory, or test development, where the investigator does not manipulate subjects' behavior and the research will not involve stress to subjects.

(10) Research on drugs or devices for which an investigational new drug exemption or an investigational device exemption is not required.

Source: 46 FR 8392; January 26, 1981.

PUBLIC LAW 103-43—JUNE 10, 1993

NATIONAL INSTITUTES OF HEALTH REVITALIZATION ACT OF 1993

TITLE I—GENERAL PROVISIONS REGARDING TITLE IV OF PUBLIC HEALTH SERVICE ACT

Subtitle A—Research Freedom

PART II—RESEARCH ON TRANSPLANTATION OF FETAL TISSUE

SEC. 111. ESTABLISHMENT OF AUTHORITIES.

Part G of title IV of the Public Health Service Act (42 U.S.C. 289 et seq.) is amended by inserting after section 498 the following section:

"RESEARCH ON TRANSPLANTATION OF FETAL TISSUE

"SEC. 498A. (a) ESTABLISHMENT OF PROGRAM.—

"(1) IN GENERAL.—The Secretary may conduct or support research on the transplantation of human fetal tissue for therapeutic purposes.

"(2) SOURCE OF TISSUE.—Human fetal tissue may be used in research carried out under paragraph (1) regardless of whether the tissue is obtained pursuant to a spontaneous or induced abortion or pursuant to a stillbirth.

"(b) INFORMED CONSENT OF DONOR.—

"(1) IN GENERAL.—In research carried out under subsection (a), human fetal tissue may be used only if the woman providing the tissue makes a statement, made in writing and signed by the woman, declaring that—

"(A) the woman donates the fetal tissue for use in research described in subsection (a);

"(B) the donation is made without any restriction regarding the identity of individuals who may be the recipients of transplantations of the tissue; and

"(C) the woman has not been informed of the identity of any such individuals.

"(2) ADDITIONAL STATEMENT.—In research carried out under subsection (a), human fetal tissue may be used only if the attending physician with respect to obtaining the tissue from the woman involved makes a statement, made in writing and signed by the physician, declaring that—

"(A) in the case of tissue obtained pursuant to an induced abortion—

"(i) the consent of the woman for the abortion was obtained prior to requesting or obtaining consent for a donation of the tissue for use in such research;

"(ii) no alteration of the timing, method, or procedures

used to terminate the pregnancy was made solely for the purposes of obtaining the tissue; and

"(iii) the abortion was performed in accordance with applicable State law;

(B) the tissue has been donated by the woman in accordance with paragraph (1); and

"(C) full disclosure has been provided to the woman with regard to—

"(i) such physician's interest, if any, in the research to be conducted with the tissue; and

"(ii) any known medical risks to the woman or risks to her privacy that might be associated with the donation of the tissue and that are in addition to risks of such type that are associated with the woman's medical care.

"(c) INFORMED CONSENT OF RESEARCHER AND DONEE.—In research carried out under subsection (a), human fetal tissue may be used only if the individual with the principal responsibility for conducting the research involved makes a statement, made in writing and signed by the individual, declaring that the individual—

"(1) is aware that—

"(A) the tissue is human fetal tissue;

"(B) the tissue may have been obtained pursuant to a spontaneous or induced abortion or pursuant to a stillbirth; and

"(C) the tissue was donated for research purposes;

"(2) has provided such information to other individuals with responsibilities regarding the research;

"(3) will require, prior to obtaining the consent of an individual to be a recipient of a transplantation of the tissue, written acknowledgment of receipt of such information by such recipient; and

"(4) has had no part in any decisions as to the timing, method, or procedures used to terminate the pregnancy made solely for the purposes of the research.

"(d) AVAILABILITY OF STATEMENTS FOR AUDIT.—

"(1) IN GENERAL.—In research carried out under subsection (a), human fetal tissue may be used only if the head of the agency or other entity conducting the research involved certifies to the Secretary that the statements required under subsections (b)(2) and (c) will be available for audit by the Secretary.

"(2) CONFIDENTIALITY OF AUDIT.—Any audit conducted by the Secretary pursuant to paragraph (1) shall be conducted in a confidential manner to protect the privacy rights of the individuals and entities involved in such research, including such individuals and entities involved in the donation, transfer, receipt, or transplantation of human fetal tissue. With respect to any material or information obtained pursuant to such audit, the Secretary shall—

"(A) use such material or information only for the purposes of verifying compliance with the requirements of this section;

"(B) not disclose or publish such material or information, except where required by Federal law, in which case such material or information shall be coded in a manner such that the identities of such individuals and entities are protected; and

"(C) not maintain such material or information after completion of such audit, except where necessary for the purposes of such audit.

"(e) APPLICABILITY OF STATE AND LOCAL LAW.—

"(1) RESEARCH CONDUCTED BY RECIPIENTS OF ASSISTANCE.—The Secretary may not provide support for research under subsection (a) unless the applicant for the financial assistance involved agrees to conduct the research in accordance with applicable State law.

"(2) RESEARCH CONDUCTED BY SECRETARY.—The Secretary may conduct research under subsection (a) only in accordance with applicable State and local law.

"(f) REPORT.—The Secretary shall annually submit to the Committee on Energy and Commerce of the House of Representatives, and to the Committee on Labor and Human Resources of the Senate, a report describing the activities carried out under this section during the preceding fiscal year, including a description of whether and to what extent research under subsection (a) has been conducted in accordance with this section.

"(g) DEFINITION.—For purposes of this section, the term 'human fetal tissue' means tissue or cells obtained from a dead human embryo or fetus after a spontaneous or induced abortion, or after a stillbirth."

SEC. 112. PURCHASE OF HUMAN FETAL TISSUE; SOLICITATION OR ACCEPTANCE OF TISSUE AS DIRECTED DONATION FOR USE IN TRANSPLANTATION.

Part G of title IV of the Public Health Service Act, as amended by section 111 of this Act, is amended by inserting after section 498A the following section:

"PROHIBITIONS REGARDING HUMAN FETAL TISSUE

"SEC. 498B. (a) PURCHASE OF TISSUE.—It shall be unlawful for any person to knowingly acquire, receive, or otherwise transfer any human fetal tissue for valuable consideration if the transfer affects interstate commerce.

"(b) SOLICITATION OR ACCEPTANCE OF TISSUE AS DIRECTED DONATION FOR USE IN TRANSPLANTATION.—It shall be unlawful for any person to solicit or knowingly acquire, receive, or accept a donation of human fetal tissue for the purpose of transplantation of such tissue into another person if the donation affects interstate commerce, the tissue will be or is obtained pursuant to an induced abortion, and—

"(1) the donation will be or is made pursuant to a promise to the donating individual that the donated tissue will be transplanted into a recipient specified by such individual;

"(2) the donated tissue will be transplanted into a relative of the donating individual; or

"(3) the person who solicits or knowingly acquires, receives, or accepts the donation has provided valuable consideration for the costs associated with such abortion.

"(c) CRIMINAL PENALTIES FOR VIOLATIONS.—

"(1) IN GENERAL.—Any person who violates subsection (a) or (b) shall be fined in accordance with title 18, United States Code, subject to paragraph (2), or imprisoned for not more than 10 years, or both.

"(2) PENALTIES APPLICABLE TO PERSONS RECEIVING CONSIDERATION. —With respect to the imposition of a fine under paragraph (1), if the person involved violates subsection (a) or (b)(3), a fine shall be imposed in an amount not less than twice the amount of the valuable consideration received.

"(d) DEFINITIONS.—For purposes of this section:

"(1) The term 'human fetal tissue' has the meaning given such term in section 498A(f).

"(2) The term 'interstate commerce' has the meaning given such term in section 201(b) of the Federal Food, Drug, and Cosmetic Act.

"(3) The term 'valuable consideration' does not include reasonable payments associated with the transportation, implantation, processing, preservation, quality control, or storage of human fetal tissue."

SEC. 113. NULLIFICATION OF MORATORIUM.

(a) IN GENERAL.—Except as provided in subsection (c), no official of the executive branch may impose a policy that the Department of Health and Human Services is prohibited from conducting or supporting any research on the transplantation of human fetal tissue for therapeutic purposes. Such research shall be carried out in accordance with section 498A of the Public Health Service Act (as added by section 111 of this Act), without regard to any such policy that may have been in effect prior to the date of the enactment of this Act.

(b) PROHIBITION AGAINST WITHHOLDING OF FUNDS IN CASES OF TECHNICAL AND SCIENTIFIC MERIT.—

(1) IN GENERAL.—Subject to subsection (b)(2) of section 492A of the Public Health Service Act (as added by section 101 of this Act), in the case of any proposal for research on the transplantation of human fetal tissue for therapeutic purposes, the Secretary of Health and Human Services may not withhold funds for the research if—

(A) the research has been approved for purposes of subsection (a) of such section 492A;

(B) the research will be carried out in accordance with section 498A of such Act (as added by section 111 of this Act); and

(C) there are reasonable assurances that the research will not utilize any human fetal tissue that has been obtained in violation of section 498B(a) of such Act (as added by section 112 of this Act).

(2) STANDING APPROVAL REGARDING ETHICAL STATUS.—In the case of any proposal for research on the transplantation of human fetal tissue for therapeutic purposes, the issuance in December 1988 of the Report of the Human Fetal Tissue Transplantation Research Panel shall be seemed to be a report—

(A) issued by an ethics advisory board pursuant to section 492A(b)(5)(B)(ii) of the Public Health Service Act (as added by section 101 of this Act); and

(B) finding, on a basis that is neither arbitrary nor capricious, that the nature of the research is such that it is not unethical to conduct or support the research.

(c) AUTHORITY FOR WITHHOLDING FUNDS FROM RESEARCH.—In the case of any research on the transplantation of human fetal tissue for therapeutic purposes, the Secretary of Health and Human Services may withhold funds for the research if any of the conditions specified in any of subparagraphs (A) through (C) of subsection (b)(1) are not met with respect to the research.

(d) DEFINITION.—For purposes of this section, the term "human fetal tissue" has the meaning given such term in section 498A(f) of the Public Health Service Act (as added by section 111 of this Act).

Appendix C:
The Belmont Report

Ethical Principles and Guidelines for the Protection of Human Subjects of Research

The National Commission for the Protection of Human Subjects of Biomedical and Behavioral Research
April 18, 1979

DEPARTMENT OF HEALTH, EDUCATION, AND WELFARE

Office of the Secretary

Protection of Human Subjects

Belmont Report: Ethical Principles and Guidelines for the Protection of Human Subjects of Research, Report of the National Commission for the Protection of Human Subjects of Biomedical and Behavioral Research

AGENCY: Department of Health, Education, and Welfare.

ACTION: Notice of Report for Public Comment.

SUMMARY: On July 12, 1974, the National Research Act (Pub. L. 93-348) was signed into law, there-by creating the National Commission for the Protection of Human Subjects of Biomedical and Behavioral Research. One of the charges to the Commission was to identify the basic ethical principles that should underlie the conduct of biomedical and behavioral research involving human subjects and to develop guidelines which should be followed to assure that such research is conducted in accordance with those principles. In carrying out the above, the Commission was directed to consider: (i) the boundaries between biomedical and behavioral research and the accepted and routine practice of medicine, (ii) the role of assessment of risk-benefit criteria in the determination of the appropriateness of research involving human subjects, (iii) appropriate guidelines for the selection of human subjects for participation in such research, and (iv) the nature and definition of informed consent in various research settings.

The Belmont Report attempts to summarize the basic ethical principles identified by the Commission in the course of its deliberations. It is the outgrowth of an intensive four-day period of discussions that were held in February 1976 at the Smithsonian Institution's Belmont Conference Center supplemented by the monthly deliberations of the Commission that were held over a period of nearly four years. It is a statement of basic ethical principles and guidelines that should assist in resolving the ethical problems that surround the conduct of research with human subjects. By publishing the Report in the **Federal Register**, and providing reprints upon request, the Secretary intends that it may be made readily available to scientists, members of Institutional Review Boards, and Federal employees. The two-volume Appendix, containing the lengthy reports of experts and specialists who assisted the Commission in fulfilling this part of its charge, is available as DHEW Publication No. (OS) 78-0013 and No. (OS) 78-0014, for sale by the Superintendent of Documents, U.S. Government Printing Office, Washington, D.C. 20402.

Unlike most other reports of the Commission, the Belmont Report does not make specific recommendations for administrative action by the Secretary of Health, Education, and Welfare. Rather, the Commission recommended that the Belmont Report be adopted in its entirety, as a statement of the Department's policy. The Department requests public comment on this recommendation.

National Commission for the Protection of Human Subjects of Biomedical and Behavioral Research

Members of the Commission

Kenneth John Ryan, M.D., Chairman, Chief of Staff, Boston Hospital for Women.
Joseph V. Brady, Ph.D., Professor of Behavioral Biology, Johns Hopkins University.
Robert E. Cooke, M.D., President, Medical College of Pennsylvania.
Dorothy I. Height, President, National Council of Negro Women, Inc.
Albert R. Jonsen, Ph.D., Associate Professor of Bioethics, University of California at San Francisco.
Patricia King, J.D., Associate Professor of Law, Georgetown University Law Center.
Karen Lebacqz, Ph.D., Associate Professor of Christian Ethics, Pacific School of Religion.
*David W. Louisell, J.D., Professor of Law, University of California at Berkeley.
Donald W. Seldin, M.D., Professor and Chairman, Department of Internal Medicine, University of Texas at Dallas.
*Eliot Stellar, Ph.D., Provost of the University and Professor of Physiological Psychology, University of Pennsylvania.
*Robert H. Turtle, L.L.B., Attorney, VomBaur, Coburn, Simmons & Turtle, Washington, D.C.

*Deceased.

Table of Contents

A. Boundaries Between Practice and Research
B. Basic Ethical Principles
   1. Respect for Persons
   2. Beneficence
   3. Justice
C. Applications
   1. Informed Consent
   2. Assessment of Risk and Benefits
   3. Selection of Subjects

Belmont Report

Ethical Principles and Guidelines for Research Involving Human Subjects

Scientific research has produced substantial social benefits. It has also posed some troubling ethical questions. Public attention was drawn to these questions by reported abuses of human subjects in biomedical experiments, especially during the Second World War. During the Nuremberg War Crime Trials, the Nuremberg code was drafted as a set of standards for judging physicians and scientists who had conducted biomedical experiments on concentration camp prisoners. This code became the prototype of many later codes[1] intended to assure that research involving human subjects would be carried out in an ethical manner.

The codes consist of rules, some general, others specific, that guide the investigators or the reviewers of research in their work. Such rules often are inadequate to cover complex situations; at times they come into conflict, and they are frequently difficult to interpret or apply. Broader ethical principles will provide a basis on which specific rules may be formulated, criticized and interpreted.

Three principles, or general prescriptive judgments, that are relevant to research involving human subjects are identified in this statement. Other principles may also be relevant. These three are comprehensive, however, and are stated at a level of generalization that should assist scientists, subjects, reviewers and interested citizens to understand the ethical issues inherent in research involving human subjects. These principles cannot always be applied so as to resolve beyond dispute particular ethical problems. The objective is to provide an analytical framework that will guide the resolution of ethical problems arising from research involving human subjects.

This statement consists of a distinction between research and practice, a discussion of the three basic ethical principles, and remarks about the application of these principles.

A. Boundaries Between Practice and Research

It is important to distinguish between biomedical and behavioral research, on the one hand, and the practice of accepted therapy on the other, in order to know what activities ought to undergo review for the protection of human subjects of research. The distinction between research and practice is blurred partly because both often occur together (as in research designed to evaluate a therapy) and partly because notable departures from standard practice are often called "experimental" when the terms "experimental" and "research" are not carefully defined.

For the most part, the term "practice" refers to interventions that are designed solely to enhance the well-being of an individual patient or client and that have a reasonable expectation of success. The purpose of medical or behavioral practice is to provide diagnosis, preventive treatment or therapy to particular

---

[1]Since 1945, various codes for the proper and responsible conduct of human experimentation in medical research have been adopted by different organizations. The best known of these codes are the Nuremberg Code of 1947, the Helsinki Declaration of 1964 (revised in 1975), and the 1971 Guidelines (codified into Federal Regulations in 1974) issued by the U.S. Department of Health, Education, and Welfare. Codes for the conduct of social and behavioral research have also been adopted, the best known being that of the American Psychological Association, published in 1973.

individuals.[2] By contrast, the term "research" designates an activity designed to test an hypothesis, permit conclusions to be drawn, and thereby to develop or contribute to generalizable knowledge (expressed, for example, in theories, principles, and statements of relationships). Research is usually described in a formal protocol that sets forth an objective and a set of procedures designed to reach that objective.

When a clinician departs in a significant way from standard or accepted practice, the innovation does not, in and of itself, constitute research. The fact that a procedure is "experimental," in the sense of new, untested or different, does not automatically place it in the category of research. Radically new procedures of this description should, however, be made the object of formal research at an early stage in order to determine whether they are safe and effective. Thus, it is the responsibility of medical practice committees, for example, to insist that a major innovation be incorporated into a formal research project.[3]

Research and practice may be carried on together when research is designed to evaluate the safety and efficacy of a therapy. This need not cause any confusion regarding whether or not the activity requires review; the general rule is that if there is any element of research in an activity, that activity should undergo review for the protection of human subjects.

B. Basic Ethical Principles

The expression "basic ethical principles" refers to those general judgments that serve as a basic justification for the many particular ethical prescriptions and evaluations of human actions. Three basic principles, among those generally accepted in our cultural tradition, are particularly relevant to the ethics of research involving human subjects: the principles of respect for persons, beneficence and justice.

1. *Respect for Persons.*—Respect for persons incorporates at least two ethical convictions: first, that individuals should be treated as autonomous agents, and second, that persons with diminished autonomy are entitled to protection. The principle of respect for persons thus divides into two separate moral requirements: the requirement to acknowledge autonomy and the requirement to protect those with diminished autonomy.

An autonomous person is an individual capable of deliberation about personal goals and of acting under the direction of such deliberation. To respect autonomy is to give weight to autonomous persons' considered opinions and choices while

---

[2]Although practice usually involves interventions designed solely to enhance the well-being of a particular individual, interventions are sometimes applied to one individual for the enhancement of the well-being of another (e.g., blood donation, skin grafts, organ transplants) or an intervention may have the dual purpose of enhacing the well-being of a particular individual, and, at the same time, providing some benefit to others (e.g., vaccination, which protects both the person who is vaccinated and society generally). The fact that some forms of practice have elements other than immediate benefit to the individual receiving an intervention, however, should not confuse the general distinction between research and practice. Even when a procedure applied in practice may benefit some other person, it remains an intervention designed to enhance the well-being of a particular individual or groups of individuals; thus, it is practice and need not be reviewed as research.

[3]Because the problems related to social experimentation may differ substantially from those of biomedical and behavioral research, the Commission specifically declines to make any policy determination regarding such research at this time. Rather, the Commission believes that the problem ought to be addressed by one of its successor bodies.

refraining from obstructing their actions unless they are clearly detrimental to others. To show lack of respect for an autonomous agent is to repudiate that person's considered judgments, to deny an individual the freedom to act on those considered judgments, or to withhold information necessary to make a considered judgment, when there are no compelling reasons to do so.

However, not every human being is capable of self-determination. The capacity for self-determination matures during an individual's life, and some individuals lose this capacity wholly or in part because of illness, mental disability, or circumstances that severely restrict liberty. Respect for the immature and the incapacitated may require protecting them as they mature or while they are incapacitated.

Some persons are in need of extensive protection, even to the point of excluding them from activities which may harm them; other persons require little protection beyond making sure they undertake activities freely and with awareness of possible adverse consequences. The extent of protection afforded should depend upon the risk of harm and the likelihood of benefit. The judgment that any individual lacks autonomy should be periodically reevaluated and will vary in different situations.

In most cases of research involving human subjects, respect for persons demands that subjects enter into the research voluntarily and with adequate information. In some situations, however, application of the principle is not obvious. The involvement of prisoners as subjects of research provides an instructive example. On the one hand, it would seem that the principle of respect for persons requires that prisoners not be deprived of the opportunity to volunteer for research. On the other hand, under prison conditions they may be subtly coerced or unduly influenced to engage in research activities for which they would not otherwise volunteer. Respect for persons would then dictate that prisoners be protected. Whether to allow prisoners to "volunteer" or to "protect" them presents a dilemma. Respecting persons, in most hard cases, is often a matter of balancing competing claims urged by the principle of respect itself.

2. *Beneficence.*—Persons are treated in an ethical manner not only by respecting their decisions and protecting them from harm, but also by making efforts to secure their well-being. Such treatment falls under the principle of beneficence. The term "beneficence" is often understood to cover acts of kindness or charity that go beyond strict obligation. In this document, beneficence is understood in a stronger sense, as an obligation. Two general rules have been formulated as complementary expressions of beneficent actions in this sense: (1) do not harm and (2) maximize possible benefits and minimize possible harms.

The Hippocratic maxim "do no harm" has long been a fundamental principle of medical ethics. Claude Bernard extended it to the realm of research, saying that one should not injure one person regardless of the benefits that might come to others. However, even avoiding harm requires learning what is harmful; and, in the process of obtaining this information, persons may be exposed to risk of harm. Further, the Hippocratic Oath requires physicians to benefit their patients "according to their best judgment." Learning what will in fact benefit may require exposing persons to risk. The problem posed by these imperatives is to decide when it is justifiable to seek certain benefits despite the risks involved, and when the benefits should be foregone because of the risks.

The obligations of beneficence affect both individual investigators and society at large, because they extend both to particular research projects and to the entire enterprise of research. In the case of particular projects, investigators and members of their institutions are obliged to give forethought to the maximization of benefits and the reduction of risk that might occur from the research investigation.

In the case of scientific research in general, members of the larger society are obliged to recognize the longer term benefits and risks that may result from the improvement of knowledge and from the development of novel medical, psycho-therapeutic, and social procedures.

The principle of beneficence often occupies a well-defined justifying role in many areas of research involving human subjects. An example is found in research involving children. Effective ways of treating childhood diseases and fostering healthy development are benefits that serve to justify research involving children —even when individual research subjects are not direct beneficiaries. Research also makes it possible to avoid the harm that may result from the application of previously accepted routine practices that on closer investigation turn out to be dangerous. But the role of the principle of beneficence is not always so unambig-uous. A difficult ethical problem remains, for example, about research that pres-ents more than minimal risk without immediate prospect of direct benefit to the children involved. Some have argued that such research is inadmissible, while others have pointed out that this limit would rule out much research promising great benefit to children in the future. Here again, as with all hard cases, the different claims covered by the principle of beneficence may come into conflict and force difficult choices.

3. *Justice.*—Who ought to receive the benefits of research and bear its bur-dens? This is a question of justice, in the sense of "fairness in distribution" or "what is deserved." An injustice occurs when some benefit to which a person is entitled is denied without good reason or when some burden is imposed unduly. Another way of conceiving the principle of justice is that equals ought to be treated equally. However, this statement requires explication. Who is equal and who is unequal? What considerations justify departure from equal distribution? Almost all commentators allow that distinctions based on experience, age, deprivation, competence, merit and position do sometimes constitute criteria justifying differ-ential treatment for certain purposes. It is necessary, then, to explain in what respects people should be treated equally. There are several widely accepted for-mulations of just ways to distribute burdens and benefits. Each formulation men-tions some relevant property on the basis of which burdens and benefits should be distributed. These formulations are (1) to each person an equal share, (2) to each person according to individual need, (3) to each person according to individual effort, (4) to each person according to societal contribution, and (5) to each person according to merit.

Questions of justice have long been associated with social practices such as punishment, taxation and political representation. Until recently these questions have not generally been associated with scientific research. However, they are foreshadowed even in the earliest reflections on the ethics of research involving human subjects. For example, during the 19th and early 20th centuries the bur-dens of serving as research subjects fell largely upon poor ward patients, while the benefits of improved medical care flowed primarily to private patients. Sub-sequently, the exploitation of unwilling prisoners as research subjects in Nazi con-centration camps was condemned as a particularly flagrant injustice. In this coun-try, in the 1940's, the Tuskegee syphilis study used disadvantaged, rural black men to study the untreated course of a disease that is by no means confined to that population. These subjects were deprived of demonstrably effective treatment in order not to interrupt the project, long after such treatment became generally available.

Against this historical background, it can be seen how conceptions of justice are relevant to research involving human subjects. For example, the selection of research subjects needs to be scrutinized in order to determine whether some classes (e.g., welfare patients, particular racial and ethnic minorities, or persons confined to institutions) are being systematically selected simply because of their easy availability, their compromised position, or their manipulability, rather than for reasons directly related to the problem being studied. Finally, whenever research supported by public funds leads to the development of therapeutic devices and procedures, justice demands both that these not provide advantages only to those who can afford them and that such research should not unduly involve persons from groups unlikely to be among the beneficiaries of subsequent applications of the research.

C. Applications

Applications of the general principles to the conduct of research leads to consideration of the following requirements: informed consent, risk/benefit assessment, and the selection of subjects of research.

1. *Informed Consent.*—Respect for persons requires that subjects, to the degree that they are capable, be given the opportunity to choose what shall or shall not happen to them. This opportunity is provided when adequate standards for informed consent are satisfied.

While the importance of informed consent is unquestioned, controversy prevails over the nature and possibility of an informed consent. Nonetheless, there is widespread agreement that the consent process can be analyzed as containing three elements: information, comprehension and voluntariness.

Information. Most codes of research establish specific items for disclosure intended to assure that subjects are given sufficient information. These items generally include: the research procedures, their purposes, risks and anticipated benefits, alternative procedures (where therapy is involved), and a statement offering the subject the opportunity to ask questions and to withdraw at any time from the research. Additional items have been proposed, including how subjects are selected, the person responsible for the research, etc.

However, a simple listing of items does not answer the question of what the standard should be for judging how much and what sort of information should be provided. One standard frequently invoked in medical practice, namely the information commonly provided by practitioners in the field or in the locale, is inadequate since research takes place precisely when a common understanding does not exist. Another standard, currently popular in malpractice law, requires the practitioner to reveal the information that reasonable persons would wish to know in order to make a decision regarding their care. This, too, seems insufficient since the research subject, being in essence a volunteer, may wish to know considerably more about risks gratuitously undertaken than do patients who deliver themselves into the hand of a clinician for needed care. It may be that a standard of "the reasonable volunteer" should be proposed: the extent and nature of information should be such that persons, knowing that the procedure is neither necessary for their care nor perhaps fully understood, can decide whether they wish to participate in the furthering of knowledge. Even when some direct benefit to them is anticipated, the subjects should understand clearly the range of risk and the voluntary nature of participation.

A special problem of consent arises where informing subjects of some pertinent aspect of the research is likely to impair the validity of the research. In many cases, it is sufficient to indicate to subjects that they are being invited to participate in research of which some features will not be revealed until the research is concluded. In all cases of research involving incomplete disclosure, such research is justified only if it is clear that (1) incomplete disclosure is truly necessary to accomplish the goals of the research, (2) there are no undisclosed risks to subjects that are more than minimal, and (3) there is an adequate plan for debriefing subjects, when appropriate, and for dissemination of research results to them. Information about risks should never be withheld for the purpose of eliciting the cooperation of subjects, and truthful answers should always be given to direct questions about the research. Care should be taken to distinguish cases in which disclosure would destroy or invalidate the research from cases in which disclosure would simply inconvenience the investigator.

Comprehension. The manner and context in which information is conveyed is as important as the information itself. For example, presenting information in a disorganized and rapid fashion, allowing too little time for consideration or curtailing opportunities for questioning, all may adversely affect a subject's ability to make an informed choice.

Because the subject's ability to understand is a function of intelligence, rationality, maturity and language, it is necessary to adapt the presentation of the information to the subject's capacities. Investigators are responsible for ascertaining that the subject has comprehended the information. While there is always an obligation to ascertain that the information about risk to subjects is complete and adequately comprehended, when the risks are more serious, that obligation increases. On occasion, it may be suitable to give some oral or written tests of comprehension.

Special provision may need to be made when comprehension is severely limited—for example, by conditions of immaturity or mental disability. Each class of subjects that one might consider as incompetent (e.g., infants and young children, mentally disabled patients, the terminally ill and the comatose) should be considered on its own terms. Even for these persons, however, respect requires giving them the opportunity to choose to the extent they are able, whether or not to participate in research. The objections of these subjects to involvement should be honored, unless the research entails providing them a therapy unavailable elsewhere. Respect for persons also requires seeking the permission of other parties in order to protect the subjects from harm. Such persons are thus respected both by acknowledging their own wishes and by the use of third parties to protect them from harm.

The third parties chosen should be those who are most likely to understand the incompetent subject's situation and to act in that person's best interest. The person authorized to act on behalf of the subject should be given an opportunity to observe the research as it proceeds in order to be able to withdraw the subject from the research, if such action appears in the subject's best interest.

Voluntariness. An agreement to participate in research constitutes a valid consent only if voluntarily given. This element of informed consent requires conditions free of coercion and undue influence. Coercion occurs when an overt threat of harm is intentionally presented by one person to another in order to obtain compliance. Undue influence, by contrast, occurs through an offer of an excessive, unwarranted, inappropriate or improper reward or other overture in order to obtain compliance. Also, inducements that would ordinarily be acceptable may become undue influences if the subject is especially vulnerable.

Unjustifiable pressures usually occur when persons in positions of authority or commanding influence—especially where possible sanctions are involved—urge a course of action for a subject. A continuum of such influencing factors exists, however, and it is impossible to state precisely where justifiable persuasion ends and undue influence begins. But undue influence would include actions such as manipulating a person's choice through the controlling influence of a close relative and threatening to withdraw health services to which an individual would otherwise be entitled.

2. *Assessment of Risks and Benefits.*—The assessment of risks and benefits requires a careful arrayal of relevant data, including, in some cases, alternative ways of obtaining the benefits sought in the research. Thus, the assessment presents both an opportunity and a responsibility to gather systematic and comprehensive information about proposed research. For the investigator, it is a means to examine whether the proposed research is properly designed. For a review committee, it is a method for determining whether the risks that will be presented to subjects are justified. For prospective subjects, the assessment will assist the determination whether or not to participate.

The Nature and Scope of Risks and Benefits. The requirement that research be justified on the basis of a favorable risk/benefit assessment bears a close relation to the principle of beneficence, just as the moral requirement that informed consent be obtained is derived primarily from the principle of respect for persons. The term "risk" refers to a possibility that harm may occur. However, when expressions such as "small risk" or "high risk" are used, they usually refer (often ambiguously) both to the chance (probability) of experiencing a harm and the severity (magnitude) of the envisioned harm.

The term "benefit" is used in the research context to refer to something of positive value related to health or welfare. Unlike "risk," "benefit" is not a term that expresses probabilities. Risk is properly contrasted to probability of benefits, and benefits are properly contrasted with harms rather than risks of harm. Accordingly, so-called risk/benefit assessments are concerned with the probabilities and magnitudes of possible harms and anticipated benefits. Many kinds of possible harms and benefits need to be taken into account. There are, for example, risks of psychological harm, physical harm, legal harm, social harm and economic harm and the corresponding benefits. While the most likely types of harms to research subjects are those of psychological or physical pain or injury, other possible kinds should not be overlooked.

Risks and benefits of research may affect the individual subjects, the families of the individual subjects, and society at large (or special groups of subjects in society). Previous codes and Federal regulations have required that risks to subjects be outweighed by the sum of both the anticipated benefit to the subject, if any, and the anticipated benefit to society in the form of knowledge to be gained from the research. In balancing these different elements, the risks and benefits affecting the immediate research subject will normally carry special weight. On the other hand, interests other those those of the subject may on some occasions be sufficient by themselves to justify the risks involved in the research, so long as the subjects' rights have been protected. Beneficence thus requires that we protect against risk of harm to subjects and also that we be concerned about the loss of the substantial benefits that might be gained from research.

The Systematic Assessment of Risks and Benefits. It is commonly said that benefits and risks must be "balanced" and shown to be "in a favorable ratio." The metaphorical character of these terms draws attention to the difficulty of making precise judgments. Only on rare occasions will quantitative techniques be available for the scrutiny of research protocols. However, the idea of systematic, nonarbitrary analysis of risks and benefits should be emulated insofar as possible. This ideal requires those making decisions about the justifiability of research to be thorough in the accumulation and assessment of information about all aspects of the research, and to consider alternatives systematically. This procedure renders the assessment of research more rigorous and precise, while making communication between review board members and investigators less subject to misinterpretation, misinformation and conflicting judgments. Thus, there should first be a determination of the validity of the presuppositions of the research; then the nature, probability and magnitude of risk should be distinguished with as much clarity as possible. The method of ascertaining risks should be explicit, especially where there is no alternative to the use of such vague categories as small or slight risk. It should also be determined whether an investigator's estimates of the probability of harm or benefits are reasonable, as judged by known facts or other available studies.

Finally, assessment of the justifiability of research should reflect at least the following considerations: (i) Brutal or inhumane treatment of human subjects is never morally justified. (ii) Risks should be reduced to those necessary to achieve the research objective. It should be determined whether it is in fact necessary to use human subjects at all. Risk can perhaps never be entirely eliminated, but it can often be reduced by careful attention to alternative procedures. (iii) When research involves significant risk of serious impairment, review committees should be extraordinarily insistent on the justification of the risk (looking usually to the likelihood of benefit to the subject—or, in some rare cases, to the manifest voluntariness of the participation). (iv) When vulnerable populations are involved in research, the appropriateness of involving them should itself be demonstrated. A number of variables go into such judgments, including the nature and degree of risk, the condition of the particular population involved, and the nature and level of the anticipated benefits. (v) Relevant risks and benefits must be thoroughly arrayed in documents and procedures used in the informed consent process.

3. *Selection of Subjects*.—Just as the principle of respect for persons finds expression in the requirements for consent, and the principle of beneficence in risk/benefit assessment, the principle of justice gives rise to moral requirements that there be fair procedures and outcomes in the selection of research subjects.

Justice is relevant to the selection of subjects of research at two levels: the social and the individual. Individual justice in the selection of subjects would require that researchers exhibit fairness: thus, they should not offer potentially beneficial research only to some patients who are in their favor or select only "undesirable" persons for risky research. Social justice requires that distinction be drawn between classes of subjects that ought, and ought not, to participate in any particular kind of research, based on the ability of members of that class to bear burdens and on the appropriateness of placing further burdens on already burdened persons. Thus, it can be considered a matter of social justice that there is an order of preference in the selection of classes of subjects (e.g., adults before children) and that some classes of potential subjects (e.g., the institutionalized mentally infirm or prisoners) may be involved as research subjects, if at all, only on certain conditions.

Injustice may appear in the selection of subjects, even if individual subjects are selected fairly by investigators and treated fairly in the course of research. Thus injustice arises from social, racial, sexual and cultural biases institutionalized in society. Thus, even if individual researchers are treating their research subjects fairly, and even if IRBs are taking care to assure that subjects are selected fairly within a particular institution, unjust social patterns may nevertheless appear in the overall distribution of the burdens and benefits of research. Although individual institutions or investigators may not be able to resolve a problem that is pervasive in their social setting, they can consider distributive justice in selecting research subjects.

Some populations, especially institutionalized ones, are already burdened in many ways by their infirmities and environments. When research is proposed that involves risks and does not include a therapeutic component, other less burdened classes of persons should be called upon first to accept these risks of research, except where the research is directly related to the specific conditions of the class involved. Also, even though public funds for research may often flow in the same directions as public funds for health care, it seems unfair that populations dependent on public health care constitute a pool of preferred research subjects if more advantaged populations are likely to be the recipients of the benefits.

One special instance of injustice results from the involvement of vulnerable subjects. Certain groups, such as racial minorities, the economically disadvantaged, the very sick, and the institutionalized may continually be sought as research subjects, owing to their ready availability in settings where research is conducted. Given their dependent status and their frequently compromised capacity for free consent, they should be protected against the danger of being involved in research solely for administrative convenience, or because they are easy to manipulate as a result of their illness or socioeconomic condition.

[FR Doc. 79-12065 Filed 4-17-79; 8:45 am]

Index

Adverse reactions
  debriefing and, 63
  termination of study for, 62–63
Advertising, 144–146
Agreements. *See also* Informed consent
  authorship and, 79–80, 81, 102, 103
  of children, 45
  consent forms as, 43
  to data sharing, 55
  formal and informal, 25
  in research planning, 24–25
  with students and staff, 102
American Psychological Association
  confidentiality and, 51
  ethical principles of, 3
Animals
  care and use of, 156
Archival data
  consent to use, 46
  unpublished, 86
Assessment
  forensic, 158
  use and interpretation of, 143
Attribution of intellectual credit, 84
Autheticity
  authorship and, 77
Authorship
  agreements regarding, 79–80, 81, 102,
    103
  collaboration in, 80–81
  credit and responsibility for, 157
  oritoria for, 76 77
  disputes and agreements and, 79–80
  function of, 76
  honorary, 78
  multiple, 78–79
  ordering conventions for, 78–79
  plagiarism and, 83, 84
  responsibilities with, 77–78
  in results reporting, 82
  student publications and, 80
  student-staff agreements and, 102
Autonomy. *See also* Respect for persons
  obligation of researcher and, 35–36
  respect for, 6
  of student participant, 32

Beneficence and nonmaleficence. *See also*
  Harm

  in Belmont Report, 199–200
  as moral principle, 6–7
  in planning, 16–17
  selection and, 27
Benefits. *See also* Risks and benefits
  assessment of, 14–16, 203, 204
  consent and, 40
  of data sharing, 91–92
  to participants and others, 16–17
Bias
  in manuscript review, 88

Censorship
  editorial, 87
  by researcher, 87
Children
  assent of, 186
  harm and, 200
  institutional review board and, 184
  parental consent for, 30–31, 45, 186
  rewards for participation, 30–31
  risk and, 185
  special considerations with, 66–67
  as wards of the State, 187
Clinical practice
  versus research, 197–198
Co authors
  author responsibility to, 77–78
  data access by, 90–91
Coercion
  versus inducement, 29–30, 41
  noncoercive disclaimer on consent form,
    41–42
  recruitment of students and, 31
  versus voluntariness, 202
Collaboration
  authorship and, 80–81
  data access and, 91
Communication
  media release, 86
  unpublished, 85–86
Community-based research
  informed consent and, 47
Compensation
  on consent form, 41
  versus exploitation, 42
  for participation, 29–30
Competence
  in assessments and interventions, 142

Competence (*continued*)
  education of students and staff for, 99–100
  informed consent and, 44–45
  legal, 44–45
  of psychologist, 134, 136
  research supervision and, 100
Comprehension
  in informed consent, 44, 202
Confidentiality
  breach of, 51, 52
  certificate of, 53
  consent form and, 40–41
  data sharing and, 92, 93
  in editorial process, 87
  exceptions to, 52
  information release and, 150–151
  informed consent and, 51
  limits of, 148–149
  of mailed questionnaires, 55–56
  new technologies and, 54–55
  subpoenas and, 53
  threats and safeguards to, 52–53
Conflicts
  personal, 138
  resolution of ethical, 8–9, 159–160
Conflicts of interest. *See also* Ethical dilemmas
  in application of moral principles, 113–114
  identification of, 114–115
  moral principles and, 119
  in researcher's roles, 109–113, 139
  between self-interest and morality, 110
Consent. *See also* Informed consent
  to data sharing, 55
  legal capacity for, 44
  of parent for child, 30–31, 45, 186
  in research design, 18
Consent form
  alternatives and, 40
  benefits and, 40
  confidentiality and, 40–41
  contact for questions and problems, 41
  financial considerations on, 41
  incomplete disclosure on, 42–43
  invitation to participate on, 38
  long form, 38–43
  noncoercive disclaimer on, 41–42
  purpose of research and, 38
  risks and discomforts on, 39–40
  selection and, 39
  short form, 38
  signatories to, 43
  significance of, 43
  study procedures and, 39

termination of participant and, 42
  withdrawal from study and, 42
Consultation
  confidentiality and, 150
  consent to, 140
  in ethical decision-making, 120–121
  in research planning, 24
  in response to differing factual patterns, 124–125
Control group
  in research design, 20
Copyright
  duplicate publication and, 85
  self-plagiarism and, 84

Data
  access to, 89, 90–91
  archival, 46
  archival of, 82
  ethical principles and, 141
  ownership of, 21, 89
  publication of, participant privacy and, 56
  retention and disposition of, 94
  withdrawal of, 64
Databases
  confidential information on, 150
Data ownership
  definition of, 88–89
  education in, 102
  institutional policies for, 89
  student-produced data and, 90
Data sharing
  agreement to, 55
  benefits of, 91–92
  concerns about, 92–93
  confidentiality and, 55, 92, 93
  of federally funded research, 93
  functions of, 91
  participant advisement of, 155
  with professionals, 157
  with public, 104
  in public-access archive, 92–93
Debriefing
  for adverse reactions, 63
  after deception study, 69–71
  as educational, 47
  effectiveness of, 70–71
  harm from, 65–66
  as harm management, 65
  learning from, 71
  monitoring of, 71
Deception
  issues in, 68
  participants' reactions to, 67–68

problems from, 68–69
procedural, 67–71
in research, 155
Deontological ethics, 4–5
Design
  confounders of, 45–46
  consent in, 18, 45–46
  control-group in, 20
  experimental *versus* epidemiological, 19
  hypotheses in, 17
  methods selection in, 18–19
  participant identifiers in, 18
  settings in, 20–22
  target population in, 17–18
  validity of, 19–20
Diagnosis
  in professional context, 142
Disclosure
  on consent form, 42–43
  consent to, 150
  continuing, 43
  informed consent to, 201–202
Dissertation
  student-supervisor co-authorship of, 103
Dissertation research
  publication and authorship of, 81

Editorial process
  censorship in, 87
  confidentiality in, 87–88
Education
  for competence, 99–100
  in ethics, 97–99
  in legal obligations, 100–101
  of public, 104–105
  of research participants, 103–104
Errata
  author correction of, 77
Ethical Advisory Boards, 179
Ethical decision-making
  across diverse research contexts, 126
  disagreements in, 125–127
  uncertainty over choice and application
    of heuristics in, 127
Ethical dilemmas. *See also* Ethical
  decision-making
  consultation in, 120–121
  ethical principles in, 117–118
  ethical standards for, 115, 116–117
  legal standards in, 119–120
  moral principles in, 118–119
  professional standards in, 120
  resolution of, 115–121
  in response to differing fact patterns,
    121–125

Ethical principles, 134–135
  application of, 201–205
  basic, 198–201
  in ethical decision-making, 117–118
  in response to differing factual patterns,
    122–124
*Ethical Principles in the Conduct of Re-
  search With Human Participants*
  American Psychological Association, 3
*Ethical Principles of Psychologists and
  Code of Conduct*, 4, 129–160
  advertising and public statements in,
    144–146
  ethical standards in, 135–142
  evaluation, assessment, or intervention
    in, 142–144
  forensic activities in, 158–159
  general principles in, 134
  privacy and confidentiality in, 149–151
  resolving ethical issues in, 159–160
  teaching, training supervision, research,
    publishing in, 151–157
  therapy in, 146–149
Ethical standards, 135–160
  in ethical decision-making, 115, 116–117
  in response to differing factual patterns,
    122
Ethical training
  for competence, 99–100
  context-based, 97–98
  courses and workshops in, 98
Ethics
  approaches to, 4–5
  conflicts in, 8–9, 159–160
  context training in, 98–99
  law and, 136
  religious and philosophical traditions in,
    4–5
Evaluation
  in professional context, 142
Exclusion. *See also* Selection
  in population sample, 32–33
Expectations
  participants', 63, 64
Exploitation
  versus inducement, 29
  justice and, 200–201
  recruitment of students and, 31–32
  researcher avoidance of, 101, 140

Fees
  ethical principles and, 141, 142
Fidelity to science
  as moral principle, 8
  in results reporting, 82

Forensic activities, 158–159
Freedom-of-information Act
  confidentiality and, 54
Funding
  implications of, 22

Harassment, 138
  sexual, 137–138
Harm. *See also* Beneficence and
  nonmalficence
  avoidance of, 138
  benefit termination as, 64
  children and, 200
  from deception, 69, 70
  prevention of, 20
  risk of, 62–64
Hypotheses
  alternative, 17

Inducement
  versus coercion, 41
  compensation as, 29–30
  informed consent and, 202
  of participants, 155
  for participation, 29–31
Information
  sufficient, 201–202
Informed consent. *See also* Agreements
  autonomy and respect for persons and,
    35–36
  for archival data use, 46
  barriers to, 43–46
  in Belmont Report, 201–203
  to community-based research, 47
  competence for, 44–45
  data sharing and, 92
  documentation of, 176
  ethical obligation in, 35–36
  for filming and recording, 154
  full disclosure and confounder in, 45–46
  institutional review board and, 171–172
  legal obligation in, 36–37
  in longitudinal studies, 46
  obtaining of, 37
  and protection of human subjects, 174–
    176
  requirements for, 36, 174–176
  to therapy, 146–147
Institutional review board. *See also* Protection of human subjects policy
  advertising plan submission to, 28
  ethical issues and, 98
  federal regulations and, 4, 9, 161–162
  functions and operations of, 171
  informed consent and, 36

membership on, 171
  protocol updates for, 65
  research approval by, 172–173
  research review by, 171–172
  submission of protocols to, 37
Integrity
  as moral principle, 8
  of psychologists, 134
Intellectual property. *See also* data
  data as, 88–94
  editorial process and, 87
Interventions
  in professional context, 142

Justice
  distributive, 7, 200, 204
  procedural, 8
  selection of subjects and, 27, 204–205
  social, 204

Law
  compliance with, 153
  ethics and, 119–120, 136
  forensic activities and, 159
Legal obligation
  informed consent and, 36–37
  training in, 100–101

Mandatory reporting
  confidentiality and, 52
Manuscripts
  review of, 87–88
Media presentations, 145
Methodology
  qualitative *versus* quantitative, 18–19
Minorities
  population representation of, 33
Misrepresentation
  in media release, 85
Monitoring
  of debriefing, 71
  of outcomes, 20
  for safety, 62
Moral principles
  conflicting, 113–114
  in ethical decision-making, 118–119
  in ethics, 5–8
  versus fidelity and scientific integrity, 8
  in response to differing factual patterns,
    124
  versus self-interest, 110

National Institutes of Health
  population sampling and, 33

Participants
  advertising for, 28
  compensation of, 29–30
  debriefing of, 65–66
  education of, 103–104
  identifiers for, 18
  inducement of, 29–31, 155
  informing of, 155–156
  maintenance of trust of, 61–62
  safety of, 62–63
  selection of, 39
Plagiarism, 157
  authorship and, 83, 84
Pregnant women
  protection of, 178–180
Principles
  disgreements over applicable, 125
Prisoners
  Belmont Report and, 197
  defined, 182
  exploitation of, 200
  informed consent of, 45
  institutional review boards and, 182–183
  recruitment of, 30
  research permitted with, 183–184
  as research subjects, protection of, 181–184
Privacy
  archival databases and, 28
  children's, 50–51
  confidentiality and, 51, 52
  consent and, 49–50
  consent form and, 51
  maintaining, 149–150
  protection of child's, 50–51
  in reporting of results, 83
  wanted and unwanted information and, 51–52
Privileged communications, 83–84
Procedures
  consent form and, 39
Professional standards
  in ethical decision-making, 120
Protection of human subjects policy. See also Institutional review board
  compliance with, 169–170
  definitions and, 168–169
Proxy consent, 44
Publication. See also Unpublished material
  credit for, 102–103, 157
  of data, 56
  duplicate, 85, 157
  piecemeal, 84–85
  as reprints, 85
Public statements, 144–145

Questionnaires
  confidentiality of, 55–56

Records
  access by third parties, 53–54
  confidentiality and privacy of, 149–150
  ethical principles and, 141
  of institutional review board, 174
  ownership of, 151
  preservation of, 151
  subpoena of, 53
  withholding for nonpayment, 151
Recruitment. See also Participants
  advertising in, 28
  inducement in
  moral principles in, 27
  of representative sample, 32–33
  screening in, 32
  of students, 31
  through databases, 28
Referral
  ethical principles and, 140
  fees and, 142
  of special populations, 67
Relationships
  couple and family in therapy, 147
  with participants, 159
Reporting of results
  accuracy in, 82–83
Research
  clinical practice versus, 197–198
  cooperative, 173
  socially sensitive, 22–24
Research assistants
  responsibilities of, 61–62
  responsibility for, 61
Research planning
  agreements in, 24–25
  beneficence and nonmaleficence in, 16–17
  consultation in, 24
  design elements in, 17–22. See also Design
  dissemination of findings and, 22–24
  ethical training during, 98–99
  Ethics Code and, 153
  funding implications in, 22
  harm and, 16
  moral principles in, 16–17
  respect for persons in, 16
  risk assessment in, 14–16
Respect for persons
  autonomy and, 6
  in Belmont Report, 198–199
  obligation of researcher and, 35–36

Respect for persons (*continued*)
  in research planning, 16
  rights and dignity of, 135
  selection and, 27
Respects for persons. *See also* Autonomy
Responsibilities
  of authorship, 77–78
  professional and scientific, 134
  of research assistants, 61–62
  of researcher, 5, 8, 153–154
  of researchers, 5
  social, 135
  of students, 61–62
Results reporting, 156
Review
  expedited procedures for, 188
  by institutional review board, 171–172
  of manuscript, 88
Reviewers, 157
Right(s)
  to refuse participation, 43
  to withdraw from study, 64
Risk. *See also* Benefits
  assessment of, 14–16, 203–204
  children and, 185
  on consent form, 39–40
  factors in, 15–16
  for harm, 62–64
  prisoners and, 182–183
  types of, 15
Role conflicts, research
  in forensic activities, 158
Role conflicts, researcher
  as clinician, 111
  as employee, 111
  as funding recipient, 112
  as member of society, 112
  as program evaluator, 112
  as teacher, 111

Safety
  of participants, 62–64
  of researcher, 21
  of students and staff, 101
Sampling, 32–33
Screening
  in recruitment, 32
Search-and-seizure
  confidentiality and, 54
Selection. *See also* Exclusion
  methods in, 18–19
  of subjects, 39, 204–205
  of target population, 17–18
Self-plagiarism, 84
  copyright and, 84
Sensitive research, 22–24

Setting
  field, 21–22
  institutional, 20–21
Sexual issues
  therapeutic relationship and, 137–138,
    147–148
Social responsibility, 135
Solicitation, 145
Special populations
  assessment of, 143
  confidentiality and, 51
  recognition of, 66–67
  risks and benefits and, 204
  selection of, 204–205
Staff
  training of, 99–100
Staff meetings
  ethical issues and, 99
Standard(s)
  compliance with, 153
  disgreements over applicable, 125
  ethical, 115, 116–117
  legal, 119–120
  professional, 120
  research and, 153
Students
  authorship issues of, 80–81
  data ownership and, 90
  responsibility to participants, 61–62
  training of, 99–100
Subpoena
  confidentialitiy and, 53
Supervision
  clarification of, 102
  competence for, 100
  of subordinates, 140–141

Target population
  selection of, 17–18
Teaching
  ethical conduct in, 152
Termination
  by participant, 63, 64
  of participant, 42
  of research support, 177
  of study, 62–63
  of therapy, 148–149
Tests
  construction of, 143
  scoring and interpretation of, 144
  use of, 143
Therapeutic relationship, 146
Therapy
  couple and family relationships in, 147
  informed consent to, 146–147

mental health services in, 147
    sexual issues in, 147–148
    termination of, 148–149
Training
    in legal obligations, 100–101
    for safety, 101
Training programs
    for competence, 99–100
    description of, 152
    design of, 151
Trust
    in experimenter–participant relationship, 8
    of participants, 61–62

Unpublished material
    ethical guidelines for, 85–86

Utilitarian ethics, 4–5

Validity
    of design, 19–20
Voluntariness
    in informed consent, 202–203

Welfare of others, 135
Withdrawal
    consent form and, 42
    of data, 43, 64
    from study, 64
Women
    recruitment of, 33
Work-for-hire
    data ownership and, 89

About the Editors

Bruce D. Sales, PhD, JD, ScD *(hc)*, is a Professor of psychology, psychiatry, sociology, and law and Director of the Psychology, Policy and Law Program at the University of Arizona. He has served on the American Psychological Association (APA) Council of Representatives and approximately 15 other APA boards and committees, including the Ethics Committee. Among his approximately 200 publications are 17 books. Dr. Sales, the first editor of the journals *Law and Human Behavior* and *Psychology, Public Policy, and Law,* is editor of two APA book series: Law and Mental Health Professionals and Law and Public Policy: Psychology and the Social Sciences. He is a Fellow of the APA and the American Psychological Society, the recipient of the Award for Distinguished Professional Contributions to Public Service from the APA and of the Award for Distinguished Contributions to Psychology and Law from the American Psychology–Law Society, and is an elected member of the American Law Institute.

Susan Folkman, PhD, PhD *(hc)*, is a Professor of medicine and Codirector of the Center for AIDS Prevention Studies at the University of California–San Francisco. She is widely recognized in the United States and abroad for theory and empirical research on stress and coping, most recently in the context of HIV/AIDS. She has served on the American Psychological Association (APA) Council of Representatives, on committees of the Institute of Medicine, as a member of review committees at the National Institute of Mental Health, as chair of an AIDS behavioral review committee at the National Institutes of Health, and on senior advisory boards of the National Institute of Mental Health. She was awarded an honorary doctorate degree from Utrecht University, the Netherlands; has served on the editorial board of a number of journals in the behavioral sciences, and is a Fellow of the APA, the American Psychological Society, and the Western Psychological Association.